TOKYO

INSIGHT *City* GUIDES

Edited and Produced by Miguel Rivas-Micoud, Joseph Zanghi
and Megumi Hirokawa

Editorial Director: Geoffrey Eu

APA
PUBLICATIONS

TOKYO

First Edition
© **1991 APA PUBLICATIONS (HK) LTD**
All Rights Reserved
Printed in Singapore by Höfer Press Pte. Ltd

ABOUT THIS BOOK

every city is unique, and Tokyo today is the scene of an ever-changing city as it mirrors changes in Japanese society, yet its cultural roots run deep. The old and the new, the old traditions and the new-age lifestyle seem to go hand in hand everywhere one looks in the city. To gain a better understanding of some of the customs, behaviors and contradictions the traveler may encounter on his/her trip to Tokyo, *Cityguide: Tokyo* focuses on exposing some of the mysteries of Japan. For those who have returned from their trip the book will help preserve the memory. And, for those interested in Japan, the book will be a valuable resource.

It was a diverse and very talented team of coordinators, editors, writers, and photographers that came together to produce this new addition to APA Publications Cityguide series.

Miguel Rivas-Micoud arrived in Japan in 1981 after spending 15 years in Europe. In Japan, he set off on a varied career of photography, copy editing, and interior design. As project director, Miguel had to maintain the energy to keep up with the demands of compiling *Cityguide: Tokyo*. Miguel has been a producer of a wide range of projects in Japan and the notion of producing a novel guidebook about Tokyo was a new challenge, and one looked upon with great enthusiasm. With the contacts and friendships developed over the years with resident accomplished writers and photographers, Miguel set about putting together a team of people who possessed knowledge and insight into Tokyo and Japanese society.

Miguel contacted an old friend and colleague **Joseph Zanghi,** who has also been working in Tokyo in photography, journalism, and video production. Joe, chief editor of an English-language magazine and involved in ZAP Productions, was designated editorial director and was to make sure that *Cityguide: Tokyo* kept continuity, style, and overall direction. Together Miguel and Joe created the editorial core, took numerous photographs and wrote several sections of the book.

From the start Miguel brought in his partner **Megumi Hirokawa** and their design consultancy MHR Planning to handle overall coordination of the project as well as editing of Japanese words, compiling the maps, checking information, coordination and communications. She also had the tedious task of sifting through the thousands of photographs that were taken for this book. Another key person in the editorial team was **Aurora Renusch** who was able to keep coherence among the writers and add her editorial suggestions and expertise. As for the writers, **John Carroll**, well-known columnist, historian and social critic, has a wealth of knowledge about Tokyo and Japan. Wry with wit and humor, John tells the history of Tokyo. **Stuart Atkin** is a 17-stone Oxford graduate who arrived in Japan for a short visit fifteen years ago. He has remained ever since and is active in theater, narration and video production. He was the main narrator for Kobayashi's epic film, *The Tokyo Trial* and has also had several books published both as a writer and photographer. **James House** has appeared as an actor on TV, film and stage in the U.K., U.S., Europe and Japan. Most of his time is spent lecturing at university, commercial narrating and writing witty articles for magazines and newspapers. He is also a regular broadcaster for NHK (the BBC of Japan).

Rivas-Micoud

Zanghi

Hirokawa

Atkin

Carroll

Jim Bowers, a Professor of English and Speech Communication at Meiji University, is also a man of the theater, having directed several theatrical productions in Tokyo, and with his knowledge about the Japanese educational system, describes the ramifications of the strong emphasis the Japanese place on education. **Kermit Carvell**, a writer and researcher with a leading advertising and marketing agency and also a lecturer at Ferris Women's University, offers insight into the family and marriage. A long-time resident of Japan Kermit also describes Tokyo's closest urban area – Yokohama. Perhaps the most objective of the writers – having been in Japan only four years – is **Guy Fisher**. A very versatile writer, set designer, and photographer – Guy wrote a number of features for *Cityguide: Tokyo*. The roving photographer **Hiroshi Isobe** scoured the nooks and crannies, and scaffolds of the city looking for the right shot. In addition, he went on many fact-finding missions which provided valuable information for the Travel Tips section. **Roman Cybriwsky** is a professor of geography and urban studies at Temple University in Tokyo. When not teaching, he writes on the urban developments in Japan and the U.S. **Robb Satterwhite**, who recently authored his own book about Japanese food and dining, provided an overview of the foods a visitor might expect to experience on his/her stay in Tokyo. **Davis Barrager**, a long-time food and beverage writer in Japan, was able to explore the various kinds of Japanese cuisine that makes one's mouth water or the stomach a tad queasy. Photographer **Ron Kucera** took a variety of contemporary shots; whether a panorama shot of Tokyo's skyline or a beaming smile, Ron captured unforgettable images that seem to be around every street corner. Photographer **June Komater** and writer **Kevin McClure** teamed up combining her trained eye and his pen highlighting several areas of the city. **Olga Cybriwsky** teaches art history at Temple University in Tokyo, and has traveled widely throughout Southeast Asia in search of the ultimate art museum. The Japanese place a great importance on sports and sports photographer **Tadashi Matsumoto** captures the young and old performing traditional and contemporary action photos. **Chris Cook**, a fashion writer for a daily newspaper in Tokyo, added a piece on Tokyo's fashion scene.

There are a number of other people that we also wish to acknowledge, who have contributed their advice and encouragement: **Gary Hunt** for his contribution on the martial arts scene, **Dennis Mulvihill** for the first introduction to the book, "To Hear the Chimes," **Timothy Minton** for compiling the language section in the Travel Tips section of the book, **Hidemi Uesugi** for assisting with the photographs, **Nancy Baxer** for editorial suggestions, and **Ryusuke Ito** for helping with the original layout.

—APA Publications

Fisher

Isobe

Renusch

House, Carvell, Bowers

McClure

CONTENTS

TRAVEL TIPS

TO HEAR THE CHIMES

Japan is often said to be a land of paradoxes: a nation populated with self-effacing, arrogant men and dominated, subservient women who control the family purse strings, keeping the husbands on a weekly allowance. How can one begin to describe it? What do you say when people ask, "How did you like Japan?" Predictably, the description is often paradoxical.

However hard you may try to avoid them, when walking in Tokyo, your path is often crowded with giggling gaggles of junior high school girls. The braver of them will venture a well-rehearsed "hello," but the gaggles will be reduced to hysterical laughter if you respond to the salutation. In contrast to the rudeness of the girls, you may subsequently encounter an old woman (*obaasan*), clad in traditional *kimono*. Her face beaming with the chance to honor and welcome this complete stranger, she will bow to you in formal deference, as if you were visiting royalty, the most honored guest. Are the girls' taunts the real Japanese response and the old woman's the inscrutable oriental face, or is the difference one of maturity? Rude or too polite, both keep the foreigner foreign, apart from the Japanese group. It takes years to establish a relationship in which you are not exceptional.

Cities are known by their buildings. The skyscrapers of Shinjuku, straight and true, dwarf the clean, curving roofs of the Meiji Shrine in the heart of Tokyo, contrasting the old and new, the serene priest and the aggressive businessman. Though simplistic, the image does capture some of one's initial disappointment in coming to Japan. Most come with many misconceptions, and have vague, undefined expectations of some kind of uniquely Japanese architecture. Though not expecting everyone to live in a temple, we are usually not ready for the ubiquitous ferro-concrete. There are numerous shrines and temples throughout Tokyo, but they seem lost and out of place in the maze of concrete rectangles. While photographs reflect the elegant simplicity of the temples and their restrained oriental roofs, *shoji* screens and *tatami* floors, the reality is the eminently practical concrete box, honey-combed with cells, filled with worker bees.

In February, just as you begin to believe that the Japanese have been successful in covering their islands with neon-lit concrete, there begins an unequalled succession of blossoms. First are the plum blossoms (*ume*), small but articulate whites and pinks heralding the anticipated spring. Daphne perfumes the March air and magnolia trees explode in clouds of white and maroon. In April, the cherry blossoms suggest a late spring snowfall. In May, azaleas bloom and wisteria drip from overhanging trellises on every park

Preceding pages: the view of Shinjuku from Akasaka with the guest palace in the foreground; the main Ginza crossing: fashionable by day, entertainment at night; *Ohanami* – living it up under the cherry blossoms; in the middle of Tokyo's crowds, a Buddhist priest begging for alms. **Left,** low city, high city – the new and the old converge.

path. Hydrangeas bloom in June and summer weekends host spectacular iris shows. In September, giant chrysanthemums, the imperial family's flower, are sold on the streets everywhere. These are only some of the steady progression of flowers. Every week brings something new until the gray backdrop seems almost intentionally drab, necessary to offset the flora.

Once accustomed to the unique writing system, or rather the combination of four completely distinctive systems used simultaneously, you begin to notice the sounds of the country and soon discover further paradoxes. Everywhere one goes in Tokyo, there are loudspeakers arranging, selling, and directing at a volume the deaf can hear. The loudspeakers are ubiquitous. They pursue you into parks to remind you to enjoy yourself and please be out by six. They follow you home. Trucks mounted with loudspeakers prowl the neighborhood collecting old newspapers or selling laundry poles, screeching their purpose. Even the holy sanctuary of the Buddhist temple is not a refuge from the loudspeaker.

The train stations are the worst. Ear-shattering bells ring to warn you the doors are going to close, whistles confirm it. Loudspeakers announce incoming trains, proclaim their arrival, bellow their destination, and trumpet their departure. And then, if it is in the high heat of summer and you listen carefully in those few seconds between trains, you will hear the tinkle of a delicate windchime, put out by the station master to help aurally alleviate the heat.

Through the early morning hours, the young Japanese straddle their beloved motorcycles and, defying authority and waking the dead, scream down every road as fast as technologically possible. After the last Suzuki has whined through its gears, a stillness sometimes prevails. In June, when the remaining rice paddies have all been flooded, and if you happen to live nearby, the voices of the Tokyo Chorus of Frogs will rise up, and, in wondrous harmony, serenade anyone who bothers to listen. Sometimes one may think the traditional Japan is being lost in the mud, paved over by the super-highways of technology. But that is not fair. You must find the paradox and see the harmony. It is difficult to hear the windchimes in the railway station, but they are there.

Right, cherry blossoms – a seasonal explosion of pink billowy buds.

THE SAMURAI TOWN

In his eloquent essay *In Praise of Shadows*, Junichirô Tanizaki, one of the giants of Japanese literature, wrote: "The quality that we call beauty, however, must always grow from the realities of life, and our ancestors, forced to live in dark rooms, presently came to discover beauty in shadows, ultimately to guide shadows towards beauty's ends."

Although he was discussing the aesthetics of Japanese architecture and indoor design, this passage could just as easily refer to the daily lifestyle of the common people of Edo when it was the capital of the Tokugawa shoguns from 1603 to 1868. Compelled to live within a social straightjacket that bound their every move, they stole for themselves a certain kind of freedom that allowed them to develop a culture unique in human history.

Three centuries and a decade before the arrival of Commodore Matthew Calbraith Perry and his armada in Edo Bay in 1853, a different group of Westerners – Portuguese traders – had arrived at the island of Tanegashima off Kyûshû to find a very different kind of Japan. It was a divided realm swept by social and political upheaval, amidst which a number of warlords struggled for hegemony, while an emperor watched impotently from the sidelines in his Kyôto palace.

Emperor Gonara was considered, by those few subjects who even knew that he existed, as the latest in an unbroken line of sovereigns that could be traced back into the mists of prehistory, back to the semi-mythical first ruler Jimmu Tennô, descendant of the Sun Goddess. But the Imperial clan nearly 1,000 years before had lost the last of its real authority, first to a fairly pacific court aristocracy much given to elaborate Buddhist ritual, and then, when the nation traded the sutra for the sword, to the samurai.

Centuries of more or less continuous warfare had led to a breakdown of the old classes, and in a historical phenomenon the

Japanese refer to as *gekokujô* ("retainers supplanting their lords"), families were constantly rising from or sinking into the churning social flux. It should be noted that these wars were limited in scale. The warriors and their families were trying to eliminate each other and generally left the peasantry alone. As a result, a surprising amount of manuscripts and art, and to a lesser degree architectural treasures, survived the wars.

A number of militant Buddhist sects and

AN OFFICER IN COURT DRESS.

independent merchant enclaves, most importantly Sakai near Osaka, lent color to the interstices of this basically feudal social fabric. Into this already heady mix, the Portuguese introduced two new and highly volatile elements – firearms and Christianity.

Eventually, one especially ruthless chieftain emerged and was able to more or less unite the central part of the country. He was Oda Nobunaga (1534-1582), who especially was known for three things. The first was his Machiavellian sense of realpolitik, which caused him to adopt with alacrity Western guns and thus gave him a march on his rivals.

Preceding pages, the days of Edo depicted in a woodblock. **Left**, ancient warrior's helmet and mask. **Right**, officer of the court.

The second was his virulent hatred for the obstreperous warrior monks who had been causing trouble for centuries – in 1571 he put three thousand buildings of the Enryaku Temple on sacred Mt. Hiei to the torch and massacred nearly all of their inhabitants. This fixation also induced him to favor the Christians, who by now were winning many converts. The last was his love of the *noh* theater.

It was in 1582, when he was away from the huge castle he built at Azuchi on the shores of Lake Biwa just north of Kyôto, that Nobunaga was attacked and slaughtered by the forces of a disgruntled vassal.

themselves to the vicissitudes of the warrior's life and to social divorcement from neighbors or remain as peasants, subservient to the warriors.

For many years Hideyoshi bemoaned his lack of a male heir and when an infant son, Hideyori, was born in the twilight of his years, he was ecstatic and became obsessed with founding a Toyotomi dynasty of warrior rulers. To this end, he established a regency council of leading vassals and allies, foremost of whom was Tokugawa Ieyasu (1542-1616) – who controlled the greatest amount of territory in the realm after Hideyoshi. Its members all swore loyalty to

Nobunaga was succeeded by Toyotomi Hideyoshi (1536-1598) a diminutive man with megalomania of gargantuan proportions, who continued the consolidation process.

The action which probably had the greatest impact on the future course of Japanese history was his "sword hunt" begun in 1588, in which all non-samurai were forced to give up their weapons and a strict class system was introduced.

In some areas this meant that rich landlords had to make a difficult choice. Declare themselves to be samurai, thereby exposing

the infant, who was only five at the time of Hideyoshi's death.

Shogunate beginnings: In the year 1600, at the very time the religious and material passions of the Reformation were reshaping the map and future of Europe, Ieyasu made his move against the coalition of mainly western daimyos who were at least feigning loyalty to the Toyotomi. And that autumn, there on the wind-lashed fields of Sekigahara near Gifu, Ieyasu made Japan his own.

When Ieyasu established his headquarters in what is now Tokyo in 1590, the area the central city occupies today was little more than a collection of scattered farming and fishing villages. The little town of Edojuku, at the mouth of the Hirakawa River, contained only about 100 thatched huts in the shadow of the ruins of an older castle. That edifice had been built in 1457 by the minor local warlord Ota Dôkan, a sophisticated poet/scholar who in 1485 was betrayed and butchered at age 55 at the behest of his own lord.

Actually, Ota built on a site which had been fortified nearly two centuries earlier by a local governor, Edo Shigenaga. These earlier Edo castles were located near the present site of the Imperial Palace and prospered throughout Japan's middle ages. Consequently, although Tokyo is far younger than Kyôto, which served as the imperial capital for roughly a millennium up until the Meiji Restoration of 1867-68, it is by no means a stripling as far as cities go.

Prefecture, at the suggestion of the then samurai supremo, Hideyoshi.

After his unalloyed triumph at the Battle of Sekigahara, it was at Edo that Ieyasu in 1603 established the de facto military government of the land, the *bakufu* (tent government) or shogunate. The real power of the emperor in Kyôto who appointed him shogun had, despite the semi-religious aura attached to his person, been practically nil from early in Japanese history.

Huge numbers of peasants, merchants and *rônin* (masterless samurai) poured into the new capital of the shogun to labor in the construction of the castle, mansions, ware-

houses and other facilities required to run his giant bureaucracy.

Ieyasu was Napoleonic in his passion for administration, and he thought of every device possible to make sure that his descendants would keep their power. The formal establishment from 1635 of the *sankin kôtai* system of alternate-year attendance at Edo for the close to 300 independent feudal lords (daimyô) left after the winnowing of the civil wars further fueled the building boom and brought tens of thousands of more residents, even though the stays of the daimyô in town were staggered.

The founder of the Tokugawa shogunate brought with him a ready-made population of considerable size when he relocated from his former base, in what is now Shizuoka

Far left, the rise of the shogun: Hideyoshi (1536-1598), and (**left**) Ieyasu (1542-1616). **Above**, Edo, the former name of Tokyo.

The Tokugawa regime directly ruled Edo, of course, along with other major cities like Osaka and Kyôto, and most of eastern Japan, and altogether directly controlled about one-fourth of the nation's entire rice, the commodity in which wealth was then measured, and one-third of its people.

Tokugawa reign: Although the Tokugawas brought peace to a long-suffering land, the new military rulers attempted to freeze the hands of the clock of time by refining the extremely rigid status system introduced by Hideyoshi, under which nearly all individuals were classified in descending order as samurai, farmers, artisans (townsmen) or

funds by the feudal lords, especially after they got a taste of the good life in Edo, led to the development of an integrated marketing and transportation system and sometimes great influence and freedom, albeit highly circumscribed, for the still officially despised merchants.

The grounds of the huge castle ordered built by Ieyasu were far greater in scale than those of today's Imperial Palace – which is roughly five kilometers in circumference – reaching on the east to about where Tokyo Station is today. The complex was not actually completed until 1640, only to be razed by fire seven short years later. Most of

merchants. Each had their own distinctive styles of speech, dress, customs and living habits.

The individual feudal lords also tied their peasants to the land, deciding what crops they could grow and how much they should pay from their rice harvests in taxes to support the parasitic class of warriors without a war – it ran to 70% of the yield in some areas! They also banned the free sale of agricultural production and trade in anything other than authorized items.

Nevertheless, a steady growth in agricultural production and endless demands for

today's castle, which retains only a small fraction of the buildings it had during the Edo period, actually dates only from 1888, and part of it burned down in a 1945 American air raid. The previous elaborate structures were reduced to ashes in May 1873, as the result of a fire started in the room of a court lady.

The main five-story donjon of the original structure towered some 240 feet above the city. It was surrounded by an intricate swirl of moats, which incorporated existing waterways, and had 36 *mitsuke*, or lookouts, some of which have left their legacy in place names like Akasaka Mitsuke.

The residences of the *hatamoto liegemen* and major lords were originally clustered right outside the castle in what today are areas like Otemachi, Marunouchi, Hibiya and Hanzômon, while the craftsmen and merchants were crammed into the remaining space in the corridor between the castle and the sea.

Low City, High City: Due to the frequent fires, the so-called "flowers of Edo," that became a symbol of the city, this residency pattern was later modified considerably and was somewhat complicated by the fact that most of the lords had at least two or three

The dichotomy between the refined, albeit somewhat enervated, culture of the *yamanote* and the robust, plebeian art and drama of the *shitamachi*, which Edward Seidensticker has so aptly dubbed respectively as the "high city" and "low city," has been a consistent feature of life in Edo and Tokyo.

Shitamachi was definitely the life of the Edo party. Japan's population hovered around 30 million for most of the Edo era; of these, less than two million, or 7% of the people, belonged to samurai families. By the Kyôho era (1716-36), when there were approximately 30 million Japanese, an estimated 1 million to 1.4 million people lived in

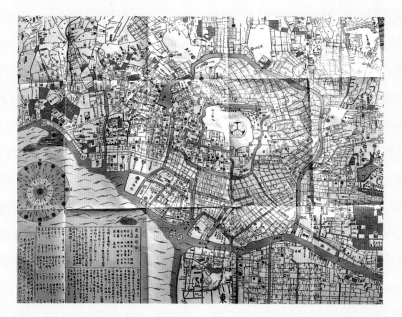

houses. In general, though, the samurai gravitated to the hilly parts, or *yamanote*, of the city, while the townsmen congregated – or were forced to congregate – in the downtown (quite literally!), or *shitamachi*, near the shore and the rivers, most famous of which is the Sumida. Almost from the start, this *shitamachi* began to encroach, through reclamation, on the waters of Tokyo Bay, a process which continues unabated today.

Left, woodblock print of Edo and revered Mt. Fuji in the distance. **Above**, map of Edo – rivers and canals were its life blood.

Edo, making it by far the largest city in the world. During the same period, Kyôto had a population of 400,000 and Osaka 300,000. In 1801, when Britain ruled the waves, London, the largest European city, had only an estimated 864,000 inhabitants.

Over half of Edo's residents, primarily townsmen, and the various social outcasts estimated to have numbered about 25,000, were crammed into the 16% of the city comprising the *shitamachi*. That amounted to an amazing population density in the area of about 70,000 people per square kilometer – more than in even the high-rise areas of

Tokyo today!

Samurai town: In its early decades, Edo was a rough-and-tumble sort of place – after all a very high percentage of its habitants were samurai or craftsmen catering to the needs of fighting men. In fact Edo all along was really more of an overblown castle town than a true city, producing and existing in its own right.

The fact that men outnumbered women many times over – two to one as late as 1721 – also probably contributed to making the boys more than a bit cantankerous.

Edo itself also soon earned the unflattering sobriquet "dumping ground of the domains." Although, technically, peasants were re-

quired to have internal passports to move to Edo or other cities, many simply absconded from the land, especially since property rights were passed on solely to the eldest son. "Younger sons eat cold rice," as the saying went. They were joined there by the riffraff of all classes.

In fact, sometimes gangs of *hatamoto yakko*, overbearing but underworked retainers of the shogun, got into sword battles with armed townsmen, often transportation workers, professional gamblers or other rough types, known as *machi yakko*. The more accomplished of the latter came to be

referred to as *otokodate* ("gallants") or *kyôkaku* ("knights of the streets").

For whatever reason, by the early 18th century, the streets had settled down a bit and these gangs had disappeared.

Lineage was all important in the Edo era. The samurai's son inherited his stipend. The merchant's son grew up playing with an abacus. The farmer's son usually died on the same land on which he was born and which he furiously tilled while alive. Even children of prostitutes in the licensed quarters usually remained there: girls to be trained from childhood for the flesh trade and boys to act as messengers and perform other odd jobs.

Ideology: Whether in Edo or the countryside, every individual knew exactly what his or her position in the general scheme of things was and how they were to behave. The stress on obedience and the maintenance of proper social relations between superior and inferior extolled by the officially supported doctrine of Confucianism filtered down over time to the lowest strata of society.

But in reality, the Tokugawa ideology was only about 20% Confucianism and the balance samurai-ism; in other words – a *bushidô* sundae with a dollop of Confucianism on top. Ieyasu himself was a fervent Buddhist, but his less capable successors felt more affinity for Confucianism; its respect for a strict hierarchy in social and personal relationships.

In fact, it was cheeky of Hideyoshi and the Tokugawas to call all of this Confucianism at all. They had borrowed the four-class social structure from China, but substituted the warrior for the scholar/bureaucrat.

The shogunate ruthlessly sought to root out Christianity, which had been introduced by St. Francis Xavier and other missionaries in the mid-1500s and which it considered a subversive threat to social stability. The "creed of the Galilean" was banned from 1606 and the country culturally imploded because of seclusion decrees issued between 1633 and 1639, which eliminated almost all outside trade and political relations. No ocean-worthy vessels were allowed to be built and no Japanese who journeyed abroad were allowed to return.

Even in the capital, the shogun's troops

ferreted out Christians. Groups of converts and missionaries who refused to apostatize were on more than one occasion burned at the stake on a bluff overlooking the Tokaidô highway or crucified upside down at the tideline along the coast at Shibaura.

It should be noted, however, that the suppression of Christianity does not seem to have been primarily an expression of xenophobia or fear of foreign invasion. Militant Buddhist sects and other forms of unorthodox thought, which threatened the particularism of feudalism, were also decimated. The major problem with Christianity was that it preached universal and transcendent known then as the "kitchen of the world." In fact, one of the reasons Ieyasu had chosen the area for his capital was its easy access to the sea. The ocean transport of strategic commodities such as rice, salt and lumber was controlled by authorized wholesalers. Lighters brought the cargo in from the ships to godowns lining the shores of the rivers and canals.

That is not to say that land transport along the five great highways which converged on the city was not also important. It was, especially so along the famous Tokaidô ("East Ocean Route"), along which most of the feudal lords traveled for their periodic atten-

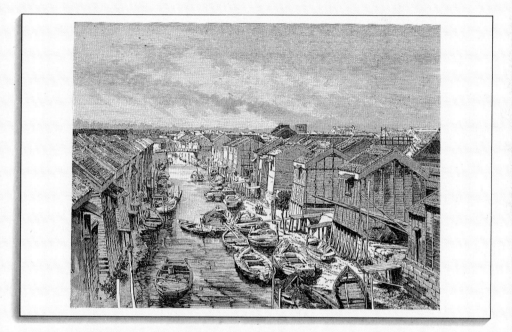

concepts. Men and women and the members of different classes, for example, were, at least theoretically, considered equal before God by the Christians.

Venice of Asia: The Shogun's capital must have been a truly beautiful city. Its many rivers, canals and other waterways made it the "Venice of Asia." It is often forgotten that the vast majority of Edo's supplies came by sea, especially from Osaka, which was

Far left, Imperial visit to Yasukuni Shrine. **Above,** warehouses in *shitamachi*, the old downtown.

dance and which formed the central artery of the city in its leg from Shinagawa to Nihombashi.

With the major lords in town, the samurai portion of the city's population probably topped 500,000 and might even have outnumbered the townsmen. They alloted to themselves, however, more than 60% of the city area. Another 20% went to the hundreds of shrines and temples – most of which formed a spiritually protective ring around the outer edges of the city – and the tens of thousands of priests who inhabited them.

The cult of the samurai culture and feudalistic thinking had an immense influence, for both bad and good on Japanese popular culture during the Edo period, and perhaps even more so during the Meiji period. Their sway has not been entirely broken to this day.

Women of Edo: Two areas in which the influence of class mimicry proved long-lasting were the treatment of women and the use of language. The strict morality elucidated for samurai wives and mothers in the *Onna Daigaku* (Great Learning for Women), attributed to the Confucian philosopher Kaibara Ekken and his wife, became the model to emulate among all classes. It reads in part: "Approach your husband as if he

rarely ventured out into society and spent most of their lives in the twilight of the home. When they did go out they wore severe dress, so as not to expose even their arms.

Likewise, the use of *keigo* or honorific language, which nearly always places the two parties to a conversation in a superior-inferior relationship, really started going out of fashion only after World War II.

Trade and craft: Most of the townsmen of Edo were segregated into neighborhoods, or *machi* (literally "towns"), according to their profession. Each of these crafts had its own unique lore and lingo. Dollmakers, fishermen, carpenters, whatever – people of the

were Heaven, since if you offend him Heaven will certainly punish you."

Naturally, the popularity of such a philosophy led to many a young wife having a very hard time, especially from her mother-in-law. But as the popular saying went, "The womb is borrowed," and marriage was considered primarily a relationship between families, not individuals. Intermarriage between members of different classes was of course strictly taboo. On the whole, it seems that wives in townsmen households were considerably freer than their social betters.

Women of the middle and upper classes

same profession usually lived together, and their neighborhoods were named accordingly.

As the Jesuit visitor João Rodriguez wrote about Edo in the first years of the 1600s, "There are all kinds of people engaged in any trade imaginable, including ones Europe hardly knows of.... Nowhere does one come across shops handling all kinds of goods mixed together." Eventually the number of

Above, a scene from a Hiroshige woodblock print.

THE WAGES OF LOYALTY

The famous story of the 47 loyal retainers, Chûshingura – the incident on which several *kabuki* plays were based, took place in 1703. In the public mind , it was perhaps the most spectacular event of the whole Edo period and depicts how peaceful as a whole these two and a half centuries were. Come to Japan in December and you will be treated to the story in many forms: *kabuki* (undoubtedly the most popular of all *kabuki* plays is *Kanadehon Chûshingura*), movies, TV dramas

that capital offense, he was ordered to commit ritual disembowelment (*seppuku*), otherwise known as *hara-kiri*.

In addition, his lands were confiscated and all his vassals turned out to fend for themselves as *rônin*. Almost two years later, the loyal retainers took revenge by attacking Kira's mansion in the Honjo area near the Sumida River, chopping off the old man's head and taking it to their lord's grave so that his spirit could finally rest in peace. They, in

A JAPANESE GOVERNOR.

and even spoofs.

The basic events on which the Chûshingura (Treasury of the Loyal Retainers) story is freely based are simple. In 1701, Lord Asano of the small fief of Akô near Hiroshima, became angered at what would be called today the *ijime,* or taunting, by the *hatamoto*, Lord Kira, who had been assigned to teach him the proper etiquette for receiving an envoy from the emperor. Asano drew his sword and wounded Kira. For

Above, bowing to one's seniors is a time-honored tradition.

turn, were ordered by the *bakufu* to commit *seppuku*. Brave men they were, samurai in the true sense of the term – "he who serves in life and death" – and also victims of the merciless demands of the feudal code.

Duty and honor are, of course, the themes of the play. In the story, no matter what media form it may be presented in, the scene in which Asano, in the "flower of youth," slits his stomach is played to the hilt, with falling cherry blossoms galore. If you go to the *kabuki*, watch out for the slippery floors, tears run like mountain torrents, not only from the mothers in the crowd.

these towns grew to some 2,000, each of which had its own head responsible for whatever happened there. The neighborhoods were more or less sealed off from each other at 10 p.m. when their gates shut.

But the castle was the focus of activities (unlike today) especially in what is now the park area on its northeast side. Here worked the thousands of samurai bureaucrats. Remarkably, most of the shoguns also appear to have been quite industrious; their working day usually began at 6 a.m.

The main donjon was a beehive of activity, too, especially considering the fact that the Great Interior, where the shogun was the

fession – no punishment could be carried out without a confession, although torture certainly could be – and then carry out the sentence as soon as possible.

The city's two main execution grounds were at Kozukappara near Senju, where an estimated 200,000 people were executed during the Edo period, and Suzugamori just off the Tokkaido, near Omori. The punishment for arson was burning at the stake. Murder or robbery rated a crucifixion. Killing of a master in any social class rated two days in the pillory, with two handsaws placed conveniently next to the neck, which had been marked off with notches, in case

only man allowed – with the exception of a few officials, bodyguards and servants – reportedly had 4,000 concubines and other females (surely an exaggeration) in it!

Law and order: Edo was a well-policed city. The *yoriki* deputies of the city magistrates – who went on horseback, the *dôshin* – lowranking samurai under them – who carried a single sword, and the underling townsmen with their truncheon and chain were a familiar and not totally unwelcome sight, when they policed the city streets.

Not many people were kept in the prison at Kodenmachô. The theory was to get a con-

any outraged bypasser cared to express his indignation by sawing a few inches. Then it was off for a parade through the streets, topped off by the crucifixion.

Culture: Edo culture was above all a performance culture, a show culture – in the way a gallant flipped his kimono sleeve, in the manner a meal was served, and more than anything else, in the *kabuki*. *Kabuki* was a sensual, not an intellectual experience. In that respect, it was a perfect symbol for Edo culture in general. The leading *kabuki* actors were the social lions of the city. In the theaters they, and not the soldier boys in the castle, were the lords.

Their kingdom was somewhat of a nether region, however. Although the plays were almost always staged in the daytime, the theaters were dark even then. That had its advantages though. The colors of the costumes and makeup were different from today's, and the effect of a good ghost or revenge play must have been unearthly.

Perhaps the consistently most popular type of *kabuki* play was that dealing with *shinjû*, or double love suicide. The great Chikamatsu Monzaemon (1653-1724), known to as "the Shakespeare of Japan," wrote several plays of this genre, including

restraints. So in that sense, the escape into death was a victory of the human spirit.

The shogunate tried banning the *kabuki*, especially *shinjû* plays, several times. It also tried banning prostitution several times. Unsuccessfully, of course, in both cases. In fact, it even tried banning tobacco as early as 1610 – as a fire, not a health hazard. However, the poisonous weed continued to be sold as "life-prolonging tea."

Yose was the most popular form of entertainment for the poor man. (The closest thing in the West would be the old-style vaudeville house.) Here storytellers beguiled their audiences with edifying *kôdan*, which were at

the immortal "The Love Suicides at Amijima."

Shinjû held a peculiar fascination for the people of the Edo period. Of course, it was an expression of despair – usually because the couple could not marry – and therefore defeat. But at the same time, it expressed the desire for freedom – freedom to love and freedom to live the way that the couple desired – without the ever present feudal

Left, Hideyoshi and his concubines having a party. **Above**, modern drama depicting life in Edo.

times a form of talking newspaper, and comical *rakugo* tales. There were hundreds of *yose* sprinkled throughout the city during the Edo and Meiji periods. People would drop in for an hour or two for the cheapest entertainment around. Few could afford to go to the *kabuki* on a regular basis.

The lotteries held throughout the city, usually at temples, were another source of entertainment. The *chokibune* "hog's head" boat, used for partying on the rivers, could have stood as the symbol of the city. Cherry blossom, snow and summertime fireworks viewing were other favorite pastimes.

If Victor Hugo had been born a Japanese, he could easily have set his tale about a lovestruck hunchback in Edo. The town was acrawl with *misemono* freaks of every description. Several neighborhoods, often *hirokoji* (or firebreaks), were especially well known for their freak shows, including the area behind Sensôji Temple in Asakusa, also the location of the archery booths whose young "instructresses" were renowned for their "bow-pulling" expertise; the Ekôin Temple, built to soothe the souls of the multitudes who died in the 1657 fire; and Ryôgoku Bridge, near where the Shin Kokugikan Sumo Hall stands today.

Takatoshi in 1673 – and the equally illustrious, Shirokiya. Mitsui, Mitsubishi, Sumitomo and the other major *zaibatsu* that were to have such a tremendous impact on the prewar Japanese economy mostly got their start in the Edo period.

The establishment of the shogunate caused many economic changes. After the seclusion orders, the merchants turned their attention to the development of a nationwide sophisticated domestic distribution and marketing system. The highway grid built by the Tokugawas and their standardization of weights, measures and coinage helped, of course, in this respect, even though barrier

These areas featured exotica aplenty: tantalizing peep shows, strippers, mixed-sex *sumo* matches, snake men, glassblowers, mountebanks, magicians, dancing bears and dogs, rare wild animals, including imported camels, tigers, ostriches and elephants. You couldn't spit without hitting an exhibitionist of some sort: jugglers, acrobats, contortionists, sword swallowers, strongmen, geeks, fat ladies.

Economy: Just north of Nihombashi Bridge were the major dry goods stores, including the Echigoya (now Mitsukoshi Department Store) – established by Mitsui Hachirobei

stations remained everywhere.

The most famous of these was at Hakone, where eagle-eyed officials vigilantly checked for "weapons going in or women coming out" – in other words, overt signs of incipient rebellion.

All this resulted in the growth of a money economy, which, naturally, was the last thing the shogunate wanted, what with its emphasis on rice taxes as the basis of the economy and a pathological desire to preserve the status quo. The samurai continued to receive their stipends in rice; the economy ran on money. The result: the samurai borrowed from the merchants and increasingly went into debt; the merchants gained power.

Many of the wealthiest or most influential merchants hailed from the Ise area. In fact, there was a famous saying: "Edo is famous for fires, fights, and the dung of Ise and Inari (fox) shrines." As this suggests, the Ise merchants were known to be cunning shylocks. But at the same time, they were very adept at establishing political connections.

They also had a role in the boom in Ise worship, making arrangements for the pilgrims traveling to that most holy of Shinto shrines. In 1771 alone, 200,000 people made the journey, illustrating the decline of feudalism, at least in regards to freedom of movement. Evidence of this are the many *kôshinzuka* images of protective deities to be found along the major highways.

Neighbors or work groups pooled their funds so that each member could visit the shrine once. The purpose of the journey was two-fold: to worship at the shrine itself and bring home talismans for everyone in their village, and to have the time of one's life in the bawdy towns outside.

The favorite objects of worship of the merchants in Edo were the seven gods of good fortune, especially Ebisu – the god of wealth.

Meanwhile, over the centuries a revolution was occurring in the countryside. Technical improvements caused a big boost in output and population at the beginning of the 19th century after staying steady for most of the Edo period, but also increased landlordism. Under such conditions, natural disasters could take a heavy toll. The Great Tempo Famine of 1833-37 is estimated to have cost hundreds of thousands of lives, and there were even reports of cannibalism.

Farmers in the poorest areas were also increasingly forced to engage in *mabiki*, meaning literally "thinning out the plants." Actually, it was infanticide, usually of girls, who were frequently strangled or buried alive. But Japan was not a poor country in normal times; it was a question of disparity

of wealth. The shogunate's erratic fiscal policies – the old "tight money, loose money" accordion effect – also had a severe impact through dramatic price fluctuations. That did show, however, that the national economy was becoming increasingly integrated.

The manpower surplus increased tenancy and gave birth by the beginning of the 19th century to what was in effect a wage labor system, a form of proto-capitalism. Japan was ripe for an industrial revolution before Perry arrived with his single-track miniature steam engine and other trinkets.

For many farmers, life was truly a vale of

tears. The number of peasant rebellions, or *hyakushô ikki*, peaked just before and after the overthrow of the shogunate. Rice riots in Edo and other cities, sometimes involving up to 10,000 people, also became more frequent, sparked either by crop failures or wholesaler speculation. *Uchikowashi* attacks on the property of rice brokers, *sake* brewers or moneylenders, often one and the same, and the anti-feudal feeling overtly expressed in folk songs were further proof that the dilapidated superstructure of the shogunate was beginning to weaken considerably.

Left, the Imperial seal, the chrysanthemum at Yasukuni Shrine. **Above**, Ebisu – the god of wealth.

THE NECESSARY REVOLUTION

The arrival of Perry's Black Ships in 1853 was an immense psychological shock for the people of Edo; after all he was sitting right out there in their bay! During the chaotic years that followed, the period of the Meiji Restoration, shock turned to disorientation. Edo society and culture had reached a dead end in many ways, but at least people had known exactly who they were, what their place was in society and what was expected of them. Now they had lost their identity overnight, courtesy of the U.S. Navy.

To add to all of this disconcertment was the Ansei Earthquake of 1855 and the accompanying fires, which nearly wiped out the entire city. The poor children of Edo must indeed have thought the sky was falling.

When the first U.S. Consul, Townshend Harris, was allowed to enter Edo for the first time in November 1857, he was greeted by crowds in their thousands – and absolute silence.

Actually, there was panic throughout Japan; something of an irrational "the Russians are coming, the Russians are coming" mentality. But the fact is, it would have been an impossibility for any of the imperialist Western countries to have conquered Japan, if the country remained united. She had hundreds of thousands of trained fighting men under arms and had learned much from China's humbling experience in the Opium War. Millions of peasants could also be mobilized, as was to be so effectively demonstrated in the Restoration War to follow, when the Chôshû fief used peasant volunteers in its kiheitai rifle units to crush the shogunate forces.

The common people posed little danger to the shogunate, even at this stage. But western fiefs, most importantly Chôshû and Satsuma, which had been nursing grudges ever since Sekigahara, certainly did. The *Kokugaku* ("National Learning") move-

Left, a print depicting the beginnings of international trade during the Meiji Era.

ment, which stressed the importance of the imperial tradition, provided the ideological rationale for a drive to overthrow the shogunate, and Perry's arrival proved the catalyst. The Restoration took as its rallying cry the slogan "Sonnô Jôi" ("Revere the Emperor, Expel the Barbarians").

This revolution was accomplished with surprisingly little bloodshed, mainly because the last shogun, Yoshinobu (Keiki), in statesman-like fashion, retired rather than precipitate a full-scale civil war. Power was officially returned to the emperor in the fall of 1867. But still the shogunate existed in Edo, where bands of armed assassins cruised

the streets.

The Kan-eiji, a huge 119-hectare complex with nearly 100 buildings, was, along with the Zôjôji in Shiba, a mortuary temple for the shoguns. In fact, the bulk of them were buried at one of the two. Ieyasu and his grandson Iemitsu are to be found at Nikkô.

It was at Kan-eiji that 2,000 diehard Tokugawa loyalists, the Shogitai, chose to make a last futile stand in the brief but bloody one-day Battle of Ueno, which burned most of the complex to the ground. Their bodies were left to rot by the victors. Days later monks released their tortured souls into the funeral pyre. Such was the end of Ieyasu's legacy.

The sons of Edo, who had always prided themselves on sitting at the shogun's knee, lifted not a finger to fight or bury. Why should they? It was a samurai affair.

The Meiji era: As if to rub in their victory, the Meiji leaders turned the Kan-eiji grounds into the first municipal park, and in 1873, one of the first public art museums was built here. Then in 1877, the first National Industrial Exposition was held here.

At times the new government, which was dominated by lower ranking samurai from Satsuma and Chôshû – the "Satchô clique" – was incredibly cynical and "modernization" really meant promotion of the ideals of Meiji oligarchy. Still, the Meiji Restoration was one of the most intense periods of social change in Japanese history. Both the winners and losers in the Restoration War were losers in the sense that the 1871 elimination of the fiefs and the later consignment of the samurai to the dustbin of history, with little compensation involved, was perhaps the only case in history in which a class committed collective hara-kiri. It might be more accurate to say that they were finessed out of existence by the new government.

As a popular little ditty at the time topknots were outlawed in 1871 put it, "Tap a shaven topknotted pate and you'll get the sound of reaction, tap a close-cropped head and you'll hear civilization and enlightenment." The government literally shamed the people into giving up customs considered "decadent" or "reactionary." Even Emperor Meiji and the members of the imperial family helped to popularize Western clothes. The people were even exhorted to eat beef for "civilization and enlightenment."

The last gasp of the samurai came during the Satsuma Rebellion of 1877, which involved a quarter of a million troops.

After that, there was no internal threat to the government, even though there had actually been more peasant uprisings in the first years after the Restoration than at any time under the Tokugawas.

Ideology: It was more than a restoration, in fact nothing less than a "conservative revolution," as contradictory as that phrase may sound. There had been a radical strain in Restoration thinking, a mystical side to the ideology of "Sonnô Jôi," an emphasis on egalitarianism – "one Lord above, 30 million subjects below." And indeed, theoretically, the Restoration had returned "all lands and people to the Emperor." This almost anarchic thinking was anathema to the Meiji leaders, but was to resurface amidst the ranks of the radical right in the 1920s and 1930s.

Nevertheless, the Meiji government was "authoritarian," not "totalitarian." In that sense, it was the forerunner of several Asian governments of today. Like them, it believed in top-down modernization and tight bu-

stripped the city of its name and substituted Tokyo or "Eastern Capital." Furthermore, Emperor Meiji said that he would rule from there. He arrived on October 16 of the same year.

While still in Kyôto, the emperor issued an extremely important document, the Five-Article Charter Oath. Among other things it said, "Knowledge shall be sought throughout the world so as to strengthen the foundations of imperial rule"; and "Evil customs of the past shall be broken and everything based upon the just laws of Nature." This was a clear manifesto by Japan to the effect, "Watch out world, here we come."

reaucratic control. "Sonnô Jôi" gave way to "fukoku, kyôhei," ("rich country, strong military") as the guiding ideology.

For five years after the emperor was restored to power, the ban on Christianity continued to be enforced. Several prominent intellectuals became Christians during Meiji, and the influence of the foreign religion was far disproportionate to the number of believers.

On July 10, 1868, an imperial edict

Far left, Commodore Perry. **Above**, Emperor Meiji starts a new era.

The Meiji Constitution: The Meiji Constitution of 1889 was modeled on that of Prussia, since the leaders distrusted and feared unbridled democracy. Indeed, in 1898 they scrapped the 1890 Civil Code, which was patterned on French law and assumed the basic equality of people regardless of sex, in favor of one that reinstated a feudalistic patriarchal system which gave the family head nearly dictatorial powers.

This constitution was riddled with potential dangers, and the only reason they did not cause major problems during the Meiji era was that the oligarchs kept a firm hand on the helm. At that time, Japan was truly a "government of men, not laws."

Professor Tadashi Furutake of Tokyo University, famous historical novelist Ryôtarô Shiba and other prominent intellectuals have argued that Japan was never a typically "Asian" country to begin with, noting that its marriage and land-holding patterns were quite different from those in China, Korea and India.

If that is so, then the efforts of the Meiji leadership to promote emperor worship and "Eastern values" to counterbalance Westernization were to a large extent an illusion. What they did, however, was to reinforce, under the cloak of modern institutions a premodern paternalistic and at the same time feudalistic state.

There are a number of good books considering Japan's modern century from a variety of angles, and nothing can beat Edward Seidensticker's Low City, High City for an account of the physical and social changes in the city up to the Kantô Earthquake; but it should be remembered that most of the traditions we consider today as defining the Japanese people evolved or were consolidated during the Edo period. Institutionalized emperor worship was not one of them; that was a Meiji invention.

It would be fair to say that for the average Japanese, the defeat in World War II marked a far greater break in thought patterns and emotions than did the Restoration or the subsequent Meiji transformation. For intellectuals, however the confrontation came earlier. Perhaps Japan's greatest modern author, Natsume Sôseki (1867-1916) dealt with problems of alienation and the need to establish the "self" in his novels, in an age which was remarkably similar to our own in its tendency to judge "success" purely in terms of material possessions. In one of these, Mon (The Gate), the gate of a Zen temple refuses to open for the hero who is searching for the truth. That was the frustration Sôseki and many intellectuals of the day faced. They could not find the answer to the questions, "Who am I?" and "Where is Japan going?"

Death of Edo: In 1878, there were 670,000 residents in Tokyo and the city was consid-erably smaller than it had been a decade before, what with dilapidated mansions and samurai barracks standing amidst overgrowth. Tokugawa life lingered on in the back streets, a poetry of squalor, and the new Meiji culture was still only taking its first fledgling steps.

By 1897 the population had revived to 1.33 million. After that, Tokyo never looked back. Bye, bye, Edo. Actually, the death of Edo was gradual and unspectacular, a slow wasting away. The tender flower of Edo culture was designed for the shadows, not the glare of the age of electric lights. The earthquake of 1923 was only the stake driven in Edo's heart, a heart that was barely ticking anyway.

The story "Takekurabe" ("Growing Up") by Ichiyô Higuchi evocatively catches the pathos of this dying world. It is set in a neighborhood near the Yoshiwara and tells the story of a young future geisha, Midori, and her childhood chum, who is destined to become a monk. Higuchi herself, despite her brilliant talent, lived in poverty and died at age 24 in 1896.

Tokyo: a new life: While Edo was dying, a new city was growing up on top of it – Tokyo. Far more than with Edo, Tokyo's story is that of the nation as a whole. Government became much more centralized than it had ever been under the shoguns, and people flocked there from all over the country. Lovers of "Old Edo," such as Kafû and Tanizaki, bewailed this conquest by the yabo (common country folk), but could not stem it. Population tripled in the first four decades of the new century. Many of those who participated in this vast migration came in search of factory jobs and, initially at least, had to live in slum areas.

The biggest problem that the city faced at this time, in fact that it had always faced, was the lack of sufficient drinking water.

Ironically, at other times the city has been plagued by an excess of water. The reclaimed area east of the Sumida, districts like Fukagawa, Honjo and Mukôjima have frequently been underwater after flooding – the Sumida used to flood once every three years on the average – and in 1910 the northern half of the city was submerged.

The Meiji leaders were ready to try anything if they thought it would advance the cause of "fukoku kyôhei." One live wire named Arinori Mori, who for a time served as Minister of Education, seriously advocated that the Japanese should intermarry with Westerners "to improve the racial stock." He also suggested replacing the Japanese language with English. Incidentally, he was assassinated. More important was Yukichi Fukuzawa, founder of Keiô University, who argued for internationalism from the point of view of classical liberalism. Although he never held office, his influence was enormous with the Meiji oligarchy.

newspapers in Yokohama, a port which still enjoyed extraterritoriality and therefore freedom of the press, showing, for example, a monkey adjusting his tuxedo. A stupendous masked ball held in 1887, at which government ministers and their ladies impersonated Napoleon, Marie Antoinette, a shepherdess and the like, was the final straw as far as the nativists were concerned and a strong chauvinistic reaction set in.

Actually, much of this tomfoolery was understandable since Japan was forced into a semi-colonial status after the opening of the treaty ports, and it was not until 1911 that the last of the unequal treaties and tariffs with

Western mimicry: The Rokumeikan, the "Hall of the Baying Stag," opened in 1885, in what today is Uchisaiwaichô across from Hibiya Park. It became the sight of soirees, charity balls and cultural events of all kinds attended by the elite of society and government officials. Also invited were prominent foreigners like Pierre Loti. In fact the justification for these elaborate affairs was to show how "civilized" the Japanese had become.

The result was scathing cartoons in the

Above, two bestsellers from the Meiji Era pushing for Westernization and self-help.

the Western nations were eliminated.

Industrial Revolution: While all these fun and games were going on, the country was reeling through the industrialization process faster than any other nation had to date. The spinning industry provided much of the momentum in the beginning. It was based on a half-feudal labor system; in bad times, the workers returned to the countryside. Industry sweatshops boasted "our wages are lower than those in India."

Yes, Japan took to the industrial revolution with a vengeance and the work conditions were deplorable. Young unmarried women worked 15 hours or more a day with no breaks. Real wages at the time were one-sixtieth of those in the United Kingdom. Criminals were largely responsible for extracting Japan's mineral wealth. Their life expectancy was not very long. This was capitalism at its Dickensian best.

But was it really capitalism? The tremendous support the government gave to the zaibatsu and other favored companies would appear to indicate it was really "State Capitalism," but actually such an assessment can be deceiving, too. There was, in fact, a dual economic structure, the huge zaibatsu industrial and international trading combines and small home industries. This dual structure continues to this day to a certain extent.

By 1877, 20% of Tokyo's residents were involved in industry. Electric lighting was introduced in 1887, although it became available only in poor areas after the Russo-Japanese War of 1904-5.

There was a strange balance and intermingling between nationalism/internationalism and liberalism/reactionary chauvinism throughout much of the early and middle Meiji period. The aggressive side of Japanese statism only really began to win out after the country's spectacular victory in the Sino-Japanese War of 1894-5. The specter of rampant ultranationalism was then released as a result of Japan's amazing victory over Czarist Russia in the Russo-Japanese War.

Their expectations fired by government propaganda and battlefield reports, the masses did not realize just how weak Japan really was. In the riots which followed the conclusion of the Portsmouth Treaty, a giveaway in the popular mind, over 1,000 people were killed or wounded in Tokyo.

At the same time, the Meiji era marked the first occasion in which large numbers of foreigners came to live and work in Japan. Most of them were from Japan's colony of Korea, but there was also a community of several thousand Chinese in Kanda. It became a hotbed for revolution against the tottering Ch'ing Dynasty in China, and Sun Yat-sen made several stopovers in Yokohama and Tokyo. In fact, he forged ties with Japan's leading ultranationalist organization, and as a result, numerous Japanese adventurers participated in the Chinese revolution even though the Japanese government tended to support the status quo.

In 1879, an existing shrine was transformed into the Yasukuni ("Peaceful Country") Shrine, dedicated to all those who died in combat for the sake of the country from the time of, and including, the Restoration. Some years during the Meiji era, it drew up to 10 million visitors. (The souls of 2.5 million combat dead from World War II have, in fact, been enshrined.)

Critics doubt whether Yasukuni has anything to do with real Shinto at all. Even though the shrine is now privately run, it remains a symbol of State Shinto pure and simple, designed to foster belief in a transcendent Emperor. The controversy over whether the serving prime minister should visit it in his official role, or visit at all, still pops up in the papers in one guise or another nearly every year, whether or not the shrine has anything to do with ultranationalism and militarism.

Shinto had always been an intimate part of daily Japanese life, as shown by the Ise pilgrimage phenomenon. In the Edo period, there were kitchen gods, toilet gods and many other kinds of gods worshipped by the people. But none of them were represented in human form. Shinto was basically a set of simple rituals and an attitude toward living life naturally. There was also much interaction with Buddhism. It was not something people were taught by the State.

Several shrines, which like Yasukuni had nothing whatsoever to do with Tokyo's daily life or religious traditions, were established during the Meiji period or shortly thereafter, including the Meiji and Nogi shrines. They might be termed "national shrines" since they were established by and served the interests of the government. The last of the above was named in honor of General Maresuke Nogi, who committed seppuku as Emperor Meiji's funeral entourage passed nearby his home, a deed which was a big shock to prominent writers like Sôseki.

Right, fashion takes on a new look.

Tokyo was definitely ready to greet the new century – the first beer hall opened in 1899.

For most of the prewar period, the true center of Tokyo's entertainment world, at least the plebeian side of it, was still in Asakusa, as it had been during the Edo period. Saruwakachô was where most of the many *kabuki* theaters were located. Sensôji, where the Kanzeon ("Goddess of Mercy") statue – perhaps the single most beloved and most revered religious image in all Japan – is

located, lay directly between Edo and "the paddies."

In Asakusa, you could find the cinemas, the cheap cabarets, the wandering *enkashi* singers accompanying themselves on violin. The 200-feet-high, octagonal, red brick Ryôunkaku "Tower Over the Clouds" became the symbol of Asakusa.

Interesting sociologically was the "Asakusa Opera" of the 1910s and 1920s. Although the quality of the divas may not have been very high, this particular brand of singing theater attracted groups of vehement ruffian fans known as *peragoro*, who

would go at it in the parks outside the theaters.

In the 1920s, if you were out looking for a *mobo* ("modern boy"), with his Harold Lloyd glasses on, or a *moga* ("modern girl"), in the Charleston look, then you would have had to bear in mind that the Ginza was the place where they did their "*Gin-bura*" stroll. That decade showed a rapid Americanization of popular culture: baseball, jazz, vaudeville, film. The cafe society of the Taishô, symbolized by the waitress of high fashion and low morals, was, of course, primarily a glossy veneer; Japan remained essentially agricultural.

World War I had proved an enormous economic boom, since Japan leaped at the chance to enter the Asian markets vacated by the European powers, who were preoccupied with their fratricidal bloodletting, and a whole new brand of nouveau riche, the *narikin* – mostly armaments makers, emerged from it. But the inevitable deflation hit hard and there were major rice riots in 1918. The following year, politics became extremely polarized as the labor movement and left gained momentum, and a new right, which believed in the politics of assassination rather than the ballot box, emerged trance-like from the political shadows.

The series of murders of political leaders that followed over the next 15 years, including prime ministers and former prime ministers, did much to create the climate of violence that would let the military take power.

The Kanto quake: The big event of the 1920s was, of course, the Great Kantô Earthquake. By sheer ill luck, it struck just about noon on September 1, 1923, when a good percentage of the city's charcoal and gas stoves were lit up. Fire, not the quake itself, caused the most damage. Ninety per cent of Yokohama was also wiped out.

Roughly one-third of the city's fatalities occurred in one quadrant, the grounds of a military clothing depot in Honjo. Some 40,000 people had gathered there with their bedding and other personal belongings when a freak whirlwind hit, licking in sparks as it settled on their heads. Nearly every person there that day was incinerated. A disaster museum in Yokozuna Park has many photos of the holocaust.

The 1920s and 30s: The concepts of civil rights and duties, and even the words used to express these ideas – *kenri* and *gimu*, entered Japan during the Meiji period. The "Taishô Democracy" of the 1920s was only an exotic grafting, a soap bubble.

Ryôtarô Shiba has made the insightful comment that the Japan of the Meiji period and of the 1920s and 1930s were like two different countries, two different races. For again many farmers were forced to sell their daughters. Perhaps not surprisingly, the radical right found many recruits in such areas.

The famous mutiny of February 26, 1936 was one of the few instances of fighting in the long history of the city. Activist officers of the "Imperial Way" faction in the Army, who were inspired by the teachings of the ideologue Ikki Kita, leading 1,500 troops, assassinated several government officials and occupied major government facilities, and made their headquarters in the Sannô Hotel in Akasaka. After six days, the rebellion was put down at the direct order of the

all their venality and other faults, the Meiji leaders were giants, ultrarealists.

The Great Depression initially hit Japan harder than the other major economic powers, but it also recovered quicker. By that time, however, the Army had gone its own way on the Continent, occupied Manchuria and was encroaching on China proper. The rural regions of Japan, especially northeast Honshu, remained depressed, and once

Far left, Meiji school boys. **Above**, the financial institutions take on a Western look in the 1930s.

emperor.

Experimentation and social change was just as vigorously discouraged during the late 1930s as it had been during the Tokugawa period. In both cases, conformity, the harnessing of the energy of the people was to be diverted into clearly defined channels. After the Manchurian Incident of September 1931, it was a heady toboggan ride into the China Incident quagmire, undeclared war with the Soviet Union on the Manchuria-Outer Mongolia border in 1936 and eventually the most important incident of all – Pearl Harbor. The phoenix city was fated to glow once again.

Pearl Harbor: The fire bomb raids in the winter of 1944 and spring of 1945 left three-quarters of a million homes in Tokyo damaged or destroyed. The Dresden-like swath bombing on the nights of March 9-10, carefully planned to wreak maximum damage on Tokyo's small industry and poorer residential quarters, alone leveled 40% of the city and cost around 100,000 lives.

After Hiroshima and Japan's unconditional surrender, the cities were in far worse shape than the countryside, which at least offered grubs for the table. The average caloric intake for a Japanese in 1946 was

Arthur and the Occupation, of course, had a tremendous impact on Japanese institutions, and the cultural break they represented was at least as great as that of the death of Emperor Meiji in 1912. But since postwar Japan has never really had a viable two-party system, some political experts express concern at how deeply democracy has really taken root.

The huge riots of 1960 protesting the renewal of the U.S.-Japan Security Treaty and the student ultraviolent radicals and their occupation of Japan's major campuses during the late 1960s now seem like a distant and faint memory.

only 1,530 calories compared to 1,950 during the war years. One judge in Tokyo who refused to eat black market rice starved to death. The tragedy of mass starvation was avoided by food assistance from the Occupation.

This was also an exciting period, however. Nylons, chewing gum and chocolate. War crimes trials, sweeping political reform and the boogie-woogie *pan-pan* girls of Company B, who haunted the Yûrakuchô area. It was really only during the Korean War that the economy started to recover.

Postwar Japan: General Douglas Mac-

The "income doubling plan" proposed by Prime Minister Hayato Ikeda and his brain trust at the beginning of the 1960s was scoffed at by critics at the time, but achieved its goals without a hitch. Meanwhile, the millions who continued to flow into the capital, whose population had more than doubled since 1950, often found homes along the hydra-like private rail lines leading out from the main terminals like Shibuya, Shinjuku or Ikebukuro. These were usually constructed by department store firms which had major stores near the head station and branches at several locations along the line.

Real estate firms grabbed up land along the tracks and sold prefabricated "rabbit hutches" to those salarymen who had not yet abandoned the dream of owning their own home, and in the process, created a nightmare of suburbia at its worst.

A trail of changes: Such trends have been continuing for decades. How many of those who were there recall the once flourishing hippie culture of East Shinjuku in the 60s and early 70s? Times do change. Ferraris and Mercedes now jostle for curb space in Roppongi and one "fashion hotel" on the Ginza charges ¥250,000 a night for a suite. And you have to book well in advance!

Japan's economy managed to skip over the waves spawned by the oil shocks like a frisbee – after an initial dip, it gained even greater altitude.

The high land prices in central Tokyo – they jumped 10% in 1986 alone – have become a serious impediment to development plans as well as spawning numerous social problems, including the infamous *jiage* land speculators, often with underworld ties, who have resorted to strong-arm tactics, even arson and murder on occasion, to force reluctant property owners to sell out and make way for development projects. Prices moderated for 18 months from September 1987, but then began a slow rise again as real estate firms apparently judged that the market had bottomed out and it was time to start buying up land again.

In 1989, land prices in Tokyo and Yokohama rose only about 10% on the average, but the ripple effect from the capital region was having a serious impact on the rest of the country. Nationwide, land prices on the average have risen more than 20% every year from 1987, 28.7% in 1989 alone, and in six major regional cities they rose more than 50%!

Tokyo itself faces a plethora of problems, including the continuing lack of water, earthquake worries, mountains of garbage and other environmental concerns, traffic snarls, a lack of adequate housing which results in 3-4 hours of commuting each day for many office workers, and, of course, the land price imbroglio.

Private property is considered sacred in Tokyo, which has resulted in a tendency for the government to use the right of eminent domain only in the most extreme cases.

As a result, highways are frequently constructed on huge concrete stilts and double-decked, making an already ugly city an eyefright. Subways also have to be built very deep under the ground.

On more than one occasion, government leaders have floated the idea of moving the capital from Tokyo to somewhere else – the

foot of Mt. Fuji or a point roughly equidistant between Tokyo and Kansai have often been mentioned – or dispersing its functions. But these suggestions have inevitably soon disappeared like the morning mist, when the estimated price tag of tens of trillions of yen for such a move is considered.

So too has the suggestion that the Diet hold its summer sessions in Tôhoku and Hokkaidô and winter sessions in Kyûshû and Shikoku. One concept still frequently discussed is the proposal to stick the Diet, or at least a "new city within the capital", out in Tokyo Bay.

Left, two atomic bombings at Hiroshima and Nagasaki marked the end of World War II. **Above**, General MacArthur landing at Atsugi Airbase near Tokyo.

Well then, what will Tokyo in the year 2040 look like? It is always hazardous to predict the future in Japan, since the Japanese are ever ready to surprise you. Once they make up their mind to do something, no matter how outlandish it may sound at first, chances are they will figure out some way to do it. Tokyo, in particular, has demonstrated an amazing capacity to cope, born of a long history of doing just that.

With all the Buck Rogers-style plans on

the drawing boards, and more certain to follow, one thing we can say with nary a doubt – Tokyo will look considerably different 50 years hence.

One problem in devising a uniform development plan for Tokyo Bay, however, is that in addition to the national government, there are three prefectural governments and numerous local governments involved. Not surprisingly, the concepts they have been considering frequently conflict.

By the year 2000, greater Tokyo's population will probably already have surpassed the 36 million mark, and nearly one out of

every three Japanese, not to mention many hundreds of thousands of foreigners, will be living in Tokyo or its environs. At that time, some of the suburbs will be pushing the 100,000-resident level in their own right.

The concentration of wealth and influence in the capital should also continue. National government statistics show that as of 1986 around 85% of the 1,050 most important foreign-capitalized companies and over 40% of all domestic firms worth more than ¥100 million were headquartered in Tokyo. All this despite the fact that downtown office space seems to be getting scarcer by the minute.

Tokyo is also the information center of the nation, monopolizing in terms of numbers of companies the advertising (37%), information services (42%), software (48%), newspaper (30%) and publishing industries (65%). About 30% of Japan's universities and junior colleges are located in Tokyo, as are more than 25% of its high school-level educational institutions. In fact, one out of every five Tokyo residents is reportedly a student!

The future look: Under a 1976 law, huge high-rise residential complexes have been authorized in several areas of the inner city. So we can expect a reversal of the tide of population outflow. When the new 243-meter-high civic center complex is completed in west Shinjuku in 1991, its twin-towered main structure will be the tallest in Japan. Already the neighborhood boasts of the biggest selection of skyscrapers in Eastern Asia, although up until 1970 there was nothing there but a water purification plant.

Like other buildings designed for the 21st century, the concrete and glass citadels here will be energy-efficient "intelligent buildings" with computerized lighting, heating and security systems, and will boast the latest in telecommunications and office automation.

The opening of these metropolitan offices, which in artist conceptions look like they belong to the San Quentin school of architecture, is expected to have a booster effect on the already booming economy of the Shinjuku area and further increase land prices there. The design is by world-famous architect Kenzô Tange, whose Yoyogi National Gymnasium is considered a masterpiece.

Reclamation of Tokyo Bay: Much of the development in central Tokyo is slated to occur either on land belonging to the government, the JR railway system, or else reclaimed from Tokyo Bay. The bay has a surface area of around 120,000 square hectares within shores that stretch for 170 kilometers in three prefectures. Although it has a maximum depth of 70 meters, its average

two million tons buried in Tokyo each year!

Since the Meiji Restoration, numerous plans for the reclamation of the bay have been put forward by prominent citizens, like the great modernizer of the Meiji era Yukichi Fukuzawa and, later, former Tokyo governor and super-bureaucrat Shimpei Gotô. Most of them have gone nowhere or are implemented in only piecemeal fashion.

The Tokyo concept: Several plans are being bandied about today, including the "Tokyo Teleport Concept," pet project of the Tokyo government. Envisaged for the Ariake zone of the bay offshore from Shinagawa and Shibaura, where there is a ship museum

depth is only 15 meters, meaning that there are no impossible engineering bars to its development.

Reclamation has been taking place ever since the beginning of the Edo period – Tsukiji, for example, was one of the first areas to be stolen from the sea – and already roughly one-fifth of it has been filled in since then, often with garbage. In fact, well over three million tons of garbage is burned and

Preceding pages, Tokyo – a changing architectural scene. **Left**, high-rise buildings defy earthquakes. **Above**, close-quarter living, a way of life in Tokyo.

owned by a motor boat impresario and global-scale philanthropist. This 100-hectare subsidiary civic center will, of course, feature a huge teleport, not to mention a ¥1.9 trillion "international business and financial center" to compete with London and New York on a 24-hour-a-day basis. In the zone, an estimated 110,000 people will work everyday and 60,000 live on a permanent basis. Convention facilities, ritzy restaurants and cultural attractions will also naturally abound. It will start opening in stages from 1993.

Perhaps the most ambitious plan is the

"Tokyo Bay Cosmopolis Concept," being pushed by the powerful Ministry of International Trade and Industry, which calls for the construction of four huge islands, totaling 10,000 square hectares, that would be home to a mixed bag of commercial, industrial, cultural, research and other facilities, and would accommodate up to 1.3 million residents and another 700,000 commuting workers. The offices of several government ministries would also be moved out into the bay and a new Diet Building constructed there! Estimated construction costs are ¥5.5 trillion.

Business cum cultural and recreational

already in progress is the metropolitan government's state-of-the-art Edo Tokyo Museum, scheduled to open in 1992, which will help bridge the historical knowledge gap among the residents.

Changes around Tokyo: Of course, development is proceeding at a feverish pace along areas of the bay in Chiba Prefecture to Tokyo's northeast and Yokohama to its south. In 1989, the huge Makuhari Messe convention complex, the largest in East Asia, opened its doors, and the Minato Mirai 21 (MM21) and other projects are giving a major facelift to the historic old port of Yokohama, which in recent years has grown

"mini-cities" are to be erected on a smaller scale in several other districts of Tokyo, including Ikebukuro, in Sumida Ward, Ebisu, Oimachi and major stops along the Yamanote loop line. All of this is part of the municipality's $100 billion urban renewal plan, known as "My Town Tokyo," to be dispersed in a fairly equal manner throughout the city's business and shopping districts.

If all goes as planned, then land prices for riverfront and bayfront property should become astronomical and *shitamachi* may see a true renaissance. One intriguing project

to have the second largest population of any community in Japan.

A one-million square meter "Telecom Island" in Chiba Prefecture will be the nerve center for a sophisticated communications network that will include fiber optic cable lines linking the onshore and offshore business neighborhoods of the city and telecommunications satellites. A proposal has also been made to build a 1,500-hectare international airport with a 6,000-meter runway off Yokohama, capable of handling supersonic aircraft or "space shuttles" and the "space planes" being developed by the Science and

Technology Agency for transport of cargo and passengers at over 27 times the speed of sound to and from space.

An intricate transportation grid of subways, highways and bridges spanning the bay is being created to tie all of these separate developments together. "Water buses," along the lines of New York's Staten Island Ferry, capable of carrying 500-2,000 passengers each are also to ply the waters between central Tokyo and the newly developed areas.

But the fact that the six-year construction of a 3.5 km suspension bridge, scheduled to be completed in 1992, and related highways

are already running 50% or more over budget due to several factors – most importantly because the softness of the ocean floor was grossly underestimated – does not augur well for the ambitious plans being laid for the bay.

Demographics: In 1945, Tokyo had only three million people; in 1985, it boasted of 11.1 million and leapfrogged New York in the resident population derby. Since then it has been overtaken by Mexico City, but most

Left, Shibuya shoppers create a sea of umbrellas. **Above**, the future is now.

demographers still count it as the largest urban unit conglomeration.

Whether Tokyo's population will totally stop growing in the near future, as some population experts predict, is very debatable. It seems more likely the inflow will continue, although at a diminished pace, once the promised new housing and amenities start becoming available. It should be noted in this regard that Tokyoites at present have a 22% higher income than the national average, but there is still a severe labor shortage, especially regarding young workers.

Perhaps the biggest problem Tokyo and Japan face are their rapidly aging populations and the need for new social services to care for the aged. By the year 2025, an estimated 31.5 million Japanese, or 23.4% of the entire population, will be 65 or older. The working population, an increasingly smaller proportion of the total population, will have to bear an ever greater burden to support those elders who achieved Japan's postwar economic miracle.

All indications are that many younger people in Japan are into "me-ism" and more interested in enjoying their wealth than sharing it. Will these so-called *shinjinrui* ("new human") really be willing to listen to "guidance from above" as their elders have?

Other industrialized nations, and even many of the developing nations will soon share the same problem of a "graying" population, although in less acute form. Perhaps Japan can show the way in finding solutions to this demographic challenge.

Whatever plans Tokyo adopts for its future, the eyes of the world will be upon it. In many ways, the city is the model for many countries of the developing world, since the type of migration it previously experienced from rural areas is similar to what they are now undergoing.

The United Nations Population Fund estimates that by the year 2025 there will be 90 cities in the world with a population of five million or more. Some 80 of these "new Tokyos" will be in the poorer countries. By the end of the next century, 75% of humankind are expected to be living in cities or huge urban conglomerations of which Tokyo might be considered the granddaddy.

If Rome is the Eternal City, then Tokyo well merits the title of the Impermanent City. Throughout its 400-year history, including the time prior to 1868 when it was called Edo, Tokyo has on innumerable occasions been mistreated by nature and man alike. Fires have cindered it. Earthquakes have slapped it flat. Wars have pockmarked it. Floods have inundated it. Yet after each disaster, this protean glutton for punishment has sprung back up in yet a different guise.

The lack of ancient architectural delights can also be attributed to a no-nonsnese, unsentimental approach to getting rid of the old. The city often seems an exercise in planned ephemerality. As a consequence, few outsiders really have any visceral affection for Tokyo. Only those who were born and raised in Tokyo or who have looked beyond the city's painted face to the tradition-imbued beauty which lies beneath really leave their hearts in Tokyo.

Bamboo, with its intertwined root structure, is in many ways similar to the Japanese social structure. From its roots come the tree's strength and ability to survive. Similarly, the tenacity of Japanese society today has evolved out of its feudal past –the welding of thousands of clans into an empire. Today, life in Tokyo is both a mirror of its past and the country's launching pad into the nation's future.

Much has been said and written about the "uniqueness" of the Japanese people both by "outsiders" and the Japanese themselves. Group orientation, growth motivation and government participation have most often been cited as factors in Japan's "economic miracle" story. A lot is to be said too about the power of positive thinking. Living by this principle – ignoring the negative aspects of things and people around them and locking on to what is positive – the Japanese are able to endure and plod on ahead.

Preceding pages, celebrating 'Coming of Age' at Meiji Shrine; the faithful endure ice water ablution at a Tokyo Shinto Shrine. Left, tattoo art. Above, picture-taking, a Japanese pastime.

While visiting Tokyo, one is immediately struck by the realities and apparent contradictions in lifestyles – a dilapidated old wooden structure straining to stand up alongside an ultra-modern glass facade. A kimono-clad woman peering into a fashionable boutique. Militaristically-uniformed students, absorbed in their textbooks on a crowded subway, sitting across from peers garbed in leathers and jeans. From the blue-suited businessman to the subservient wife to the tofu maker to the new career woman.

There is a continual bombardment of the language. Carved on old sign boards, a history is engraved in the wood. Paint fading on metal signs point to imminent renovation. Glittering of neon lights in the night displays the city's energy and intensity.

Such a portrait of a city's inhabitants would be hard to paint and stereotyping a disservice to its people and visitors. However, a closer look into lifestyles, historical undercurrents, and changing trends in society offers additional insight into one of the world's foremost and largest cities.

Approximately two kilometers east of the Imperial Palace in the Hongô district of Tokyo's Bunkyô Ward stands a red, double-doored wooden gate roofed with gray slate tiles. A low, amber-hued brick wall stretches northeast and southwest from the gate, hiding much of what lies beyond from the casual gaze of pedestrians and motorists on the busy thoroughfare that parallels the wall along its western side. The upper stories of a number of buildings, some obviously post-1945, others from previous decades, can just be glimpsed among the trees that line the inner edge of the wall.

The gate seems but another quaint reminder of the Japan of an earlier day and yet, it is a potent symbol in the Japanese psyche of the importance of education for personal and national success and of the central role of the nation's capital in that process. The gate is called Akamon (Red Gate), and it stands at the entrance of Japan's premier institution of higher education, Tokyo University.

Japanese social institutions in general, and schools in particular, are arranged hierarchically in terms of their ability to bestow economic and social status. No institution ranks higher in this regard than Tokyo University. Since its founding in 1877, Tokyo University has supplied most of the nation's political leaders and career bureaucrats as well as the largest number of presidents of companies listed on the Tokyo Stock Exchange. The awe with which the Akamon is regarded is illustrated in tales of ambitious *kimono*-clad mothers taking their six-year-olds to visit the gate before packing them off to their first day at school. The alleged purpose of such pilgrimages is to impress upon the youngster a concrete image of the goal of education.

Cultural values toward education: Whether or not such visits as those just described actually take place, there is no doubt that the Japanese people and their political and economic leaders are united in a consensus that education is essential for social cohesion, economic prosperity, and prestige in the international arena.

In common with the people of other nations, the Japanese believe that the goals of education are the acquisition of knowledge and vocational skills, and intellectual growth. But they also believe that schools should develop character, proper moral attitudes and personal habits. Among the latter, hard work, diligence and perseverance are considered particularly appropriate to success both in school and in later life.

The education system also focuses on developing such basic Japanese values as harmonious relations with others and the fundamental expression of self through membership in a limited number of social and vocational groups.

Parents and teachers are expected to work hand in hand with schools and teachers to develop such values. National, prefectural and local governments provide the leadership and resources. Schools and teachers are expected to give equal effort and support to every learner and above all to instill in each student a desire to learn, a disciplined approach to learning, and the belief that education is important.

Education is respected in Japan, and so are educators. University professors are rated third in terms of prestige behind members of the cabinet and prefectural governors in public perceptions of occupational status.

Historical background: The development of this national consensus with regard to education, and the values and goals it seeks to achieve, have their roots in Japanese history. In the sixth century, members of the Japanese ruling class visited China, and upon their return, introduced and adopted major elements of Chinese culture. These included

from the warrior clans who seized political control of the nation in the 12th century. A brief flirtation with European trading states in the 16th and 17th centuries provided an infusion of more pragmatic subjects including medicine, mathematics, and physical sciences.

With the rise of the Tokugawa clan to power in 1603, the pursuit of Western knowledge was strictly limited and controlled, and the study of Buddhist works declined in favor of an emphasis on Confucian ethics. Both actions were in part motivated by the difficulty the Tokugawas and their immediate predecessors had experi-

writing by means of Chinese ideographs, Buddhism and Confucianism, and a Chinese-style bureaucratic system of government. The latter, in particular, has influenced education in Japan in that it was based on the meritocratic selection of talented individuals, who would then be taught to read and write the *Analects* of Confucius and works related to Buddhism. Such bureaucrats were initially drawn from the aristocracy and later

Left, prestigious Tokyo University. **Above**, university students have a distinctive look.

enced in dealing with religiously motivated rivals for political power. Each warrior clan maintained a school for the education of its retainers, but the curriculum was basically Confucian with a smattering of Western sciences.

During the feudal period, education was also available to common people in *terakoya*. *"Tera"* is the Japanese word for temple and *"koya"* refers to a small room. These one-room temple schools offered the masses instruction in the written language and certain practical subjects such as the use of the abacus and elementary arithmetic.

Texts were similar to the Chinese classics used by the warriors. Many teachers, of course, were monks. However, masterless samurai eking out a living and retired merchants with time on their hands also served.

The success of the *terakoya* and clan schools pre-empted compulsory, universal education which was introduced in 1872. By that time approximately 43 percent of the boys and 15 percent of the girls had been schooled and could read by the age of fifteen.

With the overthrow of the Tokugawas and the restoration of the Imperial household to power in 1868, the government determined that universal education would be essential

to both modernization of the nation and securing it from "Balkinization" by the European powers and the United States.

In February 1869, only four months after the new government had officially designated Tokyo as the nation's capital, the government passed legislation informing the people that all children would be required to enter elementary school upon reaching the age of eight. This policy was officially enforced from 1872, and by the turn of the century, 98 percent of all elementary age school children were in school. This is the same ratio as at present and has resulted in

giving the Japanese the highest standard of literacy in the world.

The Tokugawa government had maintained three institutions for higher education of its most elite retainers: one for Confucian studies, one for general Western studies (natural science and mathematics), and one for medical studies. In 1869, these three schools were reorganized into a university with two schools: the *Higashi Kô*, or Eastern School, and the *Minami Kô*, or Southern School. In 1877, the two schools were unified as Tokyo Imperial University with four colleges: Medicine, Law, Literature, and Natural Sciences.

Modernization of the nation and its educational system was also carried out by means of a new open door policy, in which talented young men of all classes were to be sent abroad to study in Europe and the United States, and foreign scholars and advisors would be invited to Japan. Many of the young Japanese who traveled abroad under this program were responsible for later establishing such important national institutions as the Bank of Japan and the Supreme Court. Others went into private life establishing companies in various fields of business and private schools at all levels. The great majority of the latter were in Tokyo and contributed to enhancing its standard as the nation's center of education.

In 1890, the Meiji Emperor promulgated the Imperial Rescript on Education which was to provide a philosophical basis for education until the reforms carried out under the Allied occupation in 1946. The rescript extolled Confucian virtues and exhorted the people to "pursue learning and cultivate arts, and thereby develop intellectual faculties and perfect moral powers."

Under the impetus of the imperial rescript, education continued to modernize. By 1918, when the University Law was enacted, 95 percent of the population had four or more years of education. By 1937, there were 45 public universities, the majority of which were in Tokyo. These included Tokyo Imperial University, Hitotsubashi (Tokyo Commercial University), Keiô, Waseda, Meiji, Nihon, Senshû, Hôsei, Rikkyô, Sophia, Aoyama Gakuin, Chûo and Meiji Gakuin

Universities. All but the first two are private institutions.

When the military seized effective control of the national government in the 1930's, they also took control of the nation's education system and turned it into a machine for instilling patriotic fervor in the populace. Military officers were actually assigned to schools down to the junior high school level. Ostensibly, they were physical education instructors, but their roles also included political indoctrination.

The allied victory in 1945 brought about not only the military occupation of Japan, but a total reformation of the educational system. The new model was essentially American in form. There was a 6-3-3 system of six years of elementary school, three years of junior high school, and three years of high school. The first nine years were to be compulsory education. Subject matter also reflected the content normal in American schools. There was also an effort to decentralize the administration of education, which had been under the control of the central government since 1872, by instituting a system of locally elected school boards.

Many of these reforms remain in effect today, but many were modified after Japan was restored to full sovereignty in 1952. Local school boards, for example, are now appointed and the central government through the Ministry of Education, Science and Culture still exerts a major influence on the educational system as a whole.

Besides being the center for formal education, Tokyo is also Japan's center for culture. The Kanze Noh Theater, the Kabukiza and the Kokugikan Sumo Arena are all part of the Tokyo scene. (Interestingly, the Sumo Association falls under the auspices of the Ministry of Education.)

Problems and issues: The concentration of so much of the nation's educational and cultural resources in Tokyo has its problems. Population growth is one. In fact, both the Ministry of Education and the Metropolitan Board of Education have severely restricted

the expansion of schools within the metropolitan district and even encouraged the dispersal of presently established institutions (schools and research facilities) to outlying areas.

Entrance to higher education is determined by examinations which, in principle, are administered by the individual faculties of each institution. The more prestigious a school is, the greater the number of applicants seeking admission and the more difficult the examination screening applicants. During the examination season from late January to mid-March in Tokyo nearly 2 million young men amd women sit for the

examinations to the most prestigious schools.

The excessive emphasis on entrance examinations is a cause of much national concern and debate in public forums. Reforms are being considered. The rigidity of certain facets of the formal education system and the alienation of increasing numbers of young people, along with increased awareness of violence in the schools and bullying of some pupils, are also concerns. Still, the Japanese have in less than a century produced an educational system that is the envy of many nations, and Tokyo is its showpiece.

Far left, studying at home. <u>Above</u>, elementary school girls stop for a quick bite.

"Ohayô gozaimasu," ("Good Morning") little brother's voice bellows out as the work day begins.

Replying in unison, "Good Morning," the section echoes back in similar, near militaristic, Japanese.

"Does anyone have anything they wish to report?"

Silence.

No, this is not the Japanese SDF (Self Defense Forces), but the beginning of each work day at a "typical" and rather conservative Japanese company.

The leader then repeats the company's motto for this particular year: for example, "Anticipate the needs of today and tomorrow. Seek out new fields, products, and commodities. Create better lines of communication and understanding."

Next, the morning leader (more like a youthful pep-squader than a drill sergeant) gives the "Simon-says" commands for exercises. Although it's not aerobics, the office workout does get the circulation moving, blurry eyes begin to open and last night's *sake* directed away from the brain to less essential parts of the body.

Regimentation, employee loyalty, and various facets of management in Japanese companies have been cited as reasons for Japan's "economic miracle."

The big names – nearly all headquartered in Tokyo – that seem to dominate the automotive and electronic industries are now known worldwide. There are thousands of companies that supply parts and machinery so that goods can arrive wholly in the marketplace for eager consumers.

Work hours? *Salaryman*, a name given to describe most of Tokyo's male workforce, punch in to work at around 9 a.m. and leave the office at 7 p.m. or much later.

Company benefits? Most often cited is job security. An employee typically remains with (or is retained by) the company for life. Semi-annual bonus times, usually two-to four-months salary, in lieu of higher monthly wages also add incentive to remain

with the company from bonus period to bonus period. And importantly, there is comradery. After-hours drinking with co-workers and quasi-optional company trips serve to reinforce company loyalty.

Workaholics: In the face of international criticism of the Japanese tendency to overwork, the government has been pushing a campaign in the past few years for shorter working hours. Japanese workers put in about 500 more hours a year than do their counterparts in West Germany and France, and about 200 more hours than those in the U.S. and Britain. The Japanese on average use only half their paid vacation of 15 days a year.

Experts note that many Japanese are preoccupied with the idea that hard work is a virtue and give only lukewarm support to the campaign for reducing work hours. Some workers feel a little guilty about taking time off. Others fear that if they take more than a week off at a stretch, they will lose touch with the company and fall behind their rivals in office politics.

Another reason cited as to why the Japanese are reluctant to take vacations is the fear that their absence could cause trouble for their co-workers, or would create a heavy backlog of work when they return. There is also widespread fear that taking too many vacations could ruin a worker's chances of career advancement.

However, working so hard may have a price. In a recent Labor Ministry survey, one out of five salaried workers in Japan suffers from stress or stomach trouble and over half do not get enough rest, even though 80 percent of them think they are in good health.

Many Japanese baby-boomers, now middle-aged, face a series of domestic and workshop problems. With housing and other living costs to deal with, mixed in with domestic squabbles, some gents develop physical and psychological disturbances. Attention is growing on the amazing number of Japanese office workers in middle age suffering from various syndromes, including sexual impotence.

Work never killed anybody? Cases like the 32-year-old Chiba man who suddenly collapsed while working and died five days later have generated a growing concern among the Japanese. The man, in the one month that elapsed between starting the job and his collapse, was said to have put in 129 hours of overtime.

The Japanese have given a name to such kind of deaths – *karoshi,* or death from overwork.

While some *karoshi* victims were in their late 20s, the chances of being stricken rise sharply with each decade, peaking in the 40s

making workers reexamine their "selfless devotion."

Modern office buildings, with their sterile and brightly lit offices, tend to drain employees' energy. Stress has become a big social topic, and there are companies looking into ways of providing better work environments for reducing stress. Other companies are taking steps to keep their employees happy and productive. Various plans include mandatory days off – workers should not come to the office on days off, company retreats and lodges in the countryside. One company in Tokyo, Kajima Construction has experimented with "acromapology" – systemati-

and 50s. A prime *karoshi* candidate is a middle-aged male who is in the habit of working overtime and coming to work on days off.

Statistics on deaths from overwork do not exist, and any figures are dubious since it is difficult to determine the exact role overwork plays in causing sudden death. However, *karoshi* is not new, and the recent reports are causing public concern and

Above, exchanging wealth is the name of the game.

cally piping in fragrances to enhance productivity and reduce stress at its head office.

With Japan enjoying continued business expansion, workers will be required to put in more overtime as companies try to meet surging demand for goods and services. As long as Japanese workers feel stressed out and overworked, many will continue to face "dangers" on the job – *karoshi* as well as other physical and mental disorders. And, with the topic of overwork receiving more and more attention, companies and the government will have to address the issue to alleviate public concern.

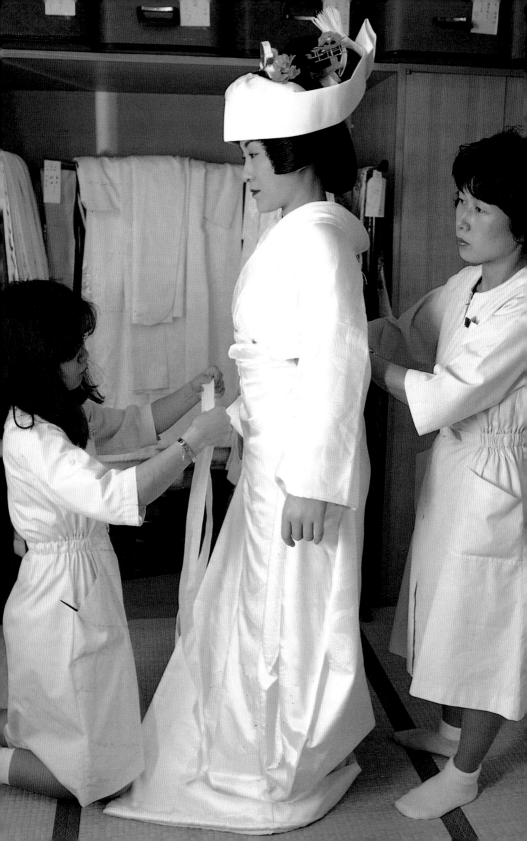

In pre-World War II Japan, a young man often got married about the time his parents reminded him that he had reached the *tekireiki,* or appropriate marriageable age. His parents took an active role in the selection of his bride, making sure she bore the markings of a good wife, wise mother, and self-sacrificing daughter-in-law.

Love rarely entered the picture. Parents knew that the couple would eventually become fond of each other. Who knows? They might even become good friends.

The majority of families in those prewar years worked on farms or operated businesses. Parents wanted a woman capable of working side by side with her husband – and still have energy enough to take care of her family.

Once married, the husband exercised authoritative control over family members and made sure that they conformed to the overall good of the family.

Individual family members hardly ever exerted private opinions or pursued personal goals that might anger him. To do so would have meant possible expulsion from the family, which was tantamount to ostracism from the society.

The wife, having severed the ties to her own family through marriage, adhered to the customs and practices of her husband's family. Throughout her upbringing and education, she was told that a woman found her greatest fulfillment in marriage. She was also told in so many words not to expect a rose garden.

Her day began before the other family members woke up when she prepared the breakfasts for her husband, children, and her husband's parents. During the day, she performed the productive activities connected with the farm or family business. Her day ended after the other family members snuggled under the *futon* covers.

Left, preparing to tie the knot. Above, after the ceremony, a change into Western dress.

The mother-in-law frequently added to the wife's burdens by complaining about her shortcomings as a housewife and mother. The wife made every effort to eliminate her "faults," though she usually despaired of ever satisfying her captious mother-in-law.

When the mother-in-law grew feeble, the wife became her caretaker. For help she could rely on other family members, and sometimes on neighbors. But the society placed the main burden squarely on her

shoulders.

Despite the hardships, the wife generally chose to stay married.

To divorce meant she had to face the censure of her own family and of the community. They almost always blamed her for the marital breakup. "You should have tried harder. After all, you owed so much to your husband."

A marriage of unequal partners: In many marriages today, the husband still maintains a higher status and exercises greater authority in the family by virtue of being the sole provider. He shows little inclination in helping around the house. Once in a while he may help to take care of the children. Basically, however, he feels that child rearing falls within the realm of motherhood.

The wife follows a similar pattern her grandmother followed in the prewar years. Getting up earlier than her husband and children, she prepares the breakfasts and makes sure everyone gets off to work or school on time.

During the day, she does the housework, goes shopping, and manages the daily household accounts. Occasionally, she takes part in activities of the neighborhood association or of her children's school. She may

the weekends or when he appears less drained.

Among the family matters that often touch off heated discussion is the wife's desire to work part-time. Conservative husbands oppose, stating that they earn enough to support the family. "Besides, what would the others think?"

His parents also express disapproval. "The children need a mother who stays home to take care of them. If money is a problem, we are willing to help out."

The wife, in the face of family opposition, gives up her desire to work. However, she keeps her resentment toward his parents'

also enjoy leisure activities such as learning a foreign language or attending aerobics classes.

At night, she and the children will eat together since her husband comes home much later in the evening. Upon his return, she will serve him his dinner and sit with him while he eats.

Sometimes his utterances at the dinner table are reduced to functional commands delivered with the force of a feudal lord: "More rice." "More tea."

The wife knows better than to discuss family matters at those times. She waits until

interference to herself, particularly if his parents provide them with financial assistance to pay for extraordinary expenses.

Like her grandmother, she feels obligated to show appreciation to the family through acquiescence and service. Unlike her grandmother, she is more willing to regain control over her own life by getting a divorce.

According to the Ministry of Health and Welfare in 1988, 154,000 Japanese couples received their final decrees of divorce. Although comparatively low, the figure reflects the growing desire of spouses to exert personal aspirations and concerns over those of the family.

Some wives file when their husbands retire from their jobs. They feel they are entitled to retire too. As part of their divorce settlement, they demand half of the husband's severance pay.

You've come a long way, baby: Today, the modern Japanese woman wants more out of marriage than just financial security. Postwar political and social reforms, a booming economy, and demographic factors have given her choices that go beyond the imagination of her grandmother.

Foremost, she wants a man not bound to his parents. She avoids forming relationships to elder sons, knowing that she might end up having to live with and eventually to take care of his mother.

After marriage, she prefers living as near as possible to her own parents. Her relationship to her parents is close, much like those of good friends. In addition, should her parents live under the same roof, her husband usually gets along well with them partly because he spends most of his day at work.

Increasingly, she is demanding to be allowed to work after marriage and after giving birth to children – a remarkable transformation of attitudes.

Under the old family system, couples married to perpetuate the family by giving birth preferably to sons. The mother devoted much of her life to rearing the children, making sacrifices so that they grew into productive offspring.

This pattern carried over into the postwar years when the mother assumed greater influence in the family. As the father worked longer hours, the mother devoted more time to the children. Her active interest in their formal education gave rise to the phenomenon of *kyôiku mama* or "education mama." The mother's success was measured by the university her children graduated from and the company they joined. The crowning achievement came when the children got married.

Young men and women today want the best for their children as well. However, they tend to place greater priority on personal goals and therefore are postponing marriage. The average age of one's first marriage in Japan is 26 for women and 29 for men, compared to 22 for American women and 25 for American men.

Toward a more equal relationship: Today, the decline in the birthrate, the aging of the population, and economic expansion have contributed to a dramatic increase of opportunities for women to work part-time and full-time.

Housewives take advantage of part-time work to help pay for the high cost of living.

The education of one child can cost as much as US$538 a month and a sack of potatoes nearly as much as a bottle of beer at a five-star hotel bar.

As Japan approaches the 21st century, the family will undergo further transformation, due in large part to the changes in attitudes of the wives. No longer just the wife and mother, and at times the self-sacrificing daughter-in-law, the wife today represents the growing number of women who want others to recognize their individuality. She expects to have a relationship with her husband that is based on equality.

Left, contemplating the future? **Above**, emphasis on the family is beginning to take hold.

It used to be that a woman with career plans in Tokyo was limited to a choice between the government bureaucracy, joining a foreign firm, or establishing a business of her own. She was rarely considered management material in the eyes of the big domestic corporations.

For years Japanese companies put new employees on one of two tracks, regardless of their education and qualifications.

The managerial track led to decision-making responsibility and was largely reserved for men. The clerical track, which led nowhere at all beyond learning telephone manner (soft and high voices preferred) and salutations (a 30-degree forward bow for most people, a 45-degree bow for special guests and executives), was the one reserved for women.

Slowly but surely, however, and from causes more economical than ideological, a growing labor shortage and a new wave of women with aspirations stretching far beyond their traditionally limited roles have made the training and utilization of woman power a major corporate issue.

Some 95 percent of Tokyo's women have been through high school, and 36 percent hold junior college or four-year college degrees. But until the late 1980s, the vast majority of these highly qualified graduates did not want careers, and they had their reasons.

For one thing, they saw little to envy in the working lives of the men. Consider: the average male white-collar worker is usually at his desk until well into the evening. From there, if he is not making the long train journey back to an area of affordable housing outside the city, he will often move on to a local watering hole either to continue a policy discussion started in the office several hours earlier or to entertain one of his company's clients. More than a few of his

weekends will be taken from him in the same way, and it is unlikely that he will take more than a week's vacation during the year.

Purchasing power: Office ladies (or OLs as they are affectionately known), on the other hand, suffer no such constraints. Even if they are denied access to marketing and operations involvement, they are still free to leave when the bell sounds at five o'clock, to do as they please with an income that is almost 100 percent disposable. (Most of Tokyo's single

girls work full-time and live rent-free with their parents.)

In fact, the pre-marriage set do so much shopping and international traveling that they have now become the country's most conspicuous consumers.

Another point: the power of tradition. Until recently, for many women the post-school stages towards full maturity were clearly set out and perfectly acceptable. One was marriage, the other was raising a family. Both were enough to stop most women from making plans for life after 30.

They still are. Nevertheless, the number of

Left, the modern-day woman has new-form freedom. **Above**, traditionally, a woman's role work was to please the man.

women subscribing to the standard pattern of a brief period of employment, followed by several years of full-time devotion to a home and children, followed by a return to the job market as a part-time or temporary worker is declining.

Oddly, a shared sense of outrage at common injustice has not been one of the major impetuses for change, even though, to many, the injustice has long been plain to see: a wage system based upon seniority and life-time employment (the one still adhered to by most corporations) forces women to re-enter the job market as poorly paid part-timers with few rights after their careers have been

interrupted by marriage; the government's annually declining childcare budget puts unfair pressure on working mothers who have to pay ever-higher fees for day nurseries; and in spite of the equal employment opportunity law passed in 1986, many companies still discourage women from joining the managerial career track because the law carries no provisions for penalties.

Terms of equality: The new law, whatever its shortcomings and whatever its dependence on the country's healthy economic climate, is still the factor largely responsible for the new numbers of women insisting on their

rights to be trained as managers. Passed in the wake of the United Nations Decade of Women observed from 1975 to 1985, the law was the first legislation to back up the equal opportunity clause built into the country's post-World War II constitution. Effectively, it has stopped companies from saying they will not hire women. Another factor behind the change has been the steadily growing labor shortage, which has accompanied government moves to strengthen the domestic economy, especially in the construction and high-tech industries.

With the arrival of new wealth and larger numbers of glamorous job opportunities in the capital, the appeal of ordinary manual labor has sunk so low that many construction companies are unable to recruit the workers they need. Out of sheer desperation they have been taking on women, who are now visible on construction sites.

Computer and new telecommunications companies are also favorite hunting grounds for the new Tokyo woman. With their reliance on sensitivity to shifts in consumer demand and new technological developments, these companies have less time to worry about traditional recruitment standards in their search for new operations and service personnel.

The most popular employers among management-minded women are those known to treat men and women equally, and it is no coincidence that the majority of the league leaders are firms like IBM Japan, NEC and Nippon Telegraph and Telephone, all operating in the high-tech sector.

Now that they have made the important first step across the corporate threshold, women are making their presence felt in ways inconceivable just a few years ago, even within the more conservative industries: car makers have had numerous success.

The effects of promotion by seniority have still to make themselves shown, of course, but one thing is certain: growing numbers of women managers and business leaders are guaranteed in the 1990s and beyond.

Above, women are now common on construction sites. **Right**, thinking about equality?

In Japan *gaijin* are a very special breed. Less than 10 years ago, we are told by old Japan hands, they were such a rare sight that when elementary school kids caught sight of them they would shout, *"Gaijin da!"* (Look, it's a *gaijin!*)

These rare and wonderful beings are usually tall (less so these days), have blue eyes (except those with brown), blonde hair (but for those with brown or black) and long noses (in Japanese, "high noses"). Yes, maybe you've guessed it, *gaijin* are foreigners. The name is particularly applied to the round-eyed, pinkish-skinned variety, and literally means, "outside person."

Other varieties may be referred to by color – *kokujin* for black person, or by nationality – *Indojin* means Indian.

While blacks may have a novelty appeal for some Japanese, and Pakistanis and other Southeast Asians are a useful, if often illegal, addition to the manual labor work force, it is the *gaijin* proper (or improper!) who still capture the imagination of the Japanese.

Gaijin, in the shape of Portuguese traders, first landed on the shores of Nippon in the 16th century. They were followed shortly after by peddlers of a different sort – the priests.

The Christian religion was seen as such a threat to the order of Japan that it was eventually banned, and horrific punishments, including crucifixion, were used to discourage adherents. Perhaps that is why even today, despite hundreds of years of missionary zeal, there are only about a million Christians in Japan.

This brings us to one of the types of *gaijin* to be found in modern Japan – the Mormon missionary. Sometimes you will spot a pair of smartly dressed college types approaching young Japanese whom they will address earnestly in good Japanese. They will thrust a pamphlet at their prey and the hapless

victim, usually caught coming out of the station, is torn between polite evasion or outright flight.

Perhaps the most common variety to be found in Tokyo – and elsewhere in Japan for that matter – is the Less-Than-Well-Paid English Conversation Teacher.

Fairly easy to spot with his dowdy plumage, this type wears ill-fitting jackets with trousers that don't match – the result of department store shopping. The top button

of the shirt is invariably undone due to the endless talking they have done to their serried ranks of silent students. They wear a haunted look at the thought of the next class they will shortly have to teach.

When approached by Japanese on the train, they begin to twitch at the thought of having to talk in English for free. Running shoes are worn to give the teaching *gaijin* the speed needed to get from one class to another near train stations all over Tokyo. Their shoulder bags are stuffed with English textbooks of the 'Required Reading' variety, but they read trashy novels on the trains.

Left, *Gaijin* – still a rare breed and something to stare at. **Above,** the foreign executive likes to mingle.

Undoubtedly one of the best perches for catching sight of *gaijin,* sometimes hordes of them, is the Hibiya line. This is the gray subway line which passes through such favorite watering holes as the Ginza, Roppongi, and Hiroo (which is also a favored habitat for the richer type of *gaijin*).

A prosperous, if short-stay, type of *gaijin* is The Model, with its sub-group, The Showgirl or The Dancer. This variety is almost exclusively female, although a small number of males do exist. Tall and skinny – to the point of being skeletal, they stand out. It should be pointed out here that The Showgirl is often more curvaceous. Usually blondes,

line holding their portfolio of latest photographs, to the undisguised amazement of the locals.

The best-fed variety of all these outside creatures is The Top Executive Businessman. Some have been imported directly from *gaikoku* (outside countries – this usually means the USA). Salaries can be as much as a million dollars for a three-year contract.

There is an interesting subgroup, however, of former English teachers who, having done time in Japan and learned the ropes, have gone away and returned in borrowed plumage passing themselves off as real busi-

they suffer from pallid skins and grumpy faces and engage in loud conversations in English on the trains.

The content of these conversations often revolves around how much work they are doing and how much they are getting paid. They show little interest in their host habitat and migrate back to their native areas when their bank accounts are full and return only when they are empty.

Fresh migrations of these exotic beasts are constantly arriving on these shores and dressed in the latest fashions – expensively tailored coal sacks – they stalk the Hibiya

nessmen.

This subgroup can do extremely well as they can exploit the system in Japan that they know so well – usually they can handle the Japanese language, and they can also appear to be fresh to Japan which is a vital asset.

Sometimes this variety can be seen on the trains although they favor the more expensive and generally slower taxis, thereby flaunting their expense account status and avoiding contact with lesser breeds. They are expensively suited and groomed and carry copies of *The Financial Times* or *The Wall Street Journal. The Japan Times* is also permitted. Generally, briefcases are shunned, but if necessary the *gaijin* exec will sometimes stoop to carrying a slim Gucci attaché case.

A slight paunch, usually disguised by clever tailoring, betrays overindulgence of the business lunch. The more motivated of the species indulge in various forms of Japanese cultural study, such as calligraphy, the martial arts or *haiku* poetry with little effect.

The student variety of *gaijin* is welcomed by most Japanese, partly out of a Confucian belief in the value of study per se and partly out of pride in their own culture which the Japanese secretly believe is the best in the world, which after all is what we all believe about our own cultures.

Student *gaijin* can be divided into two subgroups: a) The Real Thing and b) The Bogus.

The Real Thing is not very interesting as it spends all day with its nose in books on its speciality and all night in earnest conversation with fellow students in elegant Japanese.

Of far more interest is The Bogus variety, which can be anything from a Chinese cook to a Filipino bar hostess. This spends all day or all night in pursuit of its various callings and, of course, the invaluable yen.

The Bar Hostess, rich in provocative plumage, is a sight to behold. Lavishly made-up and scantily clad in tight silk, this feminine variety spends most of its time in trains (early evening) or taxis (early morning) repairing its makeup before venturing into the night on 6-inch heels. On days off she can usually be discovered in department stores in groups of two or three buying unnecessary items of clothing and accompanied by a shady-looking minder.

The Pakistani construction worker does not have a very high profile, particularly in Tokyo. He, almost exclusively male, lives in barrack-like accommodations provided by his employer or in tiny crowded apartments. His lot is clearly the least secure and least well paid of all the foreigners in Japan and as

Far left, an English teacher and his student talk things over. **Above**, foreign models are natural eye-catchers.

observed before, is not referred to by the sobriquet *"gaijin."*

What the native Japanese think of these invading species is anyone's guess, but a spot check reveals that opinions vary wildly; that is, most Japanese are wild about or with *gaijin* according to their experiences and viewpoint.

There are those, a minority, who are *gaijin*ophiles. Some members of this species are so besotted that they hang around the bases at Camp Zama.

The Sanno, the U.S. forces hotel in Hiroo, is also a place where upright military *gaijin* can be found with their Japanese admirers.

Military *gaijin*, by the way, are easy to spot because of their ill-fitting civilian clothes and their cruel crewcuts. They also tend to be about seven feet tall and built like prize fighters.

Back in the days of Shogun Tokugawa, foreigners were confined to a small island off Nagasaki called Dejima – literally "exit island." Today foreigners are kept in a kind of psychological *Dejima* and are allowed into restricted areas of Japanese life. No doubt some Japanese *gaijin* watchers would like to see the real *Dejima* back, and who can blame them?

Most people are familiar with Franglais, which is that mixture of French-type English spoken by English speakers who cannot manage the real thing such as – *"Voulez-vous un strawberry?"* More seriously English has crept into French with the use of such phrases as *"le weekend"* and *"le parking,"* and the Academie Française, the guardian of pure French, is much displeased. So much so that it has come up with alternatives which, of course, are artificial and nobody uses.

Now, Needs is you.

Japan's reaction to the influx of thousands of English words and phrases has been somewhat different. This English has become so absorbed into Japanese that it cannot usually be recognized by the uninitiated outsider. There are two reasons for this. Foreign words are usually written in a script of Japanese called *katakana,* so unless you know *katakana* you won't even be able to read it. Another reason is that Japanese people normally pronounce foreign words using *katakana* which is totally based on the pronunciation of Japanese. So, even if you hear this English, the odds are that you still

won't be able to understand it. Take for example the word "inflation," which has been shortened in Japanese (another favorite ploy which confuses those who think they know English when they see or hear it) to "inflay." Well, you could make a fair guess at the original meaning from that way of writing it, but if it is put into Japanese pronunciation, *(infuray)* how would you do? Not too well, eh?

Sophisticated Japanese who wish to show how international they are pepper their conversation with such phrases as "trouble" *(toraburu)* and "travel" *(toraberu)* – spot the difference? Japanese have great trouble distinguishing the "u" and "a" and "b" and "v" sounds, thus confusions abound. This is not the only problem. More and more complicated phrases are entering the language daily so that uninitiated Japanese find they can't even understand their own language.

Older people, for example, often cannot understand words like "director" *(direkutaa)* or "producer" *(purodyusaa)* which regularly appear on their television screens. A current example of a recently introduced phrase is "sexual harassment" *(sekuhara),* which has been much in the news lately, but which is hardly likely to mean anything to your average granny living in her little apartment in, say, the undistinguished Tokyo suburb of Magome.

Some Japanese language experts have been demanding the replacement of these terms with Japanese equivalents, not, as in France, to maintain the purity of the language, but simply to make sure that everyone knows what they are talking about and can understand each other. It is unlikely though that many of the ten thousand or so established foreign words or terms will fall out of usage, such as *arubaito,* meaning temporary employment from the German *arbeit,* which means work, or *paruto,* from the English "part-timer," or *waapuro,* from "word-processor."

There is a difference between this kind of English, which has effectively become Japanese and is part of the everyday currency of communication for many Japanese, and the attempts of Japanese to use English to communicate with foreigners or in advertising campaigns to appear international.

This other kind of English is more noticeable to foreigners illiterate in Japanese because it is written in Roman script or is directly spoken to foreigners. One example would be the dubious statement, *"I rub you"* which is probably meant to mean "I love

One of the more fruitful amusements for the visitor in Tokyo who has nothing better to do is to read the messages on T-shirts and bomber jackets. You are advised not to stare too long or laugh out loud as this will confirm in the minds of the surrounding Japanese that all foreigners are perverts or crazy or both.

In Japan, anyone who comes from the city is considered sophisticated and smart, as is anything written in a foreign language. So imagine the pride with which one young man

you." Either way the statement might excite or repulse you depending on who says it. The Japanese are famous for their difficulties with "l" and "r." During the American occupation under Supreme General MacArthur, Tokyoites wanted to show their support for the good general in his possible candidacy in an upcoming election for the presidency. A huge banner was strung across a street in central Tokyo which read: *"We play for MacArthur's erection."*

Far left and Above, they call it English, but what does it mean?

was wearing a T-shirt emblazoned with the legend: *"Shity Boy."* Who would have the heart to tell him and would he get it if they did? Similarly a teenage girl more than usually endowed was wearing a T-shirt with these words strategically stenciled on her ample bosom: *"Let's Flesh Milk!"* Let's indeed. On the back of a bomber jacket worn by a student was the message: *"University of Meiji Tennis Stuff."* Since Meiji is the name of an era in Japanese history, and not a place it should read "Meiji University Tennis Staff," but for all anyone knows about the quality of their tennis, *"stuff"* might be just the right word.

The spoken language also has many pitfalls, as when you are invited to: *"Preez shit"* for "Please sit."

One conversation went like this:

Japanese teacher: You like Japanese *basu?*

Foreigner: (Thinks) Ah! Japanese buses. Yes, very efficient.

J.T.: No *basu*, (agitated now) *basu*!

Foreigner: (Thinks again) Oh, baths. Very much.

J.T.: (Relieved) *Sankyou.*

When Mrs. Thatcher came on a visit to Japan some years ago, she was invited to an

This kind of Japanized English has been variously described as "Janglish," "Jinglish," and even "English as she is Japped," by Professor Basil Hall Chamberlain at the turn of the century; apparently, it was going on even then. But, the term which appears to have won through is "Japlish."

You might ask why after so many years of exposure to English the Japanese haven't made a better job of it. Part of the answer is education, where the system is more geared to getting highschoolers through the infamous university entrance exams than getting them to speak and understand the language, and partly it is to do with the fact that most

interview on NHK television, the equivalent of the BBC, to answer questions put to her in English by a panel of distinguished Japanese professors. One professor's pronunciation was so poor that the Iron Lady was having a hard time following him. At one point, he went completely beyond the bounds of comprehension and said: "Mrs. *Satchaa*, you are *berry* famous for *Satchaaism.*" Mrs. T. thought he said "socialism" and got very angry. Actually he meant "Thatcherism," and the professor was clearly aghast and deeply embarrassed by the ire he aroused quite innocently by his Japanese English.

Japanese still do not see English as vital to their lives, unlike the rest of Southeast Asia. But English is becoming rather passé, and the trendsetters are turning to French as the new fashionable language for Tokyo sophisticates.

Does this mean we might end up with "Nipponaise," "Japlaise," or even, heaven forfend, "Frapanese?" Now that would give the Académie Française something to get upset about, wouldn't it?

Above, with burst heads and bad threads, what's all the hype about Japanese products?

THE NIHONGO TANGO

Stepping off the plane at the New Tokyo International Airport at Narita, a recent first-time visitor to Japan commented that his first impression was that he had suddenly become completely illiterate. He was faced with waves of Chinese characters (*kanji*) phonetic scripts (*hiragana* and *katakana)* and Roman characters (*romaji*). Being an international airport, there were, of course, enough signs with English explanations that he successfully navigated himself onto a bus to Shinjuku. In Tokyo, however, most areas have signs only in Japanese. Railway stations will have some names and directions in English, but a traveler should not count on surviving with only English. By far, the greatest hurdle for the newcomer is *kanji*. These characters have a great effect on foreigners in Japan who do not have one or two years of their lives to devote to memorizing Chinese characters. Many foreigners achieve proficiency in spoken Japanese; few ever learn enough *kanji* to read a newspaper.

For the temporary resident or visitor to Tokyo learning the most important characters will be enough. Guidebooks which provide English transliterations next to the *kanji* original, such as *Tokyo Transit Guide,* are very helpful as are basic Japanese reading books. *Read Japanese Today* by Carles E. Tuttle Company is particularly helpful and easily available. However, the traveler

Above, trying to make heads or tails out of *kanji*.

should count on learning some basic *kanji*.

Communicating in Japanese: Besides difficulties posed by the written language, there are some considerations to keep in mind when attempting to communicate orally. First, English speakers will not find the similarities in grammar and vocabulary which have helped so many in tackling Romance languages. Secondly, the growing number of words borrowed from English and which are increasingly being used in lieu of the native Japanese word, offer little help. For example, *erebeitaa* (elevator), *bôifurendo* (boyfriend) and *apaato* (apartment). Despite these obvious differences, daily conversation in Japanese is not difficult to pick up. Simple daily activities, such as finding the correct train platform, buying movie tickets, and answering questions about your background ("Where are you from?"), can be done in Japanese after only a little study.

Cultural considerations, however, can interfere with communication to a far greater extent than any strictly linguistic factors. Japanese who usually face life with aplomb may suddenly become prone to stammering, fits of sweating, or nervous twitching. They are not adventurous types who seek out encounters with foreign ideas, foods, or people. On the streets of Tokyo, natives, at times, seem to run away in reply to or wave the visitor away with their hands and say *"Wakarimasen"* ("I don't understand") even when the questioner is speaking comprehensible Japanese. At other times, a question posed may receive a response in clear comprehensible English. Often though, it will solicit a response in which the Japanese person will try out his/her best English.

Most of Tokyo's top-class hotels are grouped in or nearby the city's main shopping and business districts of Akasaka, Ginza and Roppongi, with little to choose between them other than the convenience of their respective locations – the facilities, service and cuisine of the famous names are all of international standard. The single most attractive feature of the medium-range hotels, on the other hand, is their cost: almost all of them have been built within the last 20 years, and in architectural terms they are more or less identical.

Overlapping with this category are the so-called Business Hotels, which offer basic accommodation (they have very few twin or double rooms) also at lower prices. Business Hotels usually have communications facilities like facsimile, telex and modem machines, but do not always have porters, room services or restaurants. They often give special discount rates for weekly or monthly bookings.

Another hotel area, although a short distance from the city, is the Maihama-Tokyo Bay Resort City where the emphasis in on relaxation. Nearby Tokyo Disneyland, there are several international hotels located on waterfront property.

Offering a glimpse of the old Tokyo and the traditional hospitality of its neighborhood inns, there are still a few family-run *ryokan* in accessible parts of the city which are worth experiencing if your schedule does not allow for a visit to one of the hot spring hostelries outside. If you do try one, remember there are certain rules of etiquette to be observed. On entering, you should leave your shoes at the door and change into the slippers provided for you. Remove the slippers before you step onto the straw *tatami* flooring in the room or in the dining hall. You will usually be served green tea on arrival and will later find your *futon* bedding laid out

on the floor for you, along with a *yukata* robe to relax in after a bath, which you can wear in and outside the room.

In a category all their own are the Capsule Hotels. These cater almost exclusively to office workers who either because of overwork or over-consumption have missed their last train home, even to the point of renting freshly pressed suits and shirts to guests who might otherwise not pass muster the morning after. Surprisingly comfortable and well

equipped (many of them have saunas and small workout rooms), they are only of novelty interest to foreign visitors.

Luxury Class: The first Western-style hotel built in Japan, the original Imperial Hotel was designed by the venerable American architect Frank Lloyd Wright. One of the city's finest, and a premier conference venue, the new Imperial is within ten minutes' walk of the restaurants, bars and up-market shopping avenues of the famous Ginza district. There are also a number of exclusive boutiques and restaurants in the basement plaza of the hotel. In the same

Preceding pages, chefs take their culinary skills seriously. **Left**, traditional accommodation at a *ryokan*. **Above**, Akasaka Prince Hotel.

league, and almost certainly the city's best-known deluxe hotel, is the Hotel Okura. The Okura is at the center of the Akasaka business district and has long been the first choice of visiting VIPs and foreign dignitaries. It is conveniently located next door to the American embassy.

In the process of transforming itself into a self-contained urban sub-center (with its new Garden Court business tower), the vast accommodation and shopping complex of the Hotel New Otani is built around an elegant 400 year-old garden that once formed part of the feudal *samurai* domain of the Katô clan. There is a wide range of shops, restaurants, bars, sports facilities and a pool on the premises, including the only Japanese franchise of the exclusive Paris restaurant, the Tour d'Argent. The hotel is ten minutes from Ginza by subway and a few minutes' walk from the center of Akasaka.

The Akasaka Prince Hotel directly across the street is an ultra-modern 40-story tower designed by Olympic stadium architect Kenzô Tange to allow each room its own corner and an impressive view of the city – especially at night. The hotel has 12 restaurants and lounges, an executive business center and extensive meeting and banquet facilities, and, like its neighbor, prides itself on the history and scope of its landscaped gardens.

The Tokyo Hilton International in Shinjuku includes all the facilities one would expect of a Hilton chain member, among them a business center, pool, gymnasium, sauna, and numerous bars and restaurants. Although not a business and administration district of the same standing as Ginza and Akasaka, Shinjuku is set to become an important metropolitan center. This is the only area in Tokyo stable enough for the construction of skyscraper-height buildings and is the site of the new government headquarters scheduled for completion in 1991. The hotel is within a few minutes' walk of the area's shops, cinemas and infamous Kabukichô red light district.

A respectable but less glamorous hotel, the Keio Plaza Intercontinental is popular with business visitors unwilling to pay the higher dining and room rates prevalent in the Ginza-Akasaka enclave. It is one of the city's leading conference locations, designed around two well-appointed conference centers.

Medium Range: A moderately priced hotel in the center of the Ginza shopping district, the Hotel Ginza Dai-ei is just one block from the Kabukiza on Harumi Dôri. All the rooms have bath, shower, color TV, telephones and air-conditioning, and the hotel operates a pick-up service from the nearby Ginza Tokyû Hotel, the nearest stop for the Airport Limousine bus service to and from Narita. Close enough, but at a peaceful remove from Ginza and Shimbashi, the Shiba Park Hotel

and its helpful staff are a few minutes from eponymous parkland and the Zôjôji Temple across the street. The nearest Airport Limousine stop is at the Tokyo City Air Terminal. The Akasaka Shanpia Hotel, also more peaceful than many, is located on a hill in one of Akasaka's quieter sections behind the TBS television studios. It is conveniently close to the Akasaka Station on the Chiyoda Subway Line. The Holiday Inn Tokyo is also conveniently located for business travelers, but provides less surprises. It is close to the Tokyo City Air Terminal and the Tokyo Bay waterfront.

The basic but bearable Star Hotel Tokyo is very close to Shinjuku Station and the majority of the district's cinemas and nightspots. All the rooms have bath, telephone and color TV. A possible last resort in the high season might be the nearby Taishô Central Hotel, located one minute from Takadanobaba Station on the JR Yamanote (Loop) Line that circles the inner city. Shinjuku is one stop down the tracks.

Business Hotels: Shimbashi Dai-ichi Hotel is between Ginza's central district and the Imperial Palace moat, two minutes from Shimbashi Station on the JR Yamanote Line. The Airport Limousine bus stops here. The Mitsui Urban Hotel is located nearby in the center of Ginza, between Shimbashi and Ginza Stations.

Over in Roppongi, with its international business community and cosmopolitan nightlife, is the ideally situated Hotel Ibis, one of the more expensive business hotels. In contrast, the Hotel Listel Shinjuku, with more double rooms than many of its competitors, offers special weekly rates for long-stay guests. It is near Shinjuku-San-chôme Station on the Marunouchi Subway Line, a five-minute walk from the main shopping area.

A vast, slickly designed building standing among Shinjuku's tallest skyscrapers near the new government headquarters, the Shinjuku Washington Hotel is particularly popular with Japanese corporate travelers – perhaps simply because it doesn't look like a member of its class.

Ryokans: Almost certainly the best of the metropolitan traditional-style inns, Ryokan Seifûsô, in a quiet side street ten minutes from Iidabashi Station (on the JR Sôbu Line), is charming, genuinely friendly, and reasonably priced. Most rooms look out on the inn's garden and ornamental carp pond, and Kitanomaru Park and the grounds of the Yasukuni Shrine are just around the corner.

Not too far from central Tokyo, the Ryokan Sansuisô still retains an old-world atmosphere despite some modern improve-

ments. It is a five-minute walk from Gotanda Station on the JR Yamanote Line.

Located farther out in the downtown district of Asakusa – one of the last parts of Tokyo where daily life still obviously maintains its links with the past – is Mikawaya Bekkan. A cheerful place just five minutes from Asakusa Station on the Ginza Subway Line, the Mikawaya is within easy reach of the famous Sensôji Temple precincts.

Capsule Hotels: The biggest capsule hotel in the country, the Green Plaza Shinjuku is a wonder to behold. This huge complex has 600 sleeping pods (each equipped with its own radio, alarm and porno channel TV),

two sauna baths, three restaurants and bars and a multigym. Only men are admitted, and a no-blind-drunks policy means that the door staff turn away anyone incapable of standing without support. If you want to have a look at this curious phenomenon without enduring the cramped sleeping conditions, you can take an "afternoon nap" in a pod for about half the overnight price. The hotel is a two-minute walk from Shinjuku Station. Hotel White City, similar to the Green Plaza but also with regular business-style rooms, is two minutes from Ikebukuro Station on the JR Yamanote Line.

<u>Left</u>, typical love hotel. <u>Above</u>, having a rest in a capsule hotel.

When it comes to dining out, Tokyo offers a wealth of choice to the hungry traveler. To begin with, the sheer number of eating places within Tokyo is among the highest in the world. Most neighborhood train stations are surrounded by narrow shopping streets scattered with restaurants, while large office buildings often contain dozens of small eating places crammed into their basements.

Perhaps even more surprising to the visitor, though, is the degree of specialization of the restaurants here. It is not unusual to find a restaurant serving only grilled eel right next to one serving only pork cutlet, followed by a place specializing in *tempura*. Indeed, considering the high price of rents, the small size of kitchens and stiff competition, intense specialization is often a matter of economic survival.

Whatever the reason, the result is a rich variety of different types of Japanese cuisine waiting for the visitor. In addition to the anticipated *sushi* and *tempura*, the adventurous diner can also discover dozens of delicious *soba* (Japanese noodle) dishes, as well as more exotic items like *fugu*, a poisonous variety of blowfish which can only be served by specialized licensed chefs.

Tokyo also has a number of shops specializing in regional cuisines from other parts of Japan, as well as excellent restaurants serving Korean-style barbecued beef and a profusion of Chinese *ramen* noodle dishes. And for the homesick diner, Tokyo's Western-style restaurants range from super-expensive French restaurants to American fast-food hamburger outlets and their Japanese imitators.

Eating Cheap: If you've read horror stories about steak dinners in Japan that cost a week's salary, all we can say is that they're probably true. Most Japanese eat steak only rarely, though. However it is quite possible to eat inexpensively and interestingly in To-

kyo, simply by going to ordinary, everyday Japanese restaurants.

Restaurants usually post menus or price lists near the front entrance. If you're traveling "on a shoestring," but don't want to eat at McDonald's every day, among the best bargains are *soba* restaurants and *ramen* shops. Both types of noodles usually come with meat and seafood and a variety of other ingredients, and they're popular with students and ordinary workers as well as trav-

elers on a budget.

Finding a Place to Eat: A number of recommended eating places are listed at the back of this book, but if you're in the mood to explore on your own, restaurants are pretty easy to find in most neighborhoods. In major shopping districts such as Shinjuku, Ginza and Shibuya, restaurants are located on top floors of department stores as well as at ground level. One advantage of the department store restaurant floors is that you can "window shop" – comparing the menus or window displays in a number of restaurants before deciding on one.

Preceding pages, *Kaiseki* cuisine as served by Tokyo's finest, Chinzan-so in Mejiro. Left, café society – Tokyo style. Right, sushi shop master outside his restaurant.

Also, although most Japanese restaurants specialize on one type of food, department stores are more likely to also have "all-purpose" Japanese restaurants – an important consideration if you and your dining companions don't all want to eat the same thing.

Some popular department store restaurant floors include Seibu and 109 in Shibuya, Matsuya in Ginza, and all five department stores attached to Shinjuku Station (My City, Odakyû, Keiô, My Lord, and Lumine). Restaurant floors are open an hour or two later than shopping floors.

There are also a large number of restau-

rants at ground level and in basements of large office buildings. Roppongi and nearby neighborhoods probably have the greatest number of non-Japanese restaurants. In quieter, more suburban neighborhoods, most eateries can be found on streets adjacent to the local train stations.

Japanese and foreign restaurants usually serve lunch between noon and 2 p.m. Many restaurants close after lunch and open again for dinner around 6. p.m. Most places in Tokyo tend to close relatively early (usually 9 or 10, but sometimes as early as 8 p.m.). Although English-language menus are not all that common, it's perfectly acceptable to order what you want simply by pointing to the appropriate plastic food model on display in the front window of the restaurant.

Tasty Entanglements: Not all foreign entanglements are the stuff of spy thrillers. Some of them are Japanese noodle dishes, tasty entanglements indeed and always affordable and fun to eat. Unlike pasta that's turned around on a fork, Japanese noodles are drawn into the mouth with chopsticks and slurped down. Slurped down? In Japan that's how you do it, unabashedly, with total commitment.

Japanese pasta appears in the form of noodles of three main types: *soba*, *udon*, and *sômen*. Soba noodles, made of buckwheat, are thin and brownish. Udon noodles, made of wheat, are thick to very thick. Sômen noodles, also made of wheat, are thin as vermicelli. Made of the same ingredients as udon but much thinner and eaten only cold is a type called *hiyamugi* (iced noodles). Udon is usually eaten in hot dishes, and soba and sômen may be eaten hot or cold.

Although essentially Chinese, so-called *ramen* noodles are eaten so obsessively in Japan that to omit mentioning them would be conspicuously remiss. Ramen is served very hot in soy-flavored broth with savorous ingredients, most typically strips of bamboo and slices of scallion and roast pork. Since the ubiquitous ramen shops have clear glass facades, passersby can see it being cooked and served.

On a hot day, Japanese cold noodle dishes such as sômen and hiyamugi, both served in a bowl with ice, are an incomparably refreshing food. Less cold but no less a summertime favorite is *zaru soba*, served on a grill-like bamboo tray (zaru) and usually eaten with wasabi (horseradish). All Japanese cold noodle dishes are served with a small dish of sauce containing sliced scallions.

When your travel day looks long and time is short, or if you simply want a quick snack, drop into a stand-and-eat soba shop (*tachiguisobaya*). You'll see them near stations and sometimes even on the platform, and usually you can see inside. Tachiguisobaya are usually sanitary – and very inexpensive.

Prices usually range from ¥200 or less for *kakesoba* (basic soba in broth) to over ¥300 for *tendama* (soba with raw-egg and mixed ingredients fried together tempura style). Priced in between are *tempura soba*, *kitsune* (with fried tofu), *tanuki* (with tempura drippings), *tsukimi* (with raw-egg), *wakame* (with kelp), croquette, and others. At the tachiguisobaya's low prices, the quality usually is no better than satisfactory, but on a cold day hot Japanese noodle dishes are wonderfully warming.

At the other price extreme are gourmet noodle shops where a simple dish of hand-made Japanese noodles can cost 10 or 15

yourself, "What about whole suckling pig?" Would you look down your nose at it simply because it was looking down its nose at you?

Remind yourself, too, that in the tradition of Japanese cuisine the ingredients must be fresh as dawn. That's a prime requisite of good food in general, of course, together with a good recipe and a good cook. Rejoice in the fact that Japan has plenty of all three, and also an abundant variety of food products.

Though the quality of food, of course, can vary widely from place to place, in an ideal world almost all Japanese would like everything to be fresh. Unlike in the Western

times more than the tachigui prices. A rather good quality serving of Japanese noodles seldom exceeds ¥1,000 and is often less.

Dining Adventures: Gastronomic adventurism isn't as easy as it sounds, and no less in Japan. An American athlete visiting Tokyo with his teammates put it like this: "I don't eat anything that looks back at me".

If it seems that some Japanese dishes only have eyes for you, don't be deterred. Ask

Left, the plastic food, what would we do without it? **Above**, looking over the food and prices before deciding.

world, in Japan relatively few dishes are submerged in sauces, doused with gravy, and seasoned beyond recognition.

Granted, the Japanese often splash on soy sauce as impulsively as some Westerners glob on catsup. Still, the Japanese ideal – the standard they would like to live by – is to have dishes made from fresh ingredients with as much of the freshness as possible intact.

No less important than freshness is the Japanese culinary philosophy. Japanese cuisine focuses on flavor, albeit in a way quite different from the established Western perception, and on the food's appearance. Rather than create distinctive flavors with their ingredients, Japanese chefs seek above all to capture their natural flavors. And rather than alter the appearance of their ingredients, they strive to enhance their visual appeal through artful arrangements.

This is exemplified by *kaiseki ryôri*, a centuries-old form of Japanese cuisine served at restaurants in several elegant courses. Fastidiously prepared kaiseki ryôri is so aesthetically pleasing it's virtually an art form. Ideally, the visual appeal would be heightened by a room setting having artworks, flowers or flower scents, and perhaps

ing them a sense of tactile rapport with the food. Small soup bowls (*owan*) raised to the mouth with the free hand similarly convey the warmth or coolness of their ingredients.

Although Westerners may not agree that slurping and smacking sounds are desirable in the dining experience, the Japanese for the most part enjoy them. Slurping invariably accompanies the enjoyment of noodles, and smacking is prevalent even on food programs shown on Japanese television. In Japan, then, dining pleasure is also associated with the ear. Thus, in clearly evident ways, it involves all five senses.

Taste and visual pleasure also converge in

even a scenic view – all in perfect harmony with the food. Some of the better restaurants serving kaiseki ryôri have succeeded in creating exactly such an atmosphere, with brush works, flower arrangements, and views of waterfalls cascading over well-hewn rocks into placid pools reposing amidst small trees and shrubs. The effect at once elevates the senses and magnifies the singular pleasure of cuisines such as *kaiseki ryôri*.

In fact, the Japanese dining experience involves all five senses, not only sight, smell, and taste. Unlike the fork and the spoon, chopsticks (*hashi*) convey to the hand hold-

sushi and in *sashimi*, its companion dish served without rice. Although less so today than in the past, before sushi and sashimi were well known outside Japan, the Japanese are still curious about the foreigner's attitude toward these delicacies featuring raw fish, shellfish, and other ingredients, mostly from the sea. Leave your apprehensions behind, if you have any, and put sushi on your schedule. Let's consider how to enjoy this delicacy in Japan.

Unless you know someone who can accompany you to a good sushi shop (*sushiya*) and explain everything, begin your romance with *sushi* – as it usually turns out to be – at one of the *kaiten-sushiya* where small dishes containing *sushi* pass before you on a belt revolving around the counter. Some sushi aficionados might disagree with this suggestion. Still, this type of sushi dining receives a clear recommendation for those unfamiliar with *sushi*. As you watch the *sushi* go by, you'll be able to see how it looks, and en toto what it is.

Granted, in a sushi shop you can see it in the glass case, arranged in shimmering fresh magnificence, or so it should be. But in a *kaiten-sushiya* you can study it more leisurely, and sample it for less cost. Once you

horseradish), *gari* (sliced ginger), *murasaki* (soy sauce), *agari* (green tea), *nami no hana* (salt), and *otemoto* (chopsticks). Excepting wasabi, these are words applied only to *sushi*. For good sushi, the ingredients should also be of good quality. Above all, the rice should be properly vinegared and steamed and the topping should be absolutely fresh.

Those who prefer raw fish and seafood without rice order *sashimi*, served in a lacquer tray or on a plate with characteristic attention to the appearance. Be it *sushi* or *sashimi*, to leave Japan without the raw fish experience would be remiss indeed. Go back and tell others, "If you knew *sushi* like I

tend to know what you like, move up quickly to a good sushiya, armed with your newfound knowledge. It will serve you well when ordering. To dawdle apprehensively over one's order is *de rigueur* – and irritating to the *sushi* makers.

An unwritten rule of *sushi* dining is to have a good rapport with the *sushi* maker, a goal perhaps easier to achieve if you know some of *sushi*dom's special terminology: *shari* (the steamed rice used), *wasabi* (green

Left, counter dining is a way of life. **Above**, typical party fare.

knew *sushi*!" And take it from there.

Does Japan have a culinary life after "old reliables" such as *kaiseki ryôri*, *sushi*, *suki-yaki*, *tempura*, and the legendary beef steak marbled to a fine-tuned filigree? Should you stick with them? Or are you willing to wander off the center of Japan's kaleidoscopic culinary stage?

The best advice might be to seek out the old reliables and to experiment with foods you've never tried, including some you may have been certain you wouldn't try on a bet. Back home, no matter how much you may have enjoyed dishes such as *tempura*, *sushi*,

COFFEE SHOPS

Innocuous-looking chairs that vibrate in time with the music. Hitherto bland facades gaudied-up to look like medieval castles. Cups and saucers designed to look like they could be used for anything else except drinking. Yes, coffee shops in Tokyo are not beyond resorting to all manner of strange gimmicks to distinguish themselves from the competition.

The competition is quite fierce, too, since the number of coffee shops to be found cafés of Paris, they do offer a comfortable chair and welcome respite from the hustle and bustle of Tokyo.

Coffee prices range from an expensive ¥300 per cup to a very expensive ¥800 per cup, although a few discount coffee shop chains sell coffee for as little as ¥150. The quality of the coffee itself varies from shop to shop, and it's usually served with a plastic thimbleful of "milk," which is the Japanese word for non-dairy creamer (the Japanese

within Tokyo is simply enormous. Coffee shops here serve as places to escape from the office, or as convenient rendezvous points for meeting friends. For the price of a cup of coffee, one can sit for as long as one likes, reading magazines and newspapers, listening to the music, chain-smoking, and generally taking a break. (In the late afternoons, it's sometimes even possible to observe businessmen in suits taking short naps before they head back to the office.)

As a visitor, you too can try out a few of Tokyo's numerous coffee shops. While they certainly make no claim to be on par with the word for milk is *gyû-nyû*, but they probably don't have it).

There's usually some sort of food available, such as toast or sandwiches or curry rice. In the afternoon, some coffee shops also offer a "cake set" – coffee and cake, otherwise known as *keiki*, at a special price (the special price often being more expensive than an average restaurant meal outside of Tokyo).

But food, even cake, isn't the main draw. Tokyo coffee shops are basically just a place to get away from it all, and to watch everyone else doing the same.

sashimi, and *yakitori* (Japanese mini-ka-bob), chances are you'll enjoy them even more as you reflect on the day you enjoyed them in Japan.

Tempura takes on a different dimension when partaken of in a first-class tempura restaurant with live fish darting about in a large tank fed with fresh bubbling water. *Sushi*, when eaten in an inexpensive small shop in the Tsukiji fish market area, some-how seems fresher – and doubtless often is – than it does elsewhere. *Sukiyaki*, although an indifferent dish without good beef, always seems at its best on a cold day in a chilly Japanese inn. At least it does to a lot of

style pub or a large Japanese-style tavern, in Japan drinking is invariably accompanied by eating.

As you negotiate the bright-lit broadways and cozy red-lantern lanes of Japan, you'll encounter every imaginable type of estab-lishment where eating and drinking go to-gether. Among them the two that particu-larly deserve your attention are the *izakaya*, or pub, often with a string of red lanterns above its door, and the *taishû-sakaba*, a much larger tavern-like establishment that may also sport red lanterns. These red lan-terns – *akachôchin* – signify a traditional Japanese environment for eating and drink-

people.

By now you're probably asking yourself, "What's this auspicious talk about wander-ing off the center of Japan's kaleidoscopic culinary stage?" Let's pursue that. First, be mindful of what the Japanese call *kuwazu-girai*. Freely translated, it means to spurn without savoring, or to assume dislike with-out taking a taste. Secondly, consider that in Japan eating and drinking are irreducible activities. Be it a bar, a cabaret, a Japanese-

Left, cafés are where the trendy meet. **Above**, the fish shop and its friendly owner.

ing. Specialties include Japanese-style fried fish, shellfish, broiled dishes, *tofu* dishes, *ya-kitori*, fried rice-balls, simple *sashimi* dishes – that sort of thing.

It may or may not be the freshest, but the price is usually right. Don't be surprised if your presence provokes some friendly con-versation from well-oiled Japanese patrons climbing down from the city stress. They may even want to buy you a drink – and although they usually do not expect their generosity to be reciprocated, they are sin-cerely grateful when it is. Beverages usually include Japanese beer, *sake*, *shôchû* (a vodka-like spirit), and soft drinks.

Not all *izakaya* and *taishû-sakaba* are created equal. If all of them tend to be unpretentious, with service predominantly by males in shirts or long aprons, some of them serve at least a few rather offbeat dishes. In Japan the likes of octopus, squid, eel, horse-meat *sashimi*, lantern-fish liver and pot-style rice paddy locusts are not considered to be squeamishly unusual. People eat them everyday, like so many hamburgers, pizzas, and plates of spaghetti, which they also eat everyday, with a passion. What, then, is unusual in the Japanese context?

How about brazier-cooked skewered

There are many who disdain the likes of stomach, tongue, liver and heart, and others who are offended by the very thought of such things, but it can be elegant food – prepared with artful inspiration. Foie gras, after all, is goose liver – lately duck liver as well.

The most apprehensive you might get about unusual food may be if you visit a shop specializing in *mamushi*, a poisonous Japanese snake with an altogether docile flavor. Would you like your mamushi skinned before your eyes, the proprietor might ask you, as if enquiring about the size of your shoe. "By all means, yes," you might want to answer, though in fact less curious than re-

sparrow, whale testicles, and squid entrails? Or what would you say to some fermented fish entrails, fried lotuses, and beef lymph gland? In fact, all of these are but a few of the many dishes that Japanese themselves would consider unusual – albeit not necessarily offensive. You'll encounter many other unusual dishes, including some in a category that Japanese commonly refer to as "*stamina ryôri*," or dishes intended to raise your energy level and staying power. Japan, and especially Tokyo, can be pretty enervating, so "stamina restaurants" are a common phenomenon.

luctant to offend.

If you ever watch a mamushi being skinned, do it with all the detachment you can summon. From a basket containing a tangle of these venomous vipers, the cook deftly seizes one by the head, snips it off, clips the body to a cord strung along the wall, and then skins it in one swift downward motion. But no matter. Mamushi is in fact quite delicious, albeit a bit bland. And it's definitely not cheap.

If you happen to be in Tokyo between mid-November and late February, you're right in season for such game as Japanese wild boar, venison, and bear. Hunters bring it fresh from Mie, Shiga, and Hyôgo Prefectures and it is served mainly by wild game specialty restaurants. Japanese wild boar (*inoshishi*) is right at home in *sukiyaki*, the *tsukinow-aguma* bear makes fairly good steak, and venison from the Japanese deer (*Nihonjika*) is suited for steaks, *sashimi*, and pot cooking.

Wild game restaurants such as Momonjiya in Ryôgoku, near many of Tokyo's sumo stables, also serve *miso* soup containing bits of badger (*tanuki*), an un-usual but unremarkable meat. Wild game dishes served after the hunting season ends are usually made with meat that has been frozen, as most out-of-season dishes are. Wild boar, difficult to breed in captivity, have successfully crossed with domestic pigs to produce a meat called *inobuta* that sometimes appears in a pot dish called *inobuta-nabe*.

Continuing along the offbeat path, get acquainted with blowfish (*fugu*), a fish so poisonous that it may be prepared only by licensed chefs and served only in licensed restaurants. Given those two vital condi-tions, *fugu* is a great delicacy whether en-joyed as *sashimi* or in an Osaka-style *fugu* pot dish (*chirinabe*). As a food, fugu dates back to ancient times in Japan but the *tora-fugu* type used in *sashimi* gained popularity only after the mid-1950s.

Although it is known that the *fugu*'s poi-son, the nerve poison tetrodotoxin, seems to be contained in something it eats, so far no one has determined how it is accumulated in its body. Many things about the *fugu* are unknown – but how to make it safe to eat isn't one of them. Licensed cooks remove its poisonous internal organs, as well as its spiny skin, before cooking. *Fugu* for sashimi is sliced so thin that the serving dish is visible through each slice. A delicacy, indeed.

Perhaps less exotic-sounding than *fugu* dishes, but every bit as delectable, are Japa-nese dishes that use eel (*unagi*). Tradition-ally – as far back as 3,000 years ago – the Japanese antidote for dog-day blahs was

broiled eel liberally drenched in sweetish *tare* sauce. Eel, a delicacy in Japan, is rich in vitamins E and A and exceeds pork and beef in protein content, yet contains fewer calo-ries.

That's good, and what's even better is the flavor of eel in *unadon* (short for *unagi-donburi* or eel on rice in a bowl), *unajû* (similar to *unadon* but served in a box), and *kabayaki* (eel served flat on a dish without rice). All three of these dishes are cooked over charcoal and basted with a marinade of soy sauce and sweet *sake* or *mirin* (a sweet-ish fermented sauce).

If you arrive in Japan during the dog days

– *doyô no iri* – get a feel for eel. With it you might be served *kimosui*, a delicate, deli-cious clear soup containing eel organs. Japa-nese eel dishes, usually made of young eels less than two feet long, are at their best ex-traordinary.

So wide is the range of Japanese cuisine, and so unusual are some of the dishes, that one's epicurean adventure never stops and never stales. But isn't that itself the most compelling point of all? During your sojourn in Tokyo, explore the highways and byways of its inimitable cuisine with all the enthusi-asm it deserves.

Left, fried octopus for sale. **Right**, preparing for a party is an everyday event at an *izakaya*.

The common perception of the Japanese is that they are people who love to spend and presently have the yen to do so. Prices of apparel at numerous chic havens, for example, would seem to most unaccustomed foreign-currency-based visitors outlandish. However, the Japanese, though reputed for their love of high fashion and quality, do not do all their shopping in pricey stores. Day to day purchases are done for the most part in neighborhood markets.

A rapport between shopowner and customer is attained and maintained. The customer is "king" and traditionally perceived to be of higher rank than the seller. *Okyakusama* – "Oh, honorable buyer." And, service also follows. No matter which kind of shop, the customer is always greeted with *"Irasshaimase"* – "Welcome" – and often a polite bow. Upon leaving there is another bow and *"Arigatô gozaimasu"* – "Thanks a bunch." This relationship between customer and seller exists everywhere in Japan, even in the impersonal "big-city" Tokyo.

Just about every neighborhood has its shopping street. At both ends there are typically decorated arches. Shops are lined on both sides and some of these "green streets" extend for hundreds of meters. Sometimes they are covered. Anything can be purchased, from nuts to soup, from *kimono* to *ocha* (Japanese tea). These streets could be viewed as the equivalent of a Western shopping mall – Japanese style. Incidentally, the Japanese are copying mall-type complexes more and more.

Foreigners should expect the same treatment – courtesy and service – while shopping. Communicating in Japanese and trying to read the items' tags and labels, however, may give way to frustration at times. Prices are for the most part evident, although you may see the prices sometimes written in Japanese characters.

If you can't find what you're looking for in the neighborhood shops or in the gigantic department stores, or you're at your wit's end with the language barrier, you could head off to stores that cater to foreigners' needs. A number of the larger Japanese department stores have set up information centers within their stores. They have English-speaking staff on hand to assist and even lead you to the item. Isetan, Seibu, and many other large stores are promoting this "international" service.

If you are still unsatisfied, there are several stores that foreigners frequent for their fix of home goods. Thanksgiving turkeys, fine French wines, Black Sea caviar – it can all be had. In the food department, Meidi-ya and National Azabu in Hiroo are most notable. There is also Kinokuniya in the Aoyama area, up the hill from Harajuku.

In truth – or half-truth – there is nothing that can't be had in Tokyo, the largest city in the world.

Chances are that you would want to bring things back as souvenirs or as gifts. Try your luck at neighborhood shops. Or, there are stores that have a wide selection of "authentic" Japanese goods. The Oriental Bazaar in Harajuku is popular and reasonably priced. Don't expect to find bargains, except at flea markets and second-hand sales, although the prices there are rising with their increased popularity.

As for higher-ticketed items, you should know what you're buying before you actually buy it. There are a number of company showrooms which display and often allow hands-on perusal of their goods. For example, the Sony Building located at the Sukiyabashi Crossing in Ginza has on display their latest lines of audio-visual equipment. Also in Ginza, Yamaha has several showrooms boasting its technology. Most company headquarters are located in Tokyo. In the case of "buyer beware," there is ample information to make the customer aware.

Left, Tokyo is a premier fashion center. **Above**, bagging it on the Ginza.

If there is any city around the world that would qualify for the most fashionable, surely Tokyo is the top contender. Overseas, Paris is regarded as the pacesetter in trends worldwide, London's King's Road is seen as the barometer for street fashion, and New York, the melting pot of cultures in America, blends east, west and all points in between. But Tokyo has a life of its own, owed in most part to the fact that Japanese have affluence not often seen overseas. Young people can-

not afford to buy apartments, much less houses. As a result their free-spending manifests itself in high fashion, restaurants and other good things in life.

There can be no doubt that the average Japanese is amongst the world's most fashionable, able to buy designer-brand clothes at will.

Undoubtedly the place for fashion is the Harajuku-Aoyama/Shibuya area. As well as being the headquarters of Japanese fashion, the whole area draws people from far and wide at the weekend who want to shop for clothes and other articles related to fashion.

Young people come into Tokyo for the weekend from surrounding towns and cities and make a beeline for Harajuku Station, the starting point of their shopping spree.

If you ask someone what Harajuku means, they might say "boutiques, coffee shops, and young people." Another might remark on the rock 'n roll dancers on Sunday afternoons, a throwback, literally, to the great era when rock and roll became the vogue 30 or more years ago. While not displaying the latest fashion trends, their garb ranges from black leathers and greased-back hair to the 50s bebop look. Collectively they are referred to as *takenoko* dancers, or "little bamboo shoots."

A fine sunny Sunday sees Harajuku at its busiest and in Takeshita-dôri, a narrow shopping street where boutiques and restaurants jostle for space there must be more people per square meter than Ginza has ever seen. It's well worth taking a look even if you dislike being in a crowd.

While Harajuku is for the kids, Aoyama, its counterpart at the other end of Omote-sandô near Omote-sandô or Gaienmae subway stations, is more up-scale and adult-oriented. Browse the boutiques in Minami-Aoyama where Issey Miyake is king. His Issey Miyake's Men's Plantation and Issey Miyake are to be found in the same street. Comme des Garçons' fantastic flagship boutique-cum-department store features everything created by designer Rei Kawakubo. Another top Tokyo designer, Yohji Yamamoto, has both his men's and women's collections at Y's just down the street. European fashion heavyweight, are also well represented. Sonia Rykiel, Gianfranco Ferre, Emporio Armani and Gianni Versace all have boutiques here.

Clustered around Shibuya station is another horde of department stores such as Tôkyû, Seibu, Parco and related places like Seed, Quattro, and 109. It's another Shinjuku story, where floor after floor of designer wear is offered for sale to an unending horde of fashion-hungry youngsters.

FLEA MARKETS

Nomi no ichi, or flea markets, are held almost every week somewhere in or around Tokyo.

These places are good for picking up old *silk kimono, obi* (the usually silk sash that is wrapped around the *kimono* and is tied in a knot at the back), *tansu* and *hibachi,* and other such articles of traditional Japanese furniture. This is one of the few occasions when bargaining is the rule. Normally held early in the morning till dusk, weather per-

403-3591.

Arai Yakushi Temple (Nakano): Every first Sunday. Nearest station: Arai Yakushimae on the Seibu Shinjuku Line. Tel: (03) 386-1355.

Nogi Shrine (Roppongi): Every second Sunday. Nearest station: Nogizaka on the Chiyoda Subway Line. Tel: (03) 402-2181.

Roppongi (On the steps of the Roi Bldg.): Every fourth Thursday and Friday from 8 a.m. to 8 p.m., rain or shine. Nearest station:

mitting. If you are looking for some nice souvenirs, or something unique to decorate your home with, this is the place to look. However, if you are looking for real antiques, you should be careful. Most of the dealers are more like old-fashioned junk dealers than true antique dealers.

The major fairs are listed below.

Tôgô Shrine (Harajuku): Every first and fourth Sunday. Nearest station: Meiji Jingû-mae on the Chiyoda Subway Line. Tel: (03)

Left, traditional themes are always popular with fashion designers. **Above**, a mixed bag on show at a weekend flea market.

Roppongi on the Hibiya Subway Line. Tel: (03) 583-2081.

Hanazono Shrine (Shinjuku-Sanchôme): Every second and third Sunday from 7 a.m. to 5 p.m. Suspended in case of rain. Nearest station: Shinjuku Sanchôme on the Marunouchi Subway Line. Tel: (03) 200-3093.

You can also obtain flea market information after 5 p.m. from Recycle Undô Shimin no Kai at (03) 226-6800. However, this is a taped message in Japanese, so it would be advisable to have some Japanese friend make the phone call for you.

As the 1980s passed by, Japan became as health-conscious as any other nation with the time and money to worry about such things. Tokyo air is not the cleanest, and the stress involved in simply traveling around in the city every day quickly takes its toll. First came the health and fitness centers, then the joggers and the aerobics, and even a small drop in the number of smokers, if not the drinkers. Not that jogging in Tokyo will necessarily lengthen your life, although those brave souls who run right around the Imperial Palace at 6 a.m. every day (a pleasant 5 kilometers or so when there's not much traffic) presumably hope so: if Madonna and Jimmy Carter could do it, then it must be all right.

But as with any other human endeavor in Japan, if there is just a slight whiff of business potential, there's a good chance someone will make it available on a trial basis. Many such things become huge successes, such as scuba diving, windsurfing, and even, as everyone knows, golf.

Now that is a success story if ever there was one. Japan is the last country in the world, other than Liechtenstein or Hong Kong, in which golf should have become popular: there are far too many people trying to squeeze out space to live on far too little suitable land. But once out-of-shape businessmen were convinced that a bit of a walk and a friendly chat, out of the office and at the company's expense, were the only ways to do business effectively, the golf industry was off like a shot. The result? Low status businessmen and those who can't afford the several thousand dollars required to join a proper club are forced to spend their spare time at driving practice ranges. Others who can somehow manage a membership have to get up at four in the morning ready to drive a couple of hours out of Tokyo for the wonderful privilege of teeing off at 06:24. How

about that for masochism?

You might think that a squash or racquetball court in every office building would be a great idea. No chance. Those are not sufficiently "sociable" games. Tennis is all right: 20 people can practice together on the same court. Skiing is all right: all those people to join in the queue and push off moguls. Swimming is all right: a lane for each group class and one for those too mean and anti-social to join the classes. That's the way it goes. The

other thing about sports in Japan is that everyone accepts the whole business idea. If you play tennis, you wear what the stars wear and certainly don't borrow someone else's 20-year-old racket. If you go skiing, you buy this year's Rossignol skis and Salomon boots and the latest French fashion (which means buying all the magazines to find out what everyone else will also be wearing) – the only people in jeans and cowboy hats are foreigners. If you go swimming, you must have the right goggles and a brand-name costume. That's the way it goes, and that's the way the money goes, too.

Preceding pages, sumo is intimately tied to tradition. **Left**, spectators taking in the action. **Above**, warm-up exercises before a match.

But not everyone wants to *do*, many want to watch, and there's plenty of scope for that in Tokyo, from ice hockey and skating to baseball, from *karate* to rugby, from *sumo* to table tennis.

Sumo: The Power and the Glory: Some people say *sumo* is the national sport. Some would say it's the national spirit. *Sumo* wrestlers would probably say it's a long, hard grind to fleeting glory.

In fact, *sumo* is a fascinating phenomenon because it involves so many different things: physical strength, ritual developed over centuries, a huge and complicated code of behavior, religious overtones, a daunting hierarchy system, feudalistic training regimes, the clash of the physically unmatched, and for those out in the audience, a lot of drinking, eating and shouting.

Sumo wrestlers are not mountains of flab. They are immensely strong, rigorously trained mountains of muscle (often loosely covered in flab). Their way of life is still extraordinarily tough until they reach the top. To start as a young teenager up from the country means to enter a long trail of apprenticeship: little sleep, beatings, lots of dirt and sweat, constant humiliation, cooking, shopping, running errands, scrubbing backs, and the awesome task of accompanying 400 lb. senior wrestlers to the restroom.....all for just bed and board. Few youngsters hack the course.

The ones who do have two goals in mind. The first is to reach proper *"sekitori"* status (the top 50 or so wrestlers out of the more than 600 who comprise the fighting members of the Sumo Association), which means a fancy top-knot, assistants and a salary. The other goal is the ultimate one: to become a grand champion, or *"yokozuna,"* and to go down in history with a fat salary and a more-or-less assured future.

The next best thing to that is to win one of the six annual tournaments, three of which (January, May, September) are held at the Ryôgoku Kokugikan tournament hall in the Ryôgoku area in the eastern part of the city. *Sumo* is truly a case of "winner take all," and that means some amazing *sumo*-size prizes, such as a truckload of beef, a year's supply of mushrooms, a few tons of rice....in fact,

enough commodities of all kinds to keep a "stable" of hearty wrestlers and their hangers-on flatulent for years.

This feat has been achieved by foreigners only twice. Both of them were from Hawaii and blessed with king-size Samoan bodies. The first time was in 1972 when Takamiyama, reveling in the heat of Nagoya, made *sumo* history in a sport that many Japanese like to think foreigners cannot possibly ever excel at or even understand. Much admired for his gutsy approach to training and learning Japanese ways, he went on to take Japanese nationality, make a fortune from TV commercials and then run his own stable, which encourages other foreign hopefuls to come and have a go.

The second time was in the Kyûshû tournament at the end of 1989, when the mighty Konishiki (veering between 220 and 250 kilograms) overcame a series of leg problems to win the Emperor's cup. His tears of victory were testament to the immense struggle that had been involved to reach that lofty pinnacle.

Not that you have to be gigantic to win. The holder of many records, and the man who really dominated the *sumo* world in the 1980s, Chiyonofuji did so at a mere 120 kilograms. His secret was fearsome power, speed and the intense competitive drive that gave him the nickname "Wolf."

Another strange feature of *sumo* is that at the professional level it is a world unto itself. It is difficult to talk in terms of impartial judges, for example. The Sumo Association is run very much like Oxford and Cambridge Universities: to be a member of the university you have to be a member of a college; to be a member of the Sumo Association, you must belong to one of the more than 30 stables, most of which are within walking distance of the Kokugikan. This applies to all ringside attendants, referees and umpires – in fact, anyone with any official capacity.

All the major wrestlers know each other well, too. Most of the year when they are not fighting in the tournaments which determine their ranking, they are on the road with everyone else presenting demonstration tournaments, singing together on TV charity shows, or practicing together. This naturally leads to constant media debate about the possibility of fixed matches, which only serves to increase spectator interest.

Visiting the Kokugikan during one of the 15-day tournaments is certainly an experience, although it is one of the worst spectator sports if you happen to be there. There is so much to-ing and fro-ing of refreshment suppliers, so much rushing to the toilet between bouts, so much general organization of tea and beer and presents, that it is easy to miss a fight that may last less than a second (which is all it takes to sidestep and watch your opponent launch himself at high speed into the clay). If you're luckier, a fight may

glare at your opponent before hitting him headfirst.

There are several books available on all aspects of *sumo*, or if you attend a tournament you will be given a little English pamphlet and list of the day's bouts for free (usually from a burly and apparently surly ex-wrestler). Tickets go on sale on a fixed day about one month in advance, both at the Kokugikan box office and ticket outlets, at various major department stores, etc. Tickets at the Kokugikan range from about US$10 to $65. To get good seats usually means getting there really early and queueing. The same is true of tickets for sale on the

last several minutes, until one wrestler, or part of him other than his feet, touches the ground inside the 15-foot diameter *dohyô* ring, or outside it. There are a few forbidden actions, such as grabbing the hair or the private parts and punching, but otherwise it's vicious, tough, physical combat. The moment the bout is ended, politeness must return: no emotional outbursts, no arguing, no playing to the crowd other than the way you throw your purifying salt into the ring or

Above, the objective is to manoeuvre your opponent out of the ring.

day. All the best seats are already earmarked for big companies, supporters groups and so on. Business contacts may have suitable contacts, so it's a good idea to ask around.

The seats next to the ring are just that – a cushion and nothing else (along with the danger of being crushed under a flying wrestler) but all the noise and smell of sweat and pomade. Many of the other seats near the ring are called *"masu seki"* (box-seats). These are boxes designed for midgets. Long-limbed spectators, encumbered with cameras, bags, food, drink and bags of souvenirs, really do not fit. There are some comfortable chairs at the back of the auditorium with round tables, but they are rather far away from the action. Gallery seats are much more comfortable, but you can't see much without binoculars.

In the good old days before the construction of the new hall in 1985, it used to be possible to rub shoulders with the wrestlers outside, watch them exercising in the car park, and peep into the dressing rooms. All that has gone. To do that now you will have to visit the stables themselves, where practice starts at the crack of dawn. Introductions are needed to enter the practice area, and you're expected to be on your best behavior.

phere, then watching on TV is in many ways preferable. NHK shows all the major bouts from about 3.30 to 6 p.m. every day during all the tournaments. Ask a Japanese friend to explain the information about wrestlers on the screen, which includes present tournament standing, status, and details of previous encounters. Channel 10 (TV Asahi) shows a 30-minute digest version every evening around 11 p.m. and there is an English version of this on JCTV as well.

If ever a sport needed slow-motion replays, it is *sumo*: the action is so fast, and it is often impossible to see clearly what actually happened without camera shots from

Training takes place in a kind of hushed, largely humorless fashion, even though *sumo* wrestlers are immensely sociable off the job.

Demonstration tournaments are much more relaxed and give a chance to watch all the special *sumo* activities such as hairdressing (a wrestler's hair reaches right down the back and is only cut off at the formal retiring ceremony). There is one of these each year at Yasukuni Shrine in April, in memory of the war dead. You may have to travel some distance to see others.

If you are not too concerned about atmos-

several angles.

There was a period in the heady, decadent days of the Edo Period when there was women's *sumo* as well. At first they appeared just in loincloths like the men, until the law made them cover up, and the engravers of popular woodblock prints of the "Amazons" had to oblige by superimposing vests.

The only chance to see something like it these days is at one or two rooftop beer gardens in summer, when college students with outstanding proportions will tamely pretend to fight for the benefit of beer-guzzling economic animals. Traditionally, women are not allowed to step foot in the ring. This discrimination was challenged in January 1990 when Chief Cabinet Secretary Mayumi Moriyama expressed a wish to present the Prime Minister's Cup to the tournament winner. She was turned down by the conservative Sumo Association and withdrew her request.

Salaried Baseball: The real national sport, in terms of popularity and year-round interest, is the grand old Japanese game of baseball. Every time Japanese teams are thrashed by out-of-season, jet-lag weary Americans over here for a brief visit, some of the comments would make you think that baseball reached these shores only during the Occupation. In fact, it has been here since 1873 and is a major preoccupation of most Japanese boys (and softball for girls) from a tender age.

The author Robert Whiting has produced two very popular books about baseball as a social phenomenon. In these, he demonstrates how a comparison of the game played in the States and here points out a vast range of cultural trait differences.

One essential difference is that baseball players are regarded as salaried men just like anyone else and are, therefore, expected to train out of season as hard as they play during the April-October season proper.

This is the biggest bone of contention with American players who come and try their hand at the Japanese version (same rules, different attitudes): they all maintain that a short pre-season training period and 130 games is enough for anyone, and that professionals shouldn't need to have to practice techniques all winter long. The argument the other way round is that Americans on salaries bigger than their Japanese counterparts should play the game as it is played here and not cause any waves.

The media love this kind of debate and, anyway like to have training camps to cover if there are no actual games. In this way baseball devotees are kept informed and

stimulated all year long.

There are two major leagues in Japanese professional baseball, with six teams in each. They are all owned by big companies rather than being associated with cities, although there is naturally great local rivalry involved based on where each team has its home ground.

Six teams are based in or around Tokyo: the Tokyo Giants and Nippon Ham Fighters (Tokyo Dome); the Yakult Swallows (Jingûmae Ball Park); the Lotte Orions (Kawasaki Stadium); the Seibu Lions (Seibu Lions' Stadium, Tokorozawa, Saitama) and the Taiyô Whales (Yokohama Stadium).

The Tokyo Giants is the team with the biggest following around Japan by far. Perennial champions for many years, both of the Central League and the annual "Japan Series" play-offs with the champion of the Pacific League, they are the team to love with undying passion or to hate with a vengeance: the term "anti-Giants" is frequently heard. It is the team with massive financial backing from the Yomiuri Group, which includes Yomiuri Television (Channel 4) and the Yomiuri Shimbun, the largest circulation newspaper in the world, so they are not starved of publicity. The other reason for

Left, American players provide some star quality to professional baseball teams. **Above**, dreaming of the big-leagues.

their popularity is that the two players regarded as representing all that is best about Japanese baseball played together in the Giants in the 1960s and 70s: Shigeo Nagashima, the great clutch-hitter who was known as "Mr. Giants" and now appears on Japanese TV as a commentator on almost any sport, as well as coordinating Japanese Guinness Book of Records attempts; and the home-run king of the world, Sadaharu Oh, who is not technically Japanese at all, but Taiwanese.

The Seibu Lions, over in the other league, has the backing of the multi-conglomerate Seibu hotel-railway-department store-and-

shared the 50-year-old Kôrakuen Stadium next to Suidôbashi Station, a fine place for watching ball games and sipping beer on balmy summer evenings. But Kôrakuen suddenly went hi-tech with the construction of Japan's first roofed stadium, the Tokyo Dome, nicknamed the "BIG EGG" ("Big Entertainment and Golden Games"). This massive structure can hold up to 56,000 spectators, and was designed as a truly multi-purpose event space.

Both its seating capacity and distance from home plate to park screen (122 meters) make it the biggest ball park, as compared to Seibu (37,000, 120 meters), Yokohama

just-about-anything-you-can-think-of chain, which is run by the multi-millionaire Tsutsumi brothers.

The beautiful Seibu ball park just happens to be on a Seibu railway line next to the Seibu Amusement Park, to keep the whole family happy. Whenever a Seibu home-run is hit, the sky above all the Seibu property is lit up with fireworks. Display boards at the main Seibu station in Ikebukuro keep commuters informed of the latest scores, as they hurry past the massive Seibu Department Store. C'est la vie Japonaise.

Until 1988, the Giants and the Fighters

(30,000, 118 meters) and the previous largest, Jingûmae (52,000, 120 meters). Everywhere else in Japan, many baseball games have to be postponed every year because of bad weather, but the all-weather Dome has changed all that. Now all Giants and Fighters home fixtures are guaranteed to take place and there is no loss of time or revenues.

It is an exciting structure with movable stands to create all kinds of configurations: for soccer or American football, opera and rock concerts, exhibitions and conventions. During its first year of operation, the hollow egg reverberated to the sounds of Michael

Jackson, Mick Jagger and Sting, a Mike Tyson world heavyweight professional boxing title match, the opera "Aida," a "monster truck" rally and an NFL American Football game, and reeled to the fragrance of an international exhibition of orchids.

There are broad promenade areas at the back of the stands with a variety of refreshment stands and excellent views from every seat. Some baseball players from visiting teams have complained, however, about the rather heady atmosphere, and many rock concert visitors have testified to the apparent increased effect of alcohol consumed on the premises – hardly a complaint.

tainment and sports facilities designed to meet the needs of a rapidly growing leisure market.

The university baseball leagues also have tremendous following, and there are thousands of company teams as well. It is not unusual to see office workers practicing with a baseball and a glove during lunch-break out in the car park.

Rugby: Rugby has gradually gained in popularity over the past twenty years, especially in the universities, where it has now become something of a major attraction for young women supporters in particular. Major games between big universities (in-

For music it shares the old problem of the Nippon Budôkan Martial Arts Hall, where the Beatles initiated the big concert scene in Japan back in 1966 – the sound bounces back and forth across the arena. The expensive seats for concerts are actually fold-up metal chairs a long way from drinks and toilets.

The Big Egg is part of the massive Kôrakuen Leisureland complex, which includes an amusement park, pool with artificial wave generators and a whole host of enter-

Left, Japanese have a passion for golf. **Above**, physical fitness is a national obsession.

cluding Waseda, Keiô and Meiji in Tokyo) can easily fill huge-capacity stadiums such as the Olympic Stadium.

But rugby at club and inter-company level still remains a rather minor sport. It has also undergone the usual adaptation to Japanese values. Just like baseball, rugby in Japan is very much a manager's game. Several foreign commentators have pointed out that there are many talented individuals who have had great success abroad, with no lack of individual initiative, that essential element in this team game.

Unfortunately, in Japan, a team game is a

team game, and that means total submission to managers, coaches and "seniors" in universities. As a result, Japanese teams are regularly thrashed by visiting foreign teams. This is often blamed on weight and size differences and the fact that foreign rugby players tend to be very rough. Japanese players are rough in training, but often a split second too polite on the field. Nobody would think of criticizing the control of the manager, and it is always the manager who is interviewed after the game.

The Japanese image of rugby being a very serious and gentlemanly game used to mean that spectators remained very quiet during

matches. Mass student support has tended to change this, and a big game can be an exciting event, with a lot of fast play to watch. The only problem is that Japan is not a country of grass, and pitches are therefore usually extremely hard.

Skiing: For skiing, Tokyoites have a huge variety of grounds to choose from, within an hour and a half from Ueno Station by *shinkansen* (bullet train), or between three and twelve hours by road (not recommended). Many ski resorts are also hot-spring resorts and offer lots of delights whether you are really an avid skier or not.

The slopes nearest Tokyo are invariably crowded at weekends, but pleasant during the week. Most will have ski gear for rent, but boots tend to stop at 28cm, so the big-footed should check carefully before setting out. One of the great ski shopping areas is between Ochanomizu and Kanda stations, and some shops may have larger sizes. Keep hunting.

Swimming and Tennis: There are swimming and tennis facilities all over the city, but help should be sought to deal with all the details of booking procedures and so on. Major hotels have excellent pools and gyms. The Ariake Tennis Park out in the suburbs of Kôtô-ku is the biggest facility of its kind in East Asia, with excellent facilities for major tournaments.

Minor Sports and Leisure Activities: Whatever it may be, you will find it going on somewhere. For the retired, the great sport these days is a game called "gateball," which is similar to the English game of croquet. It can be seen in action on any vacant lot or spare bit of field both in the city and out in the countryside. Nobody seems to worry much about the state of the lawn – there usually isn't one.

Hiking is the great autumn and spring activity for the old and young alike, everyone equipped with knickerbockers, backpacks and boots. Within Tokyo, the **Takao** area of hills is extremely popular.

Darts is available at many bars in Tokyo, particularly those frequented by foreigners, and there is an active darts league with many top-quality Japanese players. Billiards and pool are also extremely popular, and snooker is likely to increase in popularity during the 1990s.

American football is another sport which the Japanese are gradually taking to. With its emphasis on mass group activity and cheerleading, it would appear to be a perfect game.

Cricket will never succeed in Japan, but some games are played at the Yokohama Country and Athletic Club in Yokohama, mostly by expatriates.

Left and **right**, Japanese gymnasts can compete with the best in the world.

120

THE MARTIAL ARTS

A general term for various types of fighting arts that originated in the Orient. Most martial arts practiced today came from China, Japan and Korea. They all share common techniques, but there is no one superior style.

The use of weapons is often a part of advanced training in martial arts as a way to preserve ancient tradition. In some forms of martial arts, however, weapons are part of the basic training.

Two major martial arts evolved in Japan, (1603-1867). It was made up of different systems of fighting, primarily without weapons, against either an armed or bare-handed opponent on the battlefield.

The basic principle of the *judo* technique is to utilize the strength of one's opponent to one's own advantage. It is because of this that a person of weaker physique can win over a stronger opponent. The best known *judo* hall in Japan is the Kôdôkan in Tokyo, where you can observe the judoists practice

the *bujutsu*, or ancient martial arts, and the *budô*, or new martial ways. Both are based on spiritual concepts embodied in Zen Buddhism. *Bujutsu* emphasizes combat and willingness to face death as a matter of honor. It contains the philosophy and techniques of the Japanese samurai warriors and includes such arts as *jûjutsu* and *karate-jutsu*. *Budô*, which started during the late 1800's, focuses on moral and aesthetic development. *Karate-do, judo,* and *aikidô* are all forms of *budô*.

Judo: The original form of *judo*, called *jûjutsu*, was developed in the Edo period for free from 5.00 to 7.30 p.m.

Karate: *Karate,* meaning "empty hand" in Japanese, is a form of unarmed combat in which a person kicks or strikes with the hands, elbows, knees, or feet.

In Japan *karate* developed around the 1600's on the island of Okinawa. A Japanese clan had conquered the island and passed a strict law banning the ownership of weapons. As a result, the Okinawans developed many of the unarmed techniques of modern *karate*.

Aikidô: A system of pure self-defense derived from the traditional weaponless fighting techniques of *jûjutsu* in its employment of immobilizing holds and twisting throws, whereby an attacker's own momentum and strength are made to work against him.

Since *aikidô* is primarily a self-defense system and does not require great physical strength, it has attracted many women and elderly practitioners.

By meeting rather than blocking a blow, one can redirect the flow of the opponent's *ki* (often translated as "mind" or "positive energy force"), dissipate it, and, through joint manipulation, turn it against the opponent until he or she is thrown or pinned down.

Kendô: *Kendô* (the way of the sword) is

9th century, combat on horseback led to the use of longer curved blades, and the increased length made it necessary to abandon the one-handed Chinese style of swordfighting for a two-handed style.

In 1911, *kenjutsu* was included in middle-school physical education programs, and in 1939 *kendô* became a regular course for the upper grades of primary schools. At the end of World War II, the Occupation authorities banned *kendô* on the basis of its use before the war to cultivate militarism. But following the end of the Occupation period in 1952, the All Japan Kendô Federation was established, and in 1957, the practice of *kendô* was

Japanese fencing based on the techniques of the two-handed sword of the samurai. Before the Showa period (1926-1989), it was customarily referred to as *kenjutsu* or *gekken*. *Kendô* is a relatively recent term which implies spiritual discipline as well as fencing technique.

Fencing with the single-edged, straight-blade sword was introduced from Sui (581-618) or early Tang (618-906) China. In the

returned to Japanese middle schools.

Another martial art form that developed in Japan is *ninjutsu*, which means "the art of stealing in," or espionage. People who practice *ninjutsu* are called *ninja*. Mountain mystics developed *ninjutsu* in the late 1200s. At that time, *ninja* were masters at all forms of armed and unarmed combat, including the use of disguises, bombs, and poisons. Although the rulers of Japan banned *ninjutsu* in the 1600s, the *ninja* practiced it secretly and preserved its techniques. Today, *ninja* practice their trade as a traditional martial art, with a non-violent philosophy.

Left and **above**, martial arts – a battle of both mind and body.

The Tokyo Race Course at Fuchû, on the western edge of the city, is the largest in the Far East. It covers almost 190 acres, has stands for over 35,000 people, stable accommodation for 815 horses, a dirt track, a steeplechase track, and a main course just short of 2,100 meters. Virtually all of Japan's classic races are run at the course, which holds five race meetings a year spread over a total of forty racing days.

For any visitor wanting to get an idea of

The big races are the best attended, and these are, in chronological order, the Oaks, held on the third Sunday of May; the Derby, held the Sunday following; the Autumn Emperor's Cup, held on the last Sunday in October; and the Japan Cup (the year's international meet), held at the end of November. Races of less than classic status are just as much fun and are held almost every remaining weekend in the year.

The best way to get to Fuchu is by train,

how Tokyo's ordinary working folks spend some of their precious free time and hard-earned cash, or simply looking for a moment's respite from the obligatory tour of the city's temple compounds, there are few better ways than losing a little money on the horses at the Fuchû Keiba-jô.

Tokyo's main race course (there is another one at Nakayama, 25 kilometers east of the city) never fails to attract an eclectic mix of rogues and well-behaved ruffians, and has an atmosphere completely its own, especially on a crisp, clear day when Mount Fuji is visible in the background.

either via the Keio Line (changing to the shuttle service train at Higashi Fuchû), or by the JR Musashino Line which runs to Fuchû-Hommachi. Because of the consistently heavy traffic on westbound roads and highways, travelling by car takes longer, and on some race days, particularly Derby Day, can be downright dangerous. Even in the 1990s there are plenty of drivers on the way to the track who still harbor the old superstition that their horse will be the first one home if they can just overtake all the other cars going the same way.

Inside the stadium, most of the fixtures are

the same as those in the West: long gone are the days when the start of a race was signalled by the drop of a horsehair fan.

Fuchû uses the same kind of starting gate, patrol film and totalizator system as anywhere else in the world. The rules adopted by the Japan Racing Association are based on those of the Jockey Club of England, and the Association controls all betting both on and off the course through its on-line collation network. (Bookmaking has been illegal since the sport was introduced in 1861, but goes on all the same – usually through bookies operating from the tops of upturned packing crates in downtown districts like

the country, which are often shown on the course's huge video screens in the center of the track.

Today, there are no limits on betting stakes and the proceeds from Association races are divided three ways: 75 percent goes to repayment, 15 percent is claimed by the Association, and ten percent goes to the National Treasury – but such has not always been the case.

Public betting has always been a thorny issue for the Japanese government since the early days of the Meiji restoration. Japan's first betting ticket system appeared in 1888, when administrators, with their eye on the

Asakusa and Ueno.) *De rigueur* accessories for hardened professionals are a pocket radio, a well-fingered copy of the day's race sheet and a red pencil to mark the form, all of which can be bought at the entrance gates. Casual visitors can make do with a thoughtful glance at the runners during the pre-race paddock walkaround.

Racegoers at Fuchû can also bet on races taking place on the same day in other parts of

Left, enthusiast hopes for a winner. **Above**, horse racing is becoming increasingly popular.

country's cavalry adventures, first had the thought that to encourage racing would be a way to encourage stock improvement. However, dismayed by the growth in public enthusiasm for gambling that followed, they eventually banned the sale of the tickets just 20 years later, whereupon support for the sport immediately fell away.

After 1923, and the passing of a new law designed to inject fresh blood into the sport, races up until the war were held under the sponsorship of the Horse Racing Association, and the amount of a win was limited to not more than 10 times the price of a ticket.

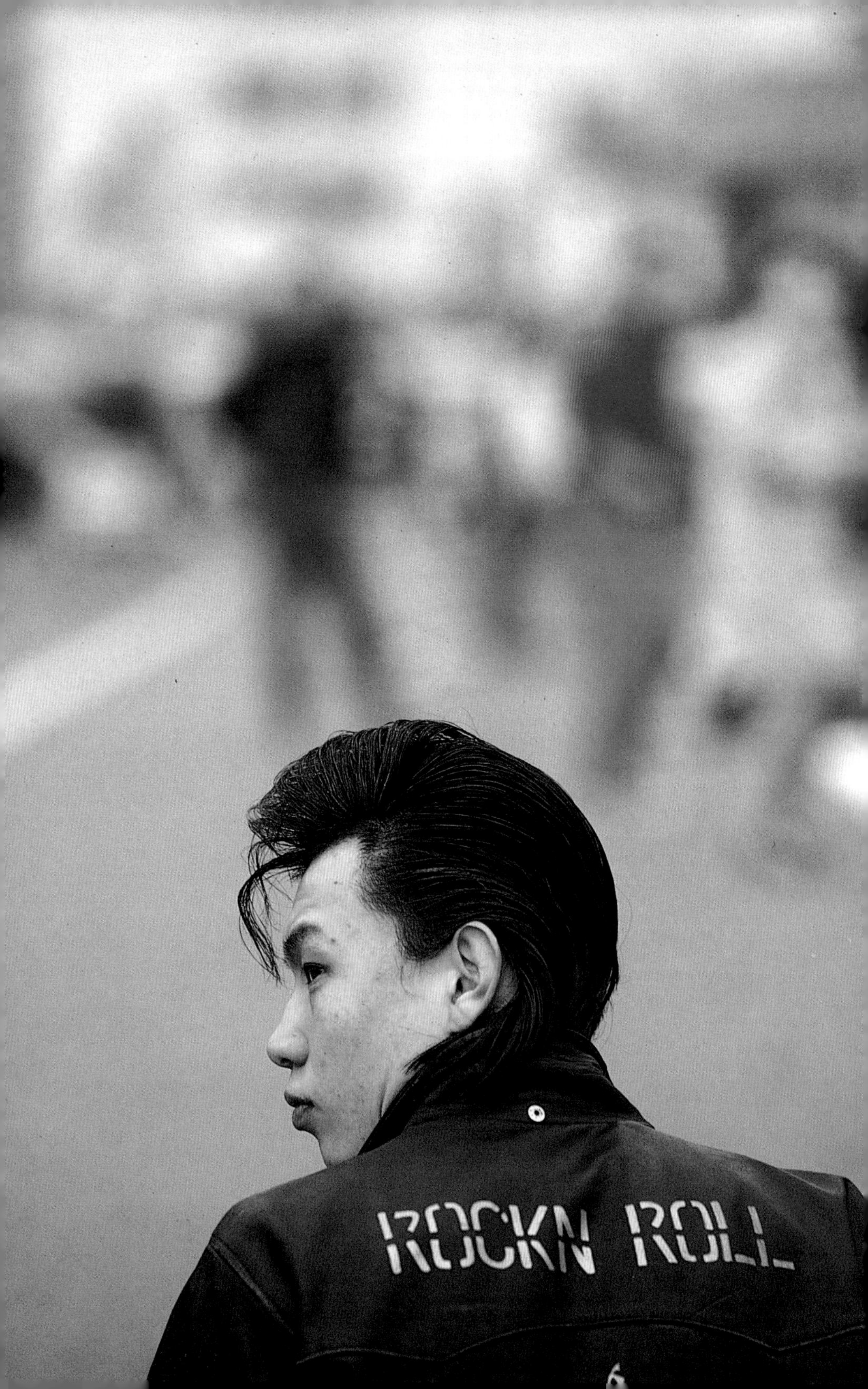
ROCKN ROLL

Attempting to describe the entertainment scene in Tokyo is rather like trying to catch snowflakes. There are flurries here, sprinklings there, different patterns constantly merging, developing, melting, being trodden under foot.

The entertainment landscape is a fascinating panoply of just about everything you ever thought of, plus a few distinctly Japanese happenings that you probably never imagined.

Everyone knows about the Japanese dedication to work and money and the pursuit of something they can never quite define. But it takes a visit to Japan to really bring home the point that the Japanese are probably the best-organized and most dedicated entertainers and impresarios in the world. If it's the same thing well packaged, it's a hit. If it's something different which no self-respecting culture-vulture could possibly avoid, it's a hit. If it's cheap, it's often a flop.

Entertainment to the Japanese is an ongoing procession of stimulation and titillation that pays little respect to time or even appropriateness. The bar people are still going home as the office workers pile on to the trains in the morning. The biggest baseball games of the year are all played in the afternoon when most of the potential audience are theoretically hard at work. *Sumo* matches stretch from 10 in the morning until six at night, but never beyond.

Concerts often start at 6 p.m. in a country where millions of people don't finish work until at least 7 p.m. Street festivals are going on somewhere day and night. Anyone with some free time during the day and at night really has the chance to cram in all kinds of sights, sounds and experiences without necessarily having to destroy too many credit ratings. Anyone bored in Tokyo doesn't deserve to be here.

Preceding pages, attending traditional Japanese drama is still a popular pastime; Kabuki – a spectacle of sight and drama. **Left**, a young man prefers Rock'n'Roll. **Above**, A *Buyô* performance.

A diary of a day that was might go something like this: "A couple of hours of *kabuki* in the morning (US$6). Department store on the Ginza for lunch ($8), souvenir shopping and an exhibition of European art. Tracked down a local festival and watched Japanese dancing. Also exhibition of *bonsai* in the shrine (free). Popped into local bar/restaurant for a drink and watched hour of *sumo* on TV. Good baby crabs (crispy) and gingko nuts (hot). Visited the all-female musical

revue for something really different. Then on to jazz club for late set – great American trio live (a bit pricey – $65 with one drink!). Met some jazz fans in suits who suggested I join them at a *karaoke* bar. Last conscious memory singing "Yesterday" with a woman in kimono. And so to tomorrow...."

With a little bit of planning, a fistful of yen and a map of the railway and subway system, Tokyo is your oyster.

Japanese life in general is designed to provide comfort and satisfaction to suit all pockets. But you can have a good time without spending a thing.

There is no better place to start than a department store (*depaato*) at 9.50 a.m. A department store for entertainment? Yes, indeed. Join the hardy band of shoppers waiting at the entrance to any major store, and you can watch the final instructions to staff being dished out – reminders on degree of bowing etc. At the stroke of 10, the doors will be opened. Walk straight through and go all the way to the top on the escalators. Behind every counter, at the end of every escalator, there will be store employees bowing and welcoming. It's the nearest humble mortals will ever get to feeling like royalty. No need to reply unless you feel like

cremes, tell them it's a present and you can watch the equally impressive art of giftwrapping, while bewailing the fate of the world's rain forests. You may even get a choice of ribbon color.

Even the big Western-style hotels can provide a lot of free entertainment. On a "lucky" day on the calendar, the lobbies will be thronged with wedding groups, a mish-mash of tails and chiffon and kimono and white suits, envelopes full of money to give and bags full of presents to take away. Marriage brokers please note that the unmarried women will be in bright colors, the married in black kimono.

raising a giggle or two. But remember *they* don't regard it as entertainment. It's strictly customer service.

There are many other free offers, too. While in the store, visit the food section in the basement, where food will be delved out generously as you pass. Not to be missed are the elevator girls in their little caps, their ritual of greeting, announcing and bowing better choreographed than most dance performances. Even the singsong style of delivery has to be rehearsed – nothing is left to chance. You might even want to buy something. Whatever it is, from silk sash to chou-

More free entertainment is available at any one of the 365 good excuses for a party that the Japanese, being essentially fun-loving and gregariously rowdy, manage to find, despite their somber international image.

Cherry-blossom viewing is a classic case of this: right through from early morning when lowly workers arrive to stake out territorial claims with cardboard and boxes ready for the arrival of everyone else when work finishes. Good will and generosity abound at such gatherings, and anyone wandering through Ueno Park on the right days could get a million offers of a glass of *sake*. Put almost any Japanese in a familiar situation with familiar faces, and all the inhibitions come tumbling down.

And to see the extraordinary fashions and ritualized dancing of the young and very young, there is always Yoyogi Park on a Sunday, now internationally famous for its transformations of demure sailor-suited high-school girls into lurid punk rockers after just a few minutes of preparation in the bushes.

But what of the heavy history of formal entertainment, rites and rituals which lies behind all these informal snippets of daily life in the big city?

Gagaku and Bugaku: If we really go back a long way, at least 1,500 years, we find a performing art form that can still be experienced much as it ever has been. This is *Gagaku* which was the special preserve of the Imperial Household. The musicians of the Music Department not only keep this eery, atonal form of music alive, they also have to provide orchestral background music, national anthems and the like for important state functions.

Gagaku literally means "elegant, authorized music," which includes not only orchestral music played on an assortment of wind and string instruments (plus gongs and drums), but also singing and dancing. *"Bugaku"* is the term used when dancing is involved. The dancing is slow, stately, symbolic and soporific and all the dancers are male. *"Kangen"* is the term used for purely instrumental pieces. Most items, barely distinguishable to the untrained ear, are based on music imported from Korea, India, China and Indo-China centuries ago.

There are performances in the Gakubu inside the Imperial Palace in spring and autumn, but you need connections to get tickets. There are, however, occasional outdoor performances in some shrines or at the National Theater which are open to anyone. *Gagaku* is likely to stimulate only the genuine musicologist, but, like climbing Mt. Fuji, it's worth trying once.

Left, a puppeteer and his *Bunraku* puppet. **Above**, Harajuku on Sundays: all made up and somewhere to go.

Noh and Kyôgen: Almost as old and even more minimal and mysterious is the theater form of *Noh*. Its origins are religious. Aristocratic patronage led to the development of its characteristic form from earlier religious plays performed in temples and shrines. The aristocrats demanded esoteric poetry, sophisticated language and the most refined simplicity of movement. And that is precisely what you can still see and hear today, six centuries later.

It is difficult to describe a *Noh* performance: words like ethereal, inaccessible, and subtle spring to mind. There is subdued passion, there is deep emotion, there is spiri-

tuality. The pace is slow and controlled, there are no lighting changes, and half the audience sleeps a lot of the time. The rest pore over their scores and mouth the words being chanted. As with so many performing arts in Japan, the audience consists mostly of those who aspire themselves to participate. Fortunately, many excellent English translations of *Noh* plays are available. Highly recommended would be any chance to see *Noh* by torchlight (*Takigi Noh*), which sometimes features in shrine festivals, particularly at Meiji Shrine.

Many people much prefer *Kyôgen*, the

comic interludes originally designed to provide light relief between *Noh* performances, but often presented now in their own right. They are very accessible if you have just the bare outline of what is going on. Some last no more than ten minutes. They present amusing situations based on folk tales and Buddhist parables. All human foibles are there and can be appreciated by almost anyone, much in the way that Shakespeare's Falstaff scenes have a universal validity. Several groups regularly perform *Kyôgen* in English, an experience not actually as weird as it may sound.

Bunraku: Puppeteers have been common in

Each major puppet is manipulated by three operators, a logistic marvel in itself. It takes many years to progress from hooded leg or left arm operator to unmasked head and right arm operator. Clearly a *Bunraku* stage is a crowded one, despite the fact that standard-bearer puppets only warrant one operator.

In theory the audience doesn't notice all the shuffling around of these silent and dedicated professionals and concentrates instead on the puppets themselves, roughly one-third human size. It is hard not to notice the head puppeteers, however, whose faces loom right behind those of their charges. Aficionados delight in the way the master's

Japan since the 7th Century. Many itinerant Chinese and Korean performers came to Japan to present semi-religious puppet plays. But the sophisticated art we now know as *Bunraku* was not consolidated until Shakespeare's time, when the puppeteers were joined by story-tellers (the art of *Jôruri*) and *shamisen* accompanists. What we are talking about here is not Punch and Judy. *Bunraku* is truly adult theater, dealing with themes as wide-ranging and profound as Shakespeare's plays: tales of revenge and sacrifice, love and rejection, reincarnation and suicide.

face mirrors that of the puppet and the way the puppet seems to control the master. Neither speak. But the puppets are constantly on the move: fingers twitch, eyebrows shoot up and down, eyeballs roll, pipes are smoked, letters are written, heads severed. Suspension of disbelief and adjustment to scale takes a few minutes, but once you get into the conventions, a *Bunraku* performance can be far more moving than one featuring walking, talking, grimacing actors. *Bunraku* children, idealized stereotypes that they are, are much more amusing than their *kabuki* counterparts.

The real tour de force, though, is perhaps given by the narrators, the *gidayu* performers, who speak, gesture and weep from a kneeling position at far stage on the left. Beside them sits an impassive *shamisen* player who keeps the tempo of the piece both musically and emotionally.

The secret is to get a seat near enough to be able to see the puppets' faces, but not so near the front that you can't easily see these amazing performers.

The small auditorium of the National Theater is the most likely place to find a *Bunraku* performance happening. Highly recommended.

Opera," and indeed troupes from both countries often perform together.

The original word *"kabuki,"* used in the early 16th century, meant "avant-garde" and referred to all-female performances often of a distinctly licentious nature. The Tokugawa regime took exception to this in 1629 and the wild women were banned. So started the all-male *kabuki* tradition, which is basically continued even today, although actresses are allowed on stage for certain special events.

Kabuki developed into its present form in the 17th and 18th centuries. This was theater for the masses. *Kabuki* actors were the rock stars of feudal Japan, immortalized in thou-

Kabuki: And so we come to that perhaps most splendid and all-encompassing theater form in Japan, *kabuki*. It is difficult to categorize. Certainly it is "theater" in the very widest sense of the word, but in many ways it also resembles opera and even ballet. In Japanese there is really no problem: *kabuki* literally translates as "song-dance-skill" with no mention of theater. It is in many ways similar to what the Chinese call "Peking

Left, *Koto* musicians produce unique and beautiful sounds. **Above**, the unique drummer group, Kodo, from Sado Island, Niigata, performs in Tokyo once a year.

sands of woodblock prints.

The older plays still performed today often began their life as puppet plays and were full of social comment, thinly disguised satire and recent news stories, again showing a similarity to Shakespeare's plays.

Silence is not golden in *kabuki,* only dramatic pauses known as *"mie."* Most of the time there are musicians on stage, sometimes with narrators as well, and always performers behind the screen stage right providing live sound effects from bird song to temple gongs. Other assistants come on stage to highlight action by banging wooden clappers. Part of the performance also takes place in the auditorium in the form of loud shouts. These are not random. Most of the shouters are paid by the actors to call out family names or professional nicknames at just the right moments. The effect is truly quadrophonic.

Actors also come into close contact with the audience by entering, exiting and posing on the *hanamichi* walkway which cuts right through the seats. They will also sometimes exit on wires to the great excitement of the hordes of kimono-clad grandmothers far below.

English programs are usually available

for big *kabuki* performances, and comfort can be gained from the fact that most of the audience can't understand all the Japanese being spoken on stage either, especially as much of it is spoken in a way unique to the *kabuki* stage.

Kabuki has so many points of interest: the extraordinary skill and femininity of the actors who play female roles (*"onnagata"*); the spectacular scenery and revolving stages; no-expenses-spared costuming; the crossover with *Bunraku, Noh, Kyôgen* and Japanese dance forms and their performers; the thrill of entering a Japan that bears little

physical relationship to what is going on outside the theater...or does it? Some commentators have noted that *kabuki* is basically presenting the emotional attitudes, relationships and obligations that are the core of the Japanese mentality now just as much as then. It is well worth going along and seeing for yourself.

The main *kabuki* theaters are the National Theater, the Kabukiza and the Shimbashi Embujô Theater. Most *kabuki* programs include various totally unrelated items spread over 10 hours or so, from late morning to evening, with generous intervals for tea-drinking, box-lunch munching and the like. The Kabukiza provides one excellent service; the chance to see only one "act," or even just part of one. There is a little box office to the left of the main entrance, charmingly inscribed "seeing act tickets." You will have to stand or sit right up at the back of the gallery, but it's a very cheap way to get at least a taste of *kabuki* if time is limited.

The National Theater: The National Theater complex is located right across the moat from the Imperial Palace. The squat, concrete design (by Hiroyuki Iwamoto) is reminiscent of an ancient Japanese storehouse, and indeed the three auditoria are repositories for all that is best about the traditional theater arts of Japan.

The main auditorium holds over 1,700 people and is designed very much according to *kabuki* principles – very wide indeed. Visibility is not particularly good, but it is worth knowing that the seats outside the *hanamichi* are much cheaper, and it is possible to get very close to the actors entering and exiting, although they rarely face in that direction. The stage machinery is complex and up-to-date. The smaller auditorium (630 seats) is used particularly for *Bunraku* and Japanese music.

There is a small auditorium at the rear of the complex which features mostly *rakugo* storytelling and other traditional Japanese entertainers. In fact, there are chances to see all kinds of events at the National Theater besides these basic forms. One stipulation, however, is that all performances there must have been tried and tested elsewhere first.

The theater also has a *kabuki* training school for people not connected by blood to major *kabuki* families, and there are special "*Kabuki* Appreciation Classrooms" in the summer which demonstrate techniques to the audiences. Although designed primarily for school groups, these are fascinating for anyone. The theater has restaurants and shops on two levels, but unfortunately, you cannot enter the complex without a ticket for a show. An English earphone guide service is available.

Rakugo: Although the Japanese have never been great joke-tellers as such, they have always had a penchant for the humorous fascinating to watch, but a considerable knowledge of formal and colloquial Japanese is required to fully appreciate the humor. However, one leading performer, Shijaku, has experimented in recent years with performances delivered mostly in English, both in Japan and the U.S. These have become very popular with foreigners and Japanese alike.

The tradition is still alive and well, and there are several small "*yose*" theaters presenting *rakugo* in Tokyo, most of them around Asakusa. The Suehirotei Theater in Shinjuku is also easy to find. Most Japanese *rakugo* fans, however, tend to watch the

story. Conversation over drinks tends to include a lot of funny stories based on real happenings. The professional version of this is *Rakugo*, a traditional storytelling form which includes old chestnuts several centuries old as well as many topical references. *Rakugo* performers deliver their stories solo from a cushion. The only props used are a fan and a towel. The voices, facial gestures and movements from a kneeling position are storytellers on TV.

Contemporary theater: The casual visitor to Japan is less likely to want to explore the byways of contemporary theater, but there is a huge amount available, including every conceivable style, performing space and price.

Translations of foreign plays and musicals are extraordinarily popular, ranging from Chekhov to *Cats*. Many major musical productions are imported more or less as they are from London or New York, with the exception that everything is performed in Japanese by Japanese dancers and singers.

Far left, watching kabuki from the balcony at the Kabukiza. **Above**, the Kabukiza Theater in Ginza.

Sometimes these are disastrous, sometimes an improvement on the original: something like *My Fair Lady* travels badly, not because of the dialect theme (Japan has plenty of those to substitute for Cockney), but because the Japanese will insist on wearing Beaton costumes, red wigs, and so on. Not that Japanese audiences seem to care. The *Man of La Mancha*, *Fiddler on the Roof*, and *The Phantom of the Opera* could probably bring in audiences forever.

There are few troupes who have been very successful in other countries. Ninagawa's troupe is one of these. Despite his alleged dislike of Shakespeare back in the days when

tacular effects is often mind-boggling. The only problem is that a lot of Japanese members of the audience and most foreigners have little idea what it's all about. But it is original. And the cosy, incestuous kind of theater world it represents provides lots of work for actors, most of them surviving only on part-time jobs. Japan is lucky in that it has no actual theater unions, which means that anyone can have a go more or less when and where they feel like it. To counteract this freedom, each group becomes tightly knit and exclusive.

If you want to see Shakespeare performed in Japanese, and many would prefer not to,

he was really rough avant-garde material, he has gone very commercial in recent years. This is most notable with his *Hamlets* and *Macbeths*, which somehow appeal to foreign audiences, despite his eclectic East-meets-West approach to staging.

The group called "Yumeno Yûminsha" has a large and devoted following in Japan and represents a peculiar facet of a lot of Japanese theatrical activity. One man, Hideki Noda, leads the troupe, directs, writes all the plays, and also gets the plum parts. His group's special acrobatic, tongue-twisting style of delivery and love of spec-

there are performances going on constantly all over Tokyo. Shakespeare's validity in translation is quite amazing. The Japanese do have one advantage, of course: some of the translations available use very modern Japanese, which means modern-dress performances have a cohesion they often lack in the original.

At the other end of the scale is the Theater of discomfort: little performing spaces often no bigger than the 6-mat living room that, in fact, they are at times, where shoes have to be taken off, capacity is exceeded by several hundred percent, and shows are delayed while the audience is constantly urged to move one buttock closer to the next person yet again. All this is accepted as part of the delight of minor-scale theater-going, but it's only for the stouthearted and flexible-limbed.

Takarazuka: For something completely different, there's nothing brighter or more entertaining than the Takarazuka Revue. This is an all-female extravaganza somewhere between Las Vegas and the London Palladium. Not an actor in sight, but lots of mustachioed and thigh-slapping dancers and singers falling in love with each other on stage while the wet-eyed young girls out in the audience fall in love with them. It's clean, it's lively and it's fun, and nobody will ever think of recommending it to foreigners.

Geisha and Buyô: Not many people would recommend *geisha* either. After generations of erotic fantasy, ideas about mysterious and exotic women slipping delicately out of kimono at the first sight of an Englishman, the *geisha* tended to drop out of the public eye until the dalliance of a certain Japanese Prime Minister came to light at the end of the Eighties. *Geisha* have, of course, been known to become mistresses of the wealthy, but then so have schoolteachers.

It has to be said again that the *geisha* are a dying breed of talented professional performers who can sing, dance, play silly games and serve drinks with more finesse than anyone else in the world, largely because it takes many years of practice. That's why they're a dying breed, and that's why someone has to pay an awful lot of money for the privilege of sharing their company.

Few foreigners really derive much pleasure from a *geisha* evening. The entertainment is designed for the hard-core middle-aged, conservative businessmen and politicians of Japan Inc., *sumo* wrestlers, and anyone else with the urge to pay over the odds. The real thing, the subdued "teahouse," of which there are still many in Tokyo, particularly east of Asakusa, is a haven for the connoisseur of the sentimental

song, the curve of a powdered neck and the liver of the angler fish. During the daytime, *geisha* are busy housewives, musicians, music teachers, organizers of gargantuan performances of Beethoven's Ninth, and generally guardians of the *Edo* spirit of friendliness and hardheadedness.

There are, however, occasional chances for lesser mortals to see the *geisha* in their finery: at special parades, such as the one in the big *Sanja* Festival in May; and at special performances of Japanese dancing (*"Buyô"*) at theaters such as the Shimbashi Embujô and the Meijiza. These sometimes also include young daughters going through

all the sophisticated adult routines with a wisdom and conviction belying their age.

Butoh: Not to be confused with *Buyô*, which everyone knows and appreciates, is the modern avant-garde dancing style known as *Butoh*. Much written about in foreign language publications, much admired abroad, particularly in France, and almost unheard of in Japan itself outside avant-garde circles, a *Butoh* performance can be a truly exotic, and sometimes erotic, experience, if at times a painfully slow one. However, its basic message seems to be to stress inhumanity, desperation, nihilism and

Left, the life and times of the past portrayed in drama. **Above**, traditional Japanese dancing.

a devotion not to the display of physical beauty and harmony, but rather ugliness and discord. Most *butoh* performers concentrate on twisting their faces, bodies and even eyes into macabre imitations of the physically handicapped. To some it is highly stimulating and thought-provoking. To others it is frankly depressing and meaningless. However, once you've seen a performance, you'll never forget it.

Noh and dance: Foreigners are often surprised by the extraordinary interest in ballet in Japan. Just as in any other country, thousands of tiny tots in tutus are put through their paces by mothers eager to see them

you can find thousands, if not millions of Japanese participating in almost any known cultural or sporting activity. Western classical music is a major passion and a massive business. It extends to musical forms which you would really not expect to find here: many universities, for example, have handbell groups and mandolin orchestras.

The latter half of the 1980s witnessed a very welcome trend towards business sponsorship of music and, to a lesser extent, theater, and the construction of many fine new auditoria. The Suntory whisky company is one enterprise actively supporting many cultural fields. The Suntory Hall is

grow up into graceful swans. Many foreign choreographers have commented on the high level of technique and dedication in Japan, but legs and arms tend to be rather too short for creating the full balletic "line." But with the rapid increase in the size of young children recently, this slight handicap may disappear.

Opera and classical music: Any mention of classical music immediately conjures up visions of the massed ranks of young violinists furiously bowing away to the dictates of the well-known Suzuki Method. It really happens. Once again, the point is proved that

much praised for its fine acoustics. Other recent halls are very European in style – Casals Hall in the university district of Ochanomizu, and the huge Bunkamura complex in Shibuya, specifically designed for the presentation of full-scale operas and symphony concerts. Casts of millions are easily accommodated in the new arenas such as the Tokyo Dome. And if you happen to be in Japan in December, there are literally hundreds of performances of Beethoven's Ninth – a curious end-of-year passion.

Foreign artists: Massive as the whole Japanese performing arts scene may be, the

1980s witnessed an inevitable trend: the willingness of foreign actors, musicians and dancers to perform in Japan as well. The market is so enormous, the prices of tickets at a world high, and the spin-off in, for example, record sales, enormous. The number of theater groups invited to Japan is still relatively small, although the situation has been much improved by the construction of the Ginza Saison Theater and the Tokyo Globe.

But musicians come in the thousands. Tokyo could well already be the finest place in the world for seeing and hearing all the greatest musicians. You will have to pay for

jazz clubs and coffee shops catering to all tastes. Many jazz performers have had great success abroad, notably the saxophonist Sadao Watanabe and the trumpeter Terumasa Hino. All the jazz greats visit Japan regularly, either to appear at sophisticated nightclubs, especially in the Roppongi area, or at one of the multitude of jazz festivals presented every year, many of them open-air. These often involve a bit of a trek out of Tokyo, but feature impressive arrays of Japanese and foreign artists. Small jazz clubs in Tokyo will generally charge between US$7 and $15 per head, others may charge much more for famous guest per-

the opportunity, of course, but whether your taste lies with chamber music, African rhythms, modern jazz, or the Birmingham Symphony Orchestra, satisfaction is guaranteed. The only problems are that concert programs tend to be dictated by Japanese taste and many performers are still jet-lagged when they are pushed onto the stage.

Jazz: Jazz is another serious field of endeavor in Japan, with hundreds of small

formers, sometimes including a free drink.

Other live houses: You should be able to satisfy any musical desire somewhere in the main centers of Tokyo: reggae, samba, country & western, blue grass, heavy metal...it's all happening. In Roppongi there are at least two different clubs providing passable imitations of the Beatles and other music from the 60s and 70s.

Discos: Tokyo likes to cater to all tastes and ages, and this is certainly true of the disco scene. The main center for foreigners and trendy Japanese is Roppongi, where some buildings are crammed full of floor after

Left, avant garde theater has its own niche. **Above**, *Butoh* expresses humanity in despair.

floor of discos, some of them open until the early morning. Most Roppongi discos are accustomed to having foreign customers, discos in other areas not so much so.

Sexual discrimination is rife: many discos charge women less than men, and unaccompanied men are often not admitted. There is also the problem that many people go to discos to dance with their friend or alone rather than to pick anyone up. There is sometimes the interesting sight of young men practicing their steps together in one corner and young girls dancing together somewhere else. There is also a passion amongst the young to indulge in group

movements to certain popular numbers and also a strange reluctance to indulge in cheek-to-cheek dancing.

The best thing is to seek the advice of residents and attempt to discover just what kind of atmosphere a particular place is likely to have as well as the type of clientele it encourages or attracts.

Discos can be lonely places for the unattached. If it's friends you want to make, many bars in the Roppongi area have a large clientele of foreigners and therefore attract Japanese who are keen to meet non-Japanese. Many Japanese discos are very high-

tech and are making the most of the cocktail and gourmet food boom of the 80s.

Do-It-Yourself live: For some reason, TV shows featuring amateur singers of all types, and in all kinds of groupings, continue to be enormously popular. Few parties remain long without a call for a song – and that can mean everybody present is expected to do their bit, whether they are willing, able and harmonious or not.

Japan is truly a land of song, ranging from old folk songs (*minyô*) and modern sentimental ballads called *enka* (the truck drivers' favorite) to *chanson* and garbled versions of Western ballads. This passion was the rea-

THE TOKYO GLOBE

One of the least likely and most conspicuous new buildings in Tokyo, which stands in the shadows of several tower blocks in the Okubo district, and is a small, almost circular pink building with unusual twin gables and cupola. At a glance, you would be forgiven for thinking that someone had decided to copy a theater from Shakespeare's time and construct it in Tokyo on a whim. It is the Tokyo Globe, one of the most exciting theater projects in Japan, if not the world, for many years.

Opened in 1988, the Tokyo Globe has already established itself as a main center for major visiting theater groups from around the world, and is, therefore, helping to fill what had previously been a great vacuum.

The Tokyo Globe is an extraordinary place that seems destined to earn the same epithet that was given to its 17th century predecessor – "the fayrest that ever was."

son for the development of *karaoke* in the 1970s. *"Kara"* means empty, as in *karate* ("empty hand"), and *"oke"* is a Japanese abbreviation of the word "orchestra." "Empty orchestra" means that a machine provides the music for you, and you become the star of the golden mic. Initially this invention deprived a lot of musicians of their work in the clubs, but the demand is now so great that many musicians are kept busy in the studio.

Karaoke is either very masochistic or very sadistic, depending on your tolerance levels and which side of the microphone you happen to be standing. Why anyone would take delight in listening to a drunken office worker failing to sing "My Way" in his very own way remains a mystery. At least it encourages drinking. The system has become quite sophisticated, with laser vision machines displaying both the words and background mood images, sometimes surprisingly erotic. It is no excuse to claim you can't sing, as patently most other people can't either. Nor can you claim ignorance of Japanese – they often have English lyrics available. If really pressed into singing, have a nice easy standard like "Yesterday" or "I Left My Heart in San Francisco" up your

providing *karaoke* rooms, like mini-studios, which can be rented by the hour for a bit of private warbling with a few friends. The only problem with those is that high-school students have found they make a perfect place for private activities of a different kind.

The international rock circus: The high decibel circus regularly comes to town in a big way. Rash is the singer or group who misses Japan during a tour. The benefits from the sales of albums, T-shirts and programs (at US$15 each) alone are considerable. When Ringo Starr appeared in Tokyo with his friends at the end of 1989, he said in a TV interview that it was a shame they hadn't

sleeve, and you will be a "star" forever. On the other hand, if you really want to sing, make the most of the chance – the charge is likely to be something like US$1 a go. And it's worth practicing anyway: *karaoke* is spreading around the world.

Karaoke can be extremely anti-social, especially to someone living right next door to a place with bad soundproofing. The latest development takes care of that problem by

Left, scantily-dressed showgirls dazzle their audience. **Above**, the modern rock scene is big business.

produced a record before the tour. The interpreter translated shame as "I am ashamed," which he well should have been!

$35 is a basic price for most rock concerts and major name groups can fill mighty spaces like the Tokyo Dome for several nights running. Many groups, feeling that the Japanese are less critical than other nations, often use the Japanese visit as a rehearsal for the rest of a world tour. That is not necessarily a wise attitude. If you have spent over $50 basic and have been waiting for a concert for months, you tend to make the most of the experience regardless. But there are many critical voices heard afterwards.

The three biggest venues in Tokyo are the Tokyo Dome, the Budôkan Martial Arts Hall and the Yoyogi Olympic Pool, where in winter you are actually sitting on an ice-rink covered with boards (thick socks needed). The sound and visibility in all three is very variable, although video screens help. Yokohama has two excellent arenas; the Yokohama Stadium (open-air) and the recently opened Yokohama Arena, which has perhaps the best visibility and seats of them all.

Tickets often have to be bought well in advance, but with the number of visiting

Snacks, soaplands, etc.: The "water trade" (*mizu shôbai*) is a massive night industry keeping thousands of waiters, hostesses, chefs, bartenders, hairdressers, clothiers and alcohol suppliers in business. Tokyo is packed with drinking establishments of all types. These range from exclusive clubs on the Ginza, where you are welcome only by appointment or with someone wearing a genuine Rolex and a genuine Pierre Cardin suit and where the very act of sitting down will cost anything from US$150 upwards, to tiny places in back streets where jovial and underpaid girls, many of them now Filipinos or Koreans, will do their best to provide

artists increasing all the time, and the size of the arenas growing, there is always a good chance of a last-minute ticket. Ticket touts are in abundance and should be treated with caution. If demand seems slight, they will often bargain right down.

Inside the arenas, security is tight and open standing areas are not allowed. When a group such as U2 appears, however, most of the audience stands all the way through anyway. For better vision and often much better sound, smaller auditoria such as the Nakano Sun Plaza or the Shibuya Kôkaidô are to be recommended.

whatever entertainment is required.

"Snack" is the word used for small bars, usually with one or two mothering young and not-so-young women in attendance, but not always.

Knowing exactly where to go and how much it might cost is best left up to friendly Japanese acquaintances. You pay for the quality of the service from the owner's point of view, not yours. The degree of titillation goes all the way from zero to total in the aptly named "Soapland" saunas-pretending-not-to-be-brothels. Actually these were called *"toruko"* (as in "Turkish bath") until there were vociferous complaints from some resident Turks. Amazingly, the *toruko* association decided to change every neon sign. Soaplands involve the use of a lot of soap at $200 a session.

Women are catered to in the much harder to find "host clubs" which seem to consist mostly of rich patronesses paying to be abused by rather greasy samples of young Japanese manhood. There is no evidence of special "soaplands" for female customers as yet. However, there is the wonderful "love hotel" phenomenon, the place to go when your liaison is predetermined. These are easily recognized by their rather gaudy ap-

as $35 for two, or far more if you want a room with video equipment, climbing frames, pool-sized bath and revolving mirror-bed. A "night" in love hotel parlance usually lasts from 10 p.m. until 10 a.m. the next morning. At other times there are special "service times" at cheap rates for two-hour liaisons, followed by rapid room-cleaning ready for the next guests.

Why are love hotels necessary? Well, it is really a question of lack of privacy. They are not only used by those involved in secret relationships; many married couples find them a wonderful way to be alone for a few hours. Most hotels provide room service and

寅さん

pearance, often without proper windows. Attempts are made to ensure privacy: there are often two separate entrances, and particularly kind establishments will cover up car number plates just in case anyone comes looking.

The love hotel system is very simple. As long as you are a couple (few places will accept anything else), you have a choice of rooms for the night. These may be as cheap

Left, *Karaoke* singing – where everyone is a star.
Above, actor Kiyoshi Atsumi brought the Tora-san character to life.

there is a trend to clean up their image by inviting women designers to add homely touches to the interiors. An interesting experience often much cheaper than real hotels.

The gay paradise: Tokyo has often been described as a paradise for homosexuals, and that is certainly a reason for many men wanting to live in Japan. Not everyone, it seems, is lured by the exotic oriental woman. A strong thread of homosexuality, sometimes overt, at other times more akin to chumminess, has always run through Japanese life. There can be few other societies where the sexes are divided so much: there is all-male theater, all-female theater, *sumo* (where no woman is allowed on the performing ring), and a very strong disassociation of the sexes in many daily activities. Boys and girls rarely mingle in university classes, there are often all-male or all-female groups on skiing holidays or even in discos.

In fact, there is a great deal of confusion as to what sex people actually are. There are many television stars who are either permanent transvestites or even famous sex-change samples. There is nothing secret about this. There are several spectacular transvestite shows at clubs in Tokyo, particularly popular with women. And un-

known to many housewives, it seems, many businessmen husbands are not in fact spending their evenings at hostess clubs, but in the warrens of gay bars in the Shinjuku 2-chôme district. By all accounts, bisexuality is rife, but rarely talked about. The same is true of lesbianism.

Oriental peeping: Voyeurism is a well-developed art in Japan and even extends to several popular photo-magazines. Areas such as Kabukichô in Shinjuku are constantly offering new varieties around the central theme: including *"no pan kissa,"* coffee shops where panties are out; topless

bars, noodle shops and curry restaurants; private peeping rooms with or without telephones for giving instructions (tissues provided); "pink salons" where action goes on under the table or elsewhere. Fashion in these activities comes and goes, but there are a thousand ways to guarantee male stimulation for money. Women are not well served in this respect.

Movies: Tokyo is well equipped with movie houses. Few of them, however, are open very late, and you have to watch films bearing Japanese subtitles, unless you really want to experience Japanese films free from sub-titles altogether. Censorship remains odd; no pubic manifestations allowed in public places. One producer has been fighting this law for many years through the medium of old erotic Japanese woodblock prints (*shunga*). These prints are widely available all over the world, but cannot be sold in Japan, nor can they be shown in movies without disfiguring alterations. He has won small battles in court, but it may take a long time.

Most major Western films come to Japan, often some time after their release somewhere else. An average ticket price would be $10.

Television: The cheapest form of popular entertainment, and in many ways the most interesting and revealing, is television. Tokyo has seven basic channels, two of them operated by NHK, the equivalent of the BBC. The other five are private channels. There are also various cable and UHF channels, including JCTV which provides English-language broadcasting to hotels. Several channels run all night, and if you really want to see what turns the nation on, you'll be surprised at the variety of fare available, from samurai dramas to singing contests, from Korean lessons to naked girls in hot springs. Some of the late-night programs are much raunchier than anywhere else in the world, others are as dry as rice crackers.

Programming on the private channels is very much controlled by the sponsors. However promising a new program might appear on paper, it will never materialize without definite sponsorship, sometimes from just one company, but usually from several. Sponsor lists appear before and after every program. One trend that has come from abroad is the huge increase in recent years of news programming.

Many bilingual and stereo programs are put out. The only problem with bilingual films (most foreign films are dubbed into Japanese, a whole industry in itself) is that most films have to be cut to fit a time slot; the film may make sense in Japanese, but if you are listening to the original soundtrack, you begin to wonder why so many actors seem to stop in mid-sentence.

Radio: Although some FM licenses were granted at the end of the 1980s, there is still age, and up to now not in great demand within the labor market. FM Japan does not restrict itself to Japanese and English, either, but often broadcasts programs in Chinese, French, Spanish, and even Russian.

The main Japanese radio channels, FM Tokyo, NHK FM and Bunka Hôsô tend to include a lot of chat and far less music. NHK includes many language lessons in its broadcasting schedules as well as classical music concerts.

There is one channel which uses no Japanese, and that is the Far East Network of the American Armed Forces Radio and Television Service. They always insist that this is

a relative dearth of radio programming in the Tokyo area. Perhaps in a country so dedicated to TV, this is not surprising, but the success of one of the new FM stations, FM Japan (or "J-Wave") suggests there is actually a big demand for radio. All of the new FM stations in the Kantô region also feature a significant development inside the Japanese media – the use of bilingual DJs and announcers, many of them of mixed parent-

Left, phone three girls and talk for an hour – ¥800. **Above**, prostitution is illegal, but what goes on behind the doors?

strictly designed to meet the needs of the U.S. forces in Japan only, and nobody else should therefore criticize what they put out. They have been somewhat superseded by the superior sound of the FM stereo stations.

Polyglots can have a wonderful time with a good radio set, picking up a mass of Korean, Chinese and Russian broadcasting. However, good shortwave equipment is needed to pick up the BBC World Service.

Beer gardens and beer halls: Beer slurping is a favorite summer pastime, and there are hundreds of rooftop beer gardens to deal with the demand. Look out for bright lanterns on the top floor and head up the nearest elevator. Some beer gardens attract customers with live bands, mud wrestling (rare), topless boxing contests (female) and the like. The beer garden with the nicest view is probably the one on top of the Kudan Kaikan, which overlooks the Nippon Budôkan and Yasukuni Shrine.

The best beer garden in a real garden is the Hanazawa Gardens near Ebisu, which was originally the home of the chairman of the Manchurian Railroad. There are covered areas for rainy days and a variety of indoor rooms are available for private parties.

Some of the larger hotels have their own

gardens, notably the Akasaka and Tokyo Prince Hotels, and the Hotel New Otani.

Tokyo also boasts various German-style beerhalls, some of them operated by Germans. The oldest and most famous is the bustling Lion Beer Hall on the main Ginza drag near the Matsuzakaya department store. Any Japanese businessman will be able to recommend a good one. One of the largest is the New Tokyo on the first floor of the building directly opposite the Seibu department store at Yûrakuchô. Since the Japan National Railways was privatized, various entertainments have helped to improve the

image of JR. These include a platform beer garden in the middle of Shinagawa Station and special alcohol promotion trains running between Tokyo and Yokohama.

Getting information: Perhaps the most important information that everyone needs is just how to get the information about what's on.

First of all, there are the four English-language daily newspapers, which provide assorted information on major cultural happenings and telephone numbers to call. You cannot guarantee getting anyone particularly fluent in English on the other end, however.

Then, there are four other publications worth consulting. The *Tour Companion* is precisely what it suggests, an up-to-date semimonthly newspaper that is particularly strong on festivals, markets and other special events. It is available free at all big hotels or from the Tourist Information Center (TIC) in Yûrakuchô, the place to go for information of all kinds. Then, there is the *Tokyo Weekender*, also free, which is more of a community paper, but covers many events appealing to foreigners.

Finally, by far the most comprehensive listings appear in the monthly magazines *The Tokyo Journal*, and *Tokyo Time Out* available at bookshops which stock foreign books and magazines, hotels, etc.

The entertainment bible for the Japanese is a magazine called *PIA*, which is a bi-weekly. Now running at about 400 pages an issue, it includes information on every type of event, details of new musical releases, books, lectures, radio and TV, and even tells you about major cultural events in the major cities of the world. The only problem is that it's all in Japanese. The publisher, PIA, has rapidly grown into the major Japanese computerized ticketing agency, with outlets all over the city, as well as a publisher of excellent guidebooks, maps, leisure guides and even venue diagrams to help you find your seat. Most of these are in Japanese only, but there are one or two bilingual publications as well.

Above, Edo Era art displayed hard and soft pornography. **Right**, numerous places to go in and have a peep.

KABUKICHO

In Tokyo, the most eminent entertainment district is now just to the north of Shinjuku Station. Its name, Kabukichô, comes from an early failed attempt to turn the area into a cultural center complete with kabuki theater. To reach it, exit from the East Exit at Shinjuku Station. Walk one block north to Yasukuni Street (Yasukunidôri) and cross. Colorful arches over the narrow streets will announce your successful entry into Kabukichô.

anything more sexual than ego massage. Hostesses, generally Japanese or foreign women who need money or have few other employment possibilities, wait on men and listen to their conversation. If both participants wish to meet outside of the club, they are, of course, free to do so.

Hostess clubs are one of the few places where Japanese women entertain men. In most of the others, the women are imported by the *yakuza* (the Japanese equivalent of the

In the area, there are many excellent restaurants featuring food from all over Asia. Kabukichô is also noted for the number and variety of theaters.

Kabukichô is most famous, however, for its sexual entertainment. Many businessmen come here to entertain clients, beginning in a restaurant and moving on to a club. The sex business manifests itself in an amazing variety of activities some of which are uniquely Japanese. These often tend to emphasize voyeurism rather than direct participation.

Probably the most common establishment is the "hostess bar." These do not involve

Mafia) from the Philippines or Thailand.

The real sexual clubs begin relatively near Yasukunidôri; the first of these are, however, rather tame. There are, for example, many signs for *nozokibeya* (peeping rooms). The patrons of these establishments sit in booths with a small window with one-way glass. They peer into a room in which a young woman, sometimes dressed in a high school uniform, performs various sexual acts.

A third popular type of business is the *terekura* or telephone club. Young men pay to sit in booths with a telephone and wait for young women to call. The women, who have found out about the club through advertising or word of mouth, call in order to have a sexual conversation with a stranger. If all goes well, the two may meet later. One or two of these clubs specialize in foreigners.

In past years, *no-pan kissa* (no panty coffee shops) have been popular, but these seem to be losing favor or moving to another district. In these coffee shops, the waitresses wear nothing under their short skirts; the floor is mirrored; the connection is easy to figure out. The coffee, incidentally, can run as high as US$7 or $8.

As the visitor penetrates deeper into Ka-

enter. Women are not allowed and the vast majority of them do not permit foreigners.

The final major sexual enterprise is the *sôpurando* (soapland). The female employees in these establishments lead their male patrons to a large bathtub or an area near a bathtub. The patron lies down on an air mattress while the female undresses and covers her body with suds. She then proceeds to scrub the man with her body. After the washing, further sexual acts can be procured for an additional fee.

In the area of Kabukichô farthest from Yasukunidôri, there are several blocks of "love hotels." In past years, the rooms

bukichô, the sexual activities become more serious. Cabarets with live sex shows become common (the word *"kyabarei"* in Japanese has a distinctly sexual connotation). Some invite the audience to come up on stage and participate in the show; others provide each visitor with a young woman to fondle.

Most of these cabarets have tough young men outside encouraging businessmen to

Left, the entrance to Kabukichô – a Tokyo hot spot. **Above**, porno shop shows what's available; topless bars and mirrored floors.

tended to be exotically decorated (pirate ships, harems, etc.). Recently, they have become more tasteful or even traditional. Always included is a bathroom with a tub large enough for two people, something which is often not available in Japanese homes.

Kabukichô can provide an entertaining evening of wandering around and gawking; it can teach the discerning visitor a great deal about modern Japanese culture. However, in the evening, especially on weekends, you should be prepared for large groups of drunken businessmen and students.

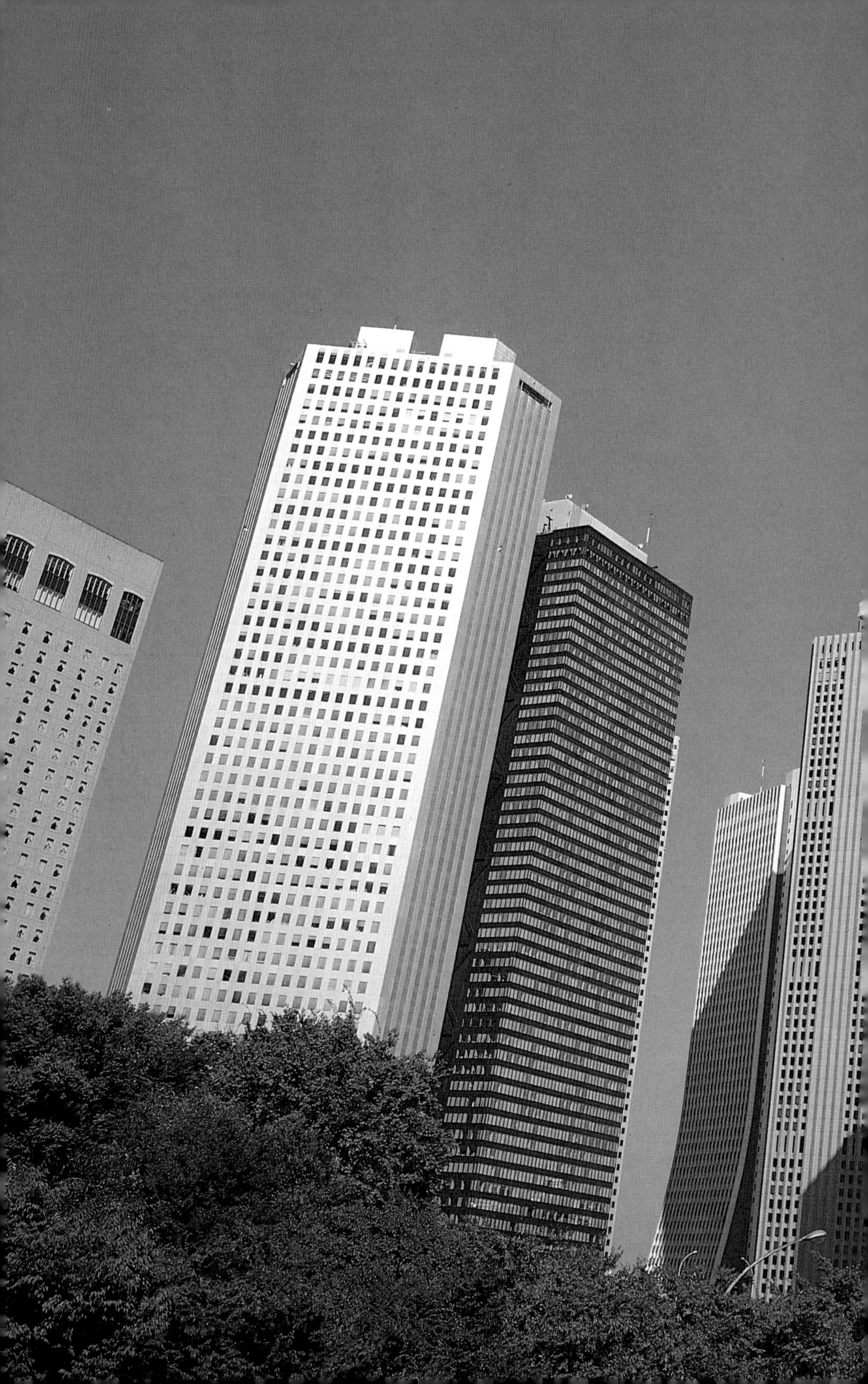

TOKYO-TO

Welcome to the world's most expensive city! If you are reading this in a downtown Tokyo coffee shop, chances are that the coffee will cost US$3 to $4 per small-sized cup, and that the space that you occupy – less than one square meter – would sell for $50,000 or more in the city's hyper-inflated land market.

There are many other examples of high prices: musk melons that cost $100 each at the supermarket; cherries that cost nearly $10 (the price to taste a *single* cherry picked at the season's beginning); a night out on the town that runs as much as $1,000; concert tickets that exceed $200, etc. These are often-repeated horror stories about Tokyo life that are true but not necessarily representative (*i.e.*, in most shops, melons and cherries are substantially cheaper).

Why the high prices? There are lots of reasons, but for many items we can point essentially to the combined effects of the great wealth nowadays of the Japanese population, the strength of the yen in comparison to other currencies, and the tendency of most business interests in Japan to charge as high a price for products and services as they can get away with.

To explain high land costs, we have to acknowledge the small size of Japan relative to the number of residents (about the size of California but five times more people), the relative scarcity of flat land for cities and farms in a country that is mostly mountainous, and the overconcentration of the population on a small fraction of the land surface (What is formally "Tokyo Metropolis" has over 11 million people (i.e., nearly 10 percent of the nation's total) on less than 1 percent of Japan's land area).

What can a budget-conscious visitor do to enjoy Tokyo? There are many ways to avoid the highest prices and stretch your yen. Keep away from the fancy restaurants and eat at small noodle and *yakitori* (skewered chicken) shops and other modest establishments frequented by working Japanese. Stay at a Japanese boarding house (*minshuku*) or inn (*ryokan*) instead of an international hotel. Walk a lot, and ride trains instead of taxis. Keep souvenir purchases to a minimum, but if you must, try shopping at one of the several Sunday flea markets that are found in the city. These sales often have lots of Japanese arts and crafts available for bargain prices. Finally, enjoy the many free attractions of Tokyo: its busy street life; the many parks, shrines, and temples; the perimeter of the Imperial Palace; the lavish department stores and other great shops (for browsing); and the many festivals of all kinds that can be found just about every week in various neighborhoods of the city.

Preceding pages: Shinjuku continues to grow – upwards!; the highway maze; Sukiyabashi crossing in Ginza; a storefront in Akihabara. **Left**, feeding the carps.

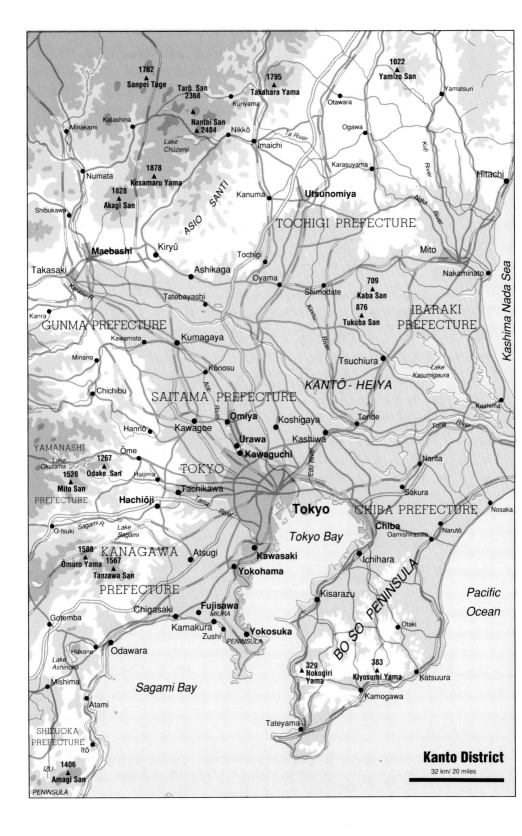

Kanto District

32 km/ 20 miles

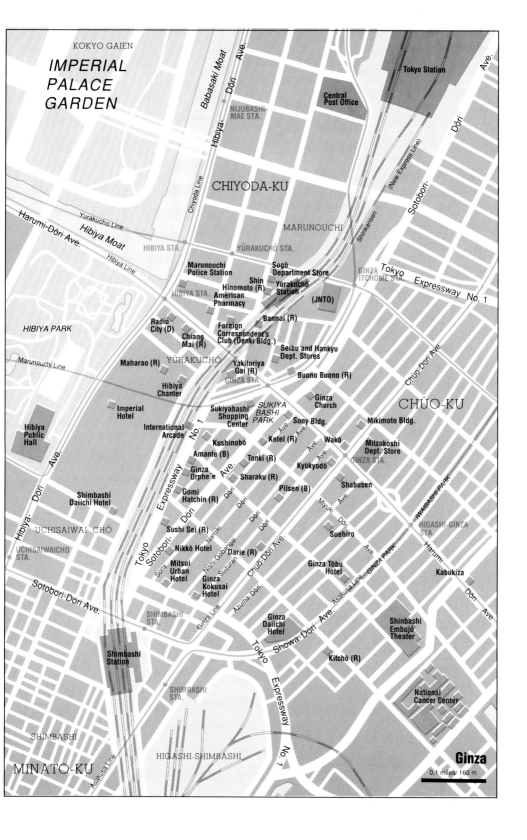

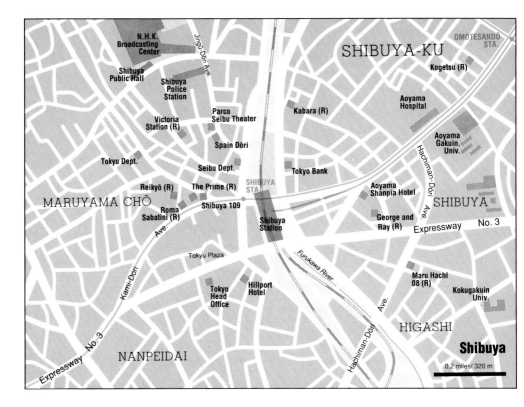

Shibuya

SHIBUYA-KU

OMOTESANDO STA.

N.H.K. Broadcasting Center

Shibuya Public Hall

Shibuya Police Station

Jingū-Dōri Ave.

Kogetsu (R)

Aoyama Hospital

Kabara (R)

Victoria Station (R)

Parco Seibu Theater

Spain Dōri

Aoyama Gakuin. Univ.

Tokyu Dept.

Seibu Dept.

Tokyo Bank

Hachiman-Dōri Ave.

Reikyō (R)

The Prime (R)

SHIBUYA STA.

MARUYAMA CHŌ

Roma Sabatini (R)

Shibuya 109

Aoyama Shanpia Hotel

SHIBUYA

George and Ray (R)

Expressway No. 3

Kami-Dōri Ave.

Shibuya Station

Tokyu Plaza

Furukawa River

Maru Hachi 08 (R)

Kokugakuin Univ.

Tokyu Head Office

Hillport Hotel

Hachiman-Dōri Ave.

HIGASHI

Expressway No. 3

NANPEIDAI

Shibuya

0,2 miles/ 320 m

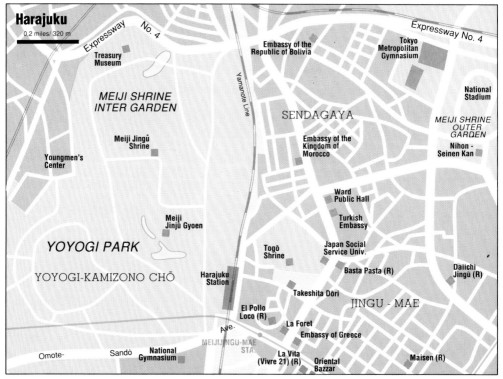

Harajuku

0,2 miles/ 320 m

Expressway No. 4

Expressway No. 4

Treasury Museum

Embassy of the Republic of Bolivia

Tokyo Metropolitan Gymnasium

MEIJI SHRINE INTER GARDEN

Yamanote Line

SENDAGAYA

National Stadium

Meiji Jingū Shrine

Embassy of the Kingdom of Morocco

MEIJI SHRINE OUTER GARDEN

Nihon - Seinen Kan

Youngmen's Center

Ward Public Hall

Turkish Embassy

YOYOGI PARK

Meiji Jinjū Gyoen

Togō Shrine

Japan Social Service Univ.

Daiichi Jingū (R)

YOYOGI-KAMIZONO CHŌ

Harajuku Station

Basta Pasta (R)

El Pollo Loco (R)

Takeshita Dōri

JINGU - MAE

La Foret

Embassy of Greece

Omote-

Sando

MEIJIJINGŪ-MAE STA.

National Gymnasium

La Vita (Vivre 21) (R)

Oriental Bazzar

Maisen (R)

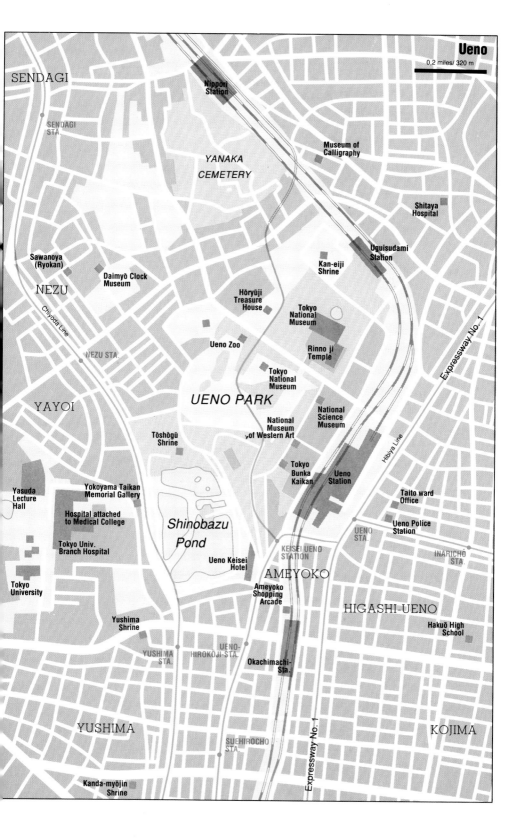

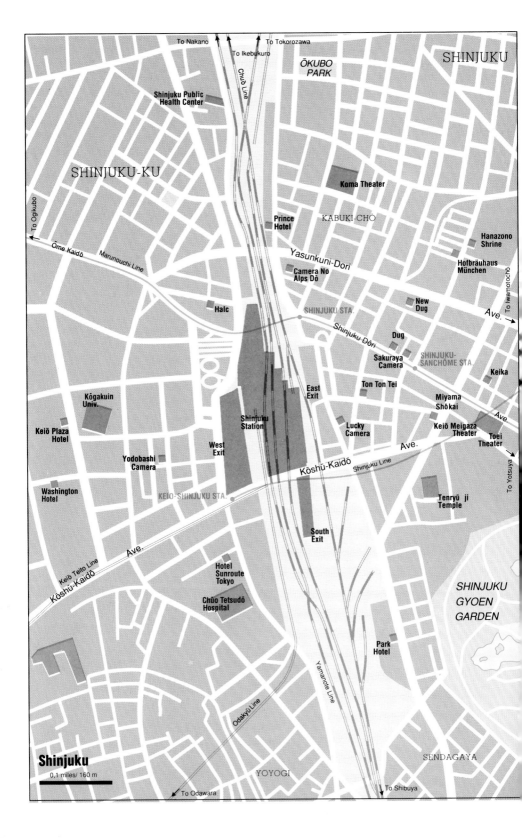

To Nakano
To Tokorozawa
To Ikebukuro

Chūō Line

ŌKUBO
PARK

SHINJUKU

Shinjuku Public
Health Center

SHINJUKU-KU

Koma Theater

Prince
Hotel

KABUKI-CHŌ

Hanazono
Shrine

Ōme Kaidō

Marunouchi Line

Yasunkuni-Dori

Hofbräuhaus
München

To Iwamotochō

Camera No
Alps Dō

Ave.

To Ogikubo

Halc

SHINJUKU STA.

New
Dug

Shinjuku Dōri

Dug

Sakuraya
Camera

SHINJUKU-
SANCHŌME STA.

Keika

Kōgakuin
Univ.

East
Exit

Ton Ton Tei

Miyama
Shōkai

Ave.

Keiō Plaza
Hotel

Shinjuku
Station

Lucky
Camera

Keiō Meigaza
Theater

Toei
Theater

Yodobashi
Camera

West
Exit

Ave.

Washington
Hotel

KEIO-SHINJUKU STA.

Kōshū-Kaidō

Shinjuku Line

Tenryū ji
Temple

South
Exit

To Yotsuya

SHINJUKU
GYOEN
GARDEN

Keiō Teito Line

Ave.

Kōshū-Kaidō

Hotel
Sunroute
Tokyo

Chūō Tetsudō
Hospital

Yamanote Line

Park
Hotel

SENDAGAYA

Shinjuku

0,1 miles/ 160 m

Odakyū Line

YOYOGI

To Odawara

To Shibuya

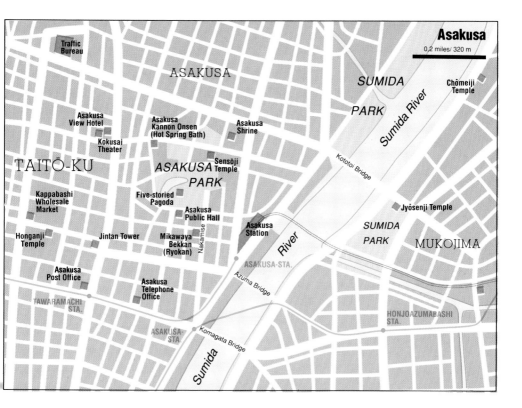

0,2 miles/ 320 m

Traffic
Bureau

ASAKUSA

SUMIDA

PARK

Sumida River

Chômeiji
Temple

Asakusa
View Hotel

Asakusa
Kannon Onsen
(Hot Spring Bath)

Asakusa
Shrine

Kokusai
Theater

Kototoi Bridge

TAITÔ-KU

ASAKUSA

Sensôji
Temple

PARK

Kappabashi
Wholesale
Market

Five-storied
Pagoda

Jyôsenji Temple

Asakusa
Public Hall

Honganji
Temple

Jintan Tower

Mikawaya
Bekkan
(Ryokan)

Nakamise

Asakusa
Station

River

SUMIDA

PARK

MUKOJIMA

Asakusa
Post Office

ASAKUSA-STA.

Asakusa
Telephone
Office

Azuma Bridge

HONJOAZUMABASHI
STA.

TAWARAMACHI
STA.

ASAKUSA-
STA

Komagata Bridge

Sumida

River

0,2 miles/ 320 m

Reinanzaka
Church

Expressway No. 3

Expressway No. 2

Defence
Agency

25

2

3

4

6

Embassy of
Finland

ROPPONGI

7 1
20
5
26

21

14

15

23

ROPPONGI
STATION

11

16

8

12 13

22

10 9

19

17

Expressway No. 3

18

Hibiya Line

MINATO-KU

Expressway No. 2

National Land
Agency

T.V. Asahi

KOKUSAI BUNKA

KAIKAN

Soviet
Embassy

1 Hotel Ibis
2 Mr. Stamps (B)
3 Chisen (R)
4 Torigin (R)
5 Bärren (B)
6 Victoria Station(R) & Haiyûza Gekijô
7 Brasserie Bernard (R)
8 Almond
9 Moti (R)
10 Azabu Police Station
11 Square Bldg. (D)
12 Serina (R)
13 Lexington Queen (D)
14 Maggie's Revenge (B)
15 Charleston (B)
16 Henry Africa's (B)
17 Roi Bldg.
18 Fukuzushi (R)
19 Tong Fu (R)
20 Body & Soul (B)
21 Cavern Club (B)
22 After Six (B)
23 Bengawan Solo (R)
24 ROPPONGI STATION
25 Bôeichô (Defence Agency)
26 Roppongi Crossing

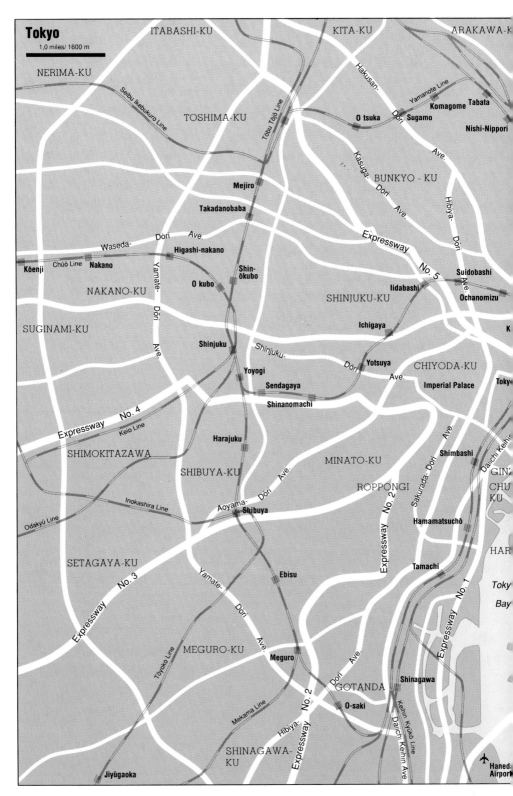

Tokyo

1,0 miles/ 1600 m

ITABASHI-KU

KITA-KU

ARAKAWA-K

NERIMA-KU

Hakusan-

Yamanote Line

Seibu Ikebukuro Line

TOSHIMA-KU

Komagome **Tabata**

O tsuka Dori **Sugamo**

Nishi-Nippori

Ave.

Kasuga-

Hibiya-

BUNKYO - KU

Mejiro

Dori Ave.

Takadanobaba

Dori

Expressway

Suidobashi

Waseda-

Dori Ave.

Higashi-nakano

No. 5

Ave.

Iidabashi

Chūō Line **Nakano**

Shin-

ōkubo

Ochanomizu

Kōenji

Yamate-

O kubo

SHINJUKU-KU

NAKANO-KU

Dori

Ichigaya

K

SUGINAMI-KU

Ave.

Shinjuku

Shinjuku-

Yotsuya

CHIYODA-KU

Dori

Yoyogi

Ave.

Imperial Palace

Toky

Sendagaya

Shinanomachi

Ave.

Shimbashi

GIN

Expressway No. 4

Harajuku

MINATO-KU

CHU

Keio Line

SHIMOKITAZAWA

Daiichi Keihin

KU

SHIBUYA-KU

ROPPONGI

Dori Ave.

Sakurada- Dori

HAR

Inokashira Line

Aoyama-

Shibuya

Hamamatsuchō

Odakyū Line

Expressway No. 2

Toky

SETAGAYA-KU

Yamate-

Ebisu

Tamachi

Bay

Expressway No. 3

Dori

No. 1

Toyoko Line

Ave.

MEGURO-KU

Meguro

Shinagawa

Hibiya-

GOTANDA

Expressway

O-saki

Keihin Kyūkō Line

Mekama Line

No. 2

Daiichi Keihin Ave.

SHINAGAWA-

Dori

KU

Expressway

✈ Haned

Jiyūgaoka

Airpor

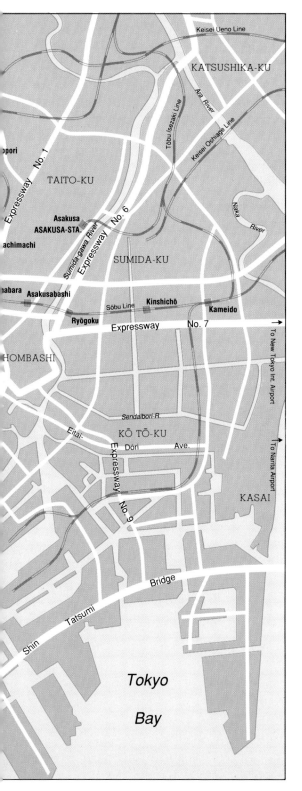

A CITY OF CITIES

Tokyo might best be viewed as a collection of many smaller sub-cities whose mini-centers are dotted along the circular **Yamanote** train line, while others lie within the railway boundary. To reach a destination on the "other side" of town may take some 45 minutes by train, and by car it could take several hours depending on traffic conditions and the person navigating.

A lot of sightseeing is done, of course, on foot. A combination of means of transport as well as mental and physical endurance is needed to adequately see the city – tolerance for the crowded subway trains and physical fitness for the numerous subway stairs and hours of walking above ground.

No place in Tokyo has officially claimed the name "Downtown Tokyo," although the *shitamachi* area, "*shita*" (down) and "*machi*" (town), was the center of Edo, Tokyo's former name. Areas of the city are divided into *ku* or Wards (23 in all). Depending on what or who resides in the *ku,* an impression of that *ku* is often transmitted. For example, **Setagaya-ku**, an affluent residential area, **Minato-ku,** nearby the **Imperial Palace**, or **Kôtô-ku,** rather industrial. Often, train station names call attention to parts of the city that have a specific atmosphere or whose area is engaged in a certain enterprise. For example, the fashionable **Ginza**, the nightlife of **Roppongi**, the business center **Otemachi**, or the electronic jungle **Akihabara**.

Like all capital cities, Tokyo is unique unto itself. However, one thing that can be said is that Tokyo is rapidly changing. Old buildings noticed a short while beforehand may seem to have been miraculously (or mysteriously) replaced by new modern structures. Along with the cranes knocking over the "old," society and lifestyle is also rapidly changing. The importance society placed on community and neighborhood is now being challenged by the environment of modern urban living.

Also perhaps unique to Tokyo is public safety. There is little need to worry about theft, let alone bodily harm in the city – day or night – though like any urban area anywhere in the world, crime does exist.

Lastly, Tokyo is said to be one of the most, if not the most, expensive cities in the world. Be ready to spend a bit more while sightseeing, for purchases, and for obtaining services.

Asakusa: Asakusa is a typical downtown amusement area where the atmosphere of Edo (old Tokyo) still remains. People love to visit the flagged street of shops in old-world **Nakamise** with the huge **Kaminarimon** (Thunder Gate), with two giant wooden guardian Diva Kings. On both sides of this street, there are almost 100 shops which sell traditional Japanese rice crackers, toys and notions. Asakusa was the common people's district of the Edo era. Here

you will experience the flavor and feeling of old Japan that is hard to find in other areas of Tokyo.

Sensôji Temple, the oldest temple in Tokyo, is one of the most worthwhile places to visit in Asakusa. Japanese people have loved to visit this temple since it was built around 1,350 years ago. Also worth seeing are the celebrated **Kannon Temple**, and the famous garden designed by Kobori Enshû. Asakusa thrives on its old legends and year-round festivals.

It's also a good idea for tourists to take a **Sumidagawa Cruise** on a boat from Asakusa to **Takeshiba** (close to Tokyo Bay) on the **Sumida River**. The water bus (*suijô*-bus) runs from Asakusa to the **Hamarikyû Garden** or **Hinode Pier**. It affords a glimpse of what is left of the old way of life along the Sumida River. You can also see several types of bridges from the boat, which departs from near the Sensôji Temple and Nakamise. Ginza or Toei Asakusa Subway Lines, Asakusa Stn.

Lanterns lead up to the temple.

164

Ueno: Like Asakusa, Ueno is one of the older, more traditional sections of Tokyo. There are two places which are especially worth visiting: one is historic **Ueno Park**, famous for its cherry blossoms in April, and the other is **Ameya Yokochô** (usually called **Ameyoko**). Ueno park is only a five-minute walk from Ueno Station, and is the largest park in Tokyo with 210 acres, containing **Ueno Zoo**, **Shinobazu Pond**, **The National Museum of Western Art** and many other museums and historical buildings.

In Ameyoko, merchants sell fresh food, dried food, clothes, and all sorts of other goods at extremely reasonable prices. At year-end, this place is crowded with year-end bargain sales. JR Yamanote Line, Ueno Stn., or Hibiya and Ginza Subway Lines, Ueno Stn.

Ginza: A glittering district with a fabled main street plus intriguing cross streets and back streets, Ginza has class and style and a magnetic personality. To

Lanterns of various establishments that have patronized the shrine.

UENO ZOO

Ueno Zoo is one of the world's largest zoos (150,000 square meters) and attracts approximately 7 million visitors a year. As Japan's first zoo, it celebrated its 100-year anniversary in 1982.

Favorite among its inhabitants are the pandas. Tong Tong, born June 1, 1986, and his cute family keep the crowds coming. Mammalians, birds, reptiles, amphibians, fish and invertebrates are all exhibited.

Shinobazu Pond is the gathering point of more than 100 species of wild birds. Great cormorants are year-round residents and some 5,000 to 9,000 wild ducks stay for the winter.

The Zoo is open from 9.30 a.m. to 4.30 p.m. (Ticket sales end at 4.00 p.m.) Admission (over 15 years old) is ¥400, junior high school students ¥100 and children under 11 years old, free. Ueno Zoo is a 4-minute walk from JR Ueno Station.

IMPERIAL PALACE

The place that is probably the single most important landmark in Tokyo and the site that a visitor to the city can least afford to miss is the **Imperial Palace.** It is the geographical and spiritual center of Tokyo, the scene of many of its most historic events, and in fact, the very reason for the city's existence.

The history of the site dates back to 1457, when a feudal lord named Ota Dôkan chose a small fishing village that was there as the place to build his castle. This is generally acknowledged as the start of the history of Tokyo, which was called Edo then.

The warlord Tokugawa Ieyasu arrived in 1590, proclaimed himself shogun, and replaced the original, comparatively small fortification with the biggest and most elaborate castle in the land. It was under his leadership and the Tokugawa shoguns who succeeded him

that Edo grew to become Japan's biggest and most powerful city. Unfortunately, Ieyasu's castle burned down during the famous "Long-Sleeves Fire" of 1657.

The next chapter in the history of the site begins in 1868, when the shogunate collapsed and imperial rule was restored to Japan. The Meiji Emperor chose the rebuilt shogunal castle to be the new imperial residence and moved there in 1869 from Kyôto, the city that had been the imperial capital for over a millennium, with his family. The city was renamed Tokyo, or "Eastern Capital." The site has remained the residence of Japan's emperors ever since.

Because the place is considered to be sacred, most of the Imperial Palace complex is closed to the public and remains secluded behind massive stone walls and old moats. The best view of the inside is from the observation windows on the 36th floor of the **Kasumigaseki Building**, a tall office tower about one kilometer south of the palace

Left, present Emperor Heisei and Empress at their wedding in 1959. Right, the late Showa Emperor Hirohito (1902-1989)

166

in the area of national government offices. Most of the 110-hectare complex is forested or given to private gardens and small ponds. The Shôwa Emperor (Hirohito), who reigned from 1926 to early 1989, was a professional biologist. So much of the inner garden area is a nature preserve. The Imperial Palace building itself is an expansive low building with a green roof. It is a new structure that was completed in 1970 to replace the imperial residence that was destroyed in an air raid in 1945.

The best approach on foot to the palace complex is from the downtown business district in the vicinity of **Hibiya Park**. One crosses a bridge over a moat, and then walks through the expanses of the **Outer Garden** (a big open area where downtown workers are supposed to go in case the city burns) to reach **Seimon Gate**, one of the main entrances to the private compound.

Nijûbashi, a distinctive bridge across an inner moat, is one of the most widely recognized landmarks of Japan.

You can often see groups of travelers, especially uniformed students on class trips, posed for obligatory group pictures in front of a scene that includes this bridge, an historic watchtower, and a small cluster of willows. On two days of the year (New Year's Day and the Emperor's birthday), the public is allowed to cross Nijûbashi and stand near the imperial residence to receive greetings from the Emperor.

Visitors are also permitted in the **East Garden** of the Imperial Palace. It is open most days and can be entered through **Kikyômon Gate,** which is a short walk from the main entrance of Tokyo Station. Inside you can examine remains of the defenses of Edo Castle and stroll among gardens and through thick stands of forest. Another public area is **Kitanomaru Park**. It is on the north side of the Imperial Palace complex and includes the **National Museum of Modern Art**, the **Science and Technology Museum,** and the **Budôkan**, a popular concert facility.

Nijûbashi bridge in the Imperial Palace grounds.

most Japanese, it has been a sort of symbol of Western culture for over a century. When, in the 1800s, Western culture first started to infiltrate into Japan, Ginza, the site of a 17th-century silver mint, became an exhibition hall of Western styles.

Several major department stores and fashionable boutiques spread throughout Ginza making it ideal for shopping. Restaurants and coffee shops abound, and for those interested in Japanese arts, there is the **Kabukiza Theater**, the pantheon of *kabuki*, a famous landmark besides being the place to watch highly entertaining and popular *kabuki* plays.

When the sun goes down, the night is lit for after-hours entertainment, and Ginza becomes the land of witty club hostesses, limousines and intoxicated company executives. Not a few business deals are clinched here after hours. A word of caution to those who may stumble into one of the clubs in **Nishi (west) Ginza:** Check the prices before you order! If there are no prices, get out

or else make sure that someone else is paying – preferably someone with an unlimited company account! Though the younger generation seem to prefer Shibuya, Shinjuku, Harajuku and Roppongi, Ginza could be called Japan's "Fifth Avenue."

The Ginza has long been the strip for fashion and entertainment. When surfacing onto the street from Ginza Station from the **TRTA's (Teito Rapid Transit Authority) Hibiya, Ginza** or **Marunouchi Subway Lines**, you will find yourself in the thick of things.

Depending on your exit onto the street, you may see the familiar McDonald's, Shakey's Pizza, and the like, or mammoth department stores – **Ginza Mitsukoshi**, **Ginza Matsuya**, **Matsuzakaya,** and others.

On foot at least it's hard to get lost. At the main intersection of Harumi Dôri (Street) and Chûo Dôri, there is the famed **Ginza police box,** whose primary, if not exclusive, job is to point the misguided in the right direction. Stop in and ask the policeman the way toward the Imperial Palace, and head in that direction. You'll soon come to another famous landmark, the **Sony Building** on the corner of Harumi Dôri and Sotobori Dôri at the Sukiyabashi crossing. Several floors of the building are devoted to displaying Sony products – an impressive array of visual, audio, and new products for the high-tech future.

On your way to the Sony Building, you'll pass by another good spot for the tired and/or bewildered. **Jena**, a four-story bookstore, is great for browsing through books and magazines, a favorite activity of the Japanese, who stand for long periods of time reading, *tachi-yomi*. Unlike many countries, in Japan you can just pick up a book or magazine off the rack and read it without any obligation to buy it.

For the artsy folks, Ginza has many well-known contemporary art galleries. If you turn left at the Sony Building and walk along the Sotobori Dôri, you'll find such galleries as the **Nichidô Gal-**

Ginza on a Sunday.

lery, the largest gallery in the Ginza area, the **Umeda Gallery,** and the **Fujii Gallerie** for Japanese paintings. Besides these and many more are the **Gallerie Tamenaga, Gallerie Tokoro, Saegusa Gallerie,** and the **Kaneko Art Gallery.**

There are also two offbeat cinemas in the neighborhood, **Ginza Bunka** and **Cine Switch Ginza.** Other theaters in the area show the more current films. However, the ticket price of ¥1,500 may seem a bit high.

Akasaka at Night: As the neon lights go on, some of the brilliant night spots in Akasaka such as popular restaurants, night clubs and discos come alive. Like Ginza, Akasaka has more of a prestigious flavor. Two of Tokyo's first-class hotels are located here, **The Akasaka Prince** and **The New Otani,** as well as several foreign embassies.

Akasaka is a traditional area for Japanese entertainment, and many exclusive Japanese restaurants called *"ryôtei"* are often patronized by gov-

ernment officials and business leaders. They find it easier to spend small fortunes on food and entertainment than does the common man, who usually heads off instead to places on the Hitotsugi Dôri and Misuji Dôri. During the day, a little bit of local color can be found at the **Hie Shrine**, also known as **Sannô Jinja**, on Sotobori Dôri. **Ginza** or **Marunouchi Subway lines, Akasaka Mitsuke Stn.**

Roppongi: Tokyo's live music scene stands to grow more forceful and diverse with the arrival of night in Roppongi. The area numbers amongst its attractions bars, night clubs and discos which have highly individual themes and decor.

Discos and live houses saty open until the wee hours of the morning. **Deja vu**, located around the corner from **Henry Africa's** is one such spot to get footloose in Roppongi. **Lexington Queen** is noted for its model clientel and is frequented by visiting foreign musicians.

Jsing the sky as a billboard lue.

Roppongi actually started as an evening playground for the many foreigners who reside in the nearby **Azabu** area, where many embassies are located. Some of the best restaurants in Tokyo can be found here, serving food from every part of the world, and prices are not really outrageous, at least not by Tokyo standards, so it remains one of the favorite night spots for Japanese and foreigners alike.

Similar to **Hachikô Square** in Shibuya, the favorite meeting spot for people in Roppongi is in front of **Almond** (*Amando* in Japanese) on one of the corners of the main **Roppongi Crossing**. When in doubt or lost, just ask for *"Amando."*

Tokyo Tower is about a fifteen-minute walk from Almond and is one of the most famous landmarks in Tokyo. The 333-meter-high steel tower is the second highest tower (without supporting steel) in the world. If you are not into walking, it can also be reached by subway on the **Toei Mita Subway Line**,

Onarimon Stn., exit A1.

One stop away on the **Hibiya Subway Line** you will arrive at **Hiroo,** which is one of Tokyo's chic Yamanote towns where embassies and high-grade mansions are concentrated. The **National Azabu Supermarket** catering to the needs of foreigners is located close to **Hiroo Station**.

Shinjuku, City Within a City: Tokyo's new sub-center is in the west side of the city. As the largest "sub-city" in Tokyo, Shinjuku represents one of the most bustling districts in all of Japan. As Shinjuku Station is always overcrowded and spreads out in all directions, it is a labyrinth to newcomers. One special feature of this area is that the atmosphere tends to change from street to street.

The east side of Shinjuku is very different from the west. **The West side of JR Shinjuku Station** has a proliferation of skyscrapers housing both office blocks and grand hotels. An underground shopping arcade leading west

Fighting for space on the crowded rush hour trains.

from the station stretches about a mile. Older Shinjuku, **the East side**, offers shopping at large department stores, large camera retail shops, boutiques, and features several exotic backstreets and alleys as well as many movie theaters. On Sundays and public holidays, you can enjoy the pedestrian mall, which bans cars from the shopping streets and makes a temporary car-free paradise.

Shinjuku Gyoen is well worth a visit. This 144.5-acre public park is well known for its great variety of cherry trees and other native Japanese flowers. It features irises in May and a chrysanthemum show in November. **Shinjuku Stn.**, exits A16 and A17.

Certain landmarks in Tokyo have become popular meeting places – from there friends join up for a day or night on the town. On the East side, the landmarks of **Kinokuniya Bookstore** and the mammoth golden screen of **Alta** are known by all. On the West side, the underground police box is surrounded by people patiently waiting, but occasionally looking down at their wristwatches.

The East side of Shinjuku, however, has the lion's share of the action. The streets are a maze of dazzling neon, where the number of lights match the number of shops and bars. People of all types are on the streets at night – all hours of the night. Some establishments especially cater to those nocturnal individuals, and to the occasional party goers that don't make their last train from Shinjuku and opt for an "all-nighter" instead of hailing a taxi.

If there is one thing to be said about Shinjuku, it is that it's the spot in town where anyone can find just about anything – fashion, food, entertainment, accommodation, drink, the overdone, the underworld, or what-have-you.

Kinokuniya Bookstore is a quiet haven from the maddening outside, a spot to leaf through pages of foreign books or pick up a book for train reading. There are the famed camera shops

People come prepared to boogie in Roppongi.

ECONOMIC GIANT

Downtown Tokyo is the nerve center of Japan's powerful economy and the best place to see the nation at work. It is headquarters for most of the country's giant multinational corporations, nearly all of its biggest banks and securities companies, the center of its government, and it's the number one center for newspaper and magazine publishing and other communications. It is a large area that covers numerous specialized districts of Chûo, Chiyoda and Minato Wards, and that is expanding quickly in all directions as new high-rises are constantly being constructed to keep pace with the city's tremendous demand for offices.

Come early in the morning to **Tokyo Station**, the city's principal train and subway terminal, to see the workday begin. Train after train arrives from the suburbs and unloads its armies of dark-

suited salarymen and young "office ladies" (OLs), who then stream out of the numerous exits and fill each of the several business districts that surround the station.

Given the huge numbers of people, it is an amazingly speechless procession. Almost no one speaks and the only sounds are of train announcements and thousands and thousands of footsteps on arrival platforms and marching down stairways and along subterranean corridors.

The main exits (west side) lead to **Marunouchi**, perhaps the most important and prestigious office area in Japan. It was first developed about 100 years ago by the powerful Mitsubishi Company and is still headquarters for many of the huge financial and manufacturing enterprises that are associated with the Mitsubishi name. It is also the center for the Tokyo Metropolitan Government, its Chamber of Commerce and Industry, and many other offices.

It is a no-nonsense district, with a geometric and a highly regimented plan for streets and the shape of buildings, and is devoted almost entirely to work. The dominant presence of the **Imperial Palace** grounds on the far side of Marunouchi from Tokyo Station adds to the sober atmosphere.

Marunouchi's neighbor to the north is **Otemachi**, the headquarters district for numerous powerful banks (Fuji, Sumitomo, Sanwa), big insurance companies (eg., Mitsui Life Insurance), the communications giant NTT, influential newspaper companies (Yomiuri, Sankei), the head office of Nippon Steel, as well as many other important concerns. It is a little more like the office districts of Manhattan in layout. To the east, on the other side of an elevated expressway that snakes along the courses of old castle moats and canals, is **Nihombashi**, the city's oldest business district.

The biggest employers include the **Bank of Japan**, the nation's central bank housed in an older (1896) stone

A young salaryman.

building and adjacent modern skyscraper; the head offices of the Bank of Tokyo, Mitsui Bank, Yasuda Trust, Nomura Securities, and numerous other leading financial institutions, and some of Japan's largest and most famous department stores (Mitsukoshi, Takashimaya, Tôkyû).

In the midst of all this is the bridge called **Nihombashi**, or "Japan Bridge," one of the city's most famous landmarks. Its history dates back to the earliest days of Edo (old Tokyo), when it served as the symbolic starting point for roads leading from the capital to feudal provinces in the countryside. The present structure is a graceful European-style reconstruction completed in 1911. Unfortunately, it is all but blocked from view by the Shuto Expressway that was built in the 1960s directly overhead. Social kibitzers like to point to this as desecration of a valuable historical landmark and evidence that modern Tokyo is too wrapped up in the affairs of big business to preserve its past or to pay attention to aesthetics in urban design.

The **Tokyo Stock Exchange** is east of Nihombashi in a downtown district called **Kabutochô**. It is open to the public during working hours Monday through Friday. There is a visitors' gallery from which you can look down on the hectic activities of the stock trading floor (trading hours are 9 a.m. -11 a.m. and 1 p.m. -3 p.m.) and listen to all of the sounds and excitement.

There is also informative Exhibition Plaza that teaches young and old alike in English and Japanese about the world of stocks. A fantastic "Hand Signal Robot" is on hand to demonstrate each of the many hand motions that are used on the trading floor. It's all free.

The Tokyo Stock Exchange is about a 20 minute-walk from Tokyo Station. Visitors can watch the frantic traders madly using hand signals for buying and selling securities on the trading floor below. It is best reached from **Kayabachô Station** on either the Tôzai or Hibiya Subway Lines (5 minutes).

The Tokyo Stock Exchange.

that sell the latest generation of cameras, equipment, and also the rest of the consumer electronics lines. Major department stores are all there, as well as many cinemas showing the roadshow films.

After dark, the **Kabukichô** section of east Shinjuku turns out to be a thriving amusement center that closely rivals Roppongi, with theaters, cabarets, bars, game arcades, etc., which draw huge throngs of evening pleasure seekers. This is the 'Latin Quarter' of Tokyo and is one of the few places where a little caution might be needed, though you will be safe enough if you act sensibly. A spin through Kabukichô is a must for any visitor, and for residents, frequency in Kabukichô depends on your nightlife orientation – a lot goes on behind some of those doors; you can get some indication by the sirens' pictures or the hawkers' "invitations."

Shinjuku is an electric house of mirrors with all the illumination of a carnival – every night. By day, the sunlight subdues Shinjuku's intensity, but not much.

Shibuya: Shibuya is Tokyo's chic center of up town residents and as such, attracts young people. The busiest parts of Shibuya extend radially along such major avenues as Dôgenzaka, Jingû-Dôri, Meiji-Dôri and Miyamasuzaka. When you come out from the north exit of the station, you will invariably come upon a mass of people standing around the statue of a little dog, waiting for someone. This is **Hachikô Square**. Hachiko is the name of a dog that, so the story goes, waited at Shibuya Station every night for his master's return for seven years, though in fact his master had passed away.

Shibuya is a transit station for several different lines which transport people between the outskirts and the center of the city. There seems to be an endless array of trendy clothing stores, restaurants and movie theaters stretching out in all directions.

Kôen Dôri, which rises up the hill

A rare clear morning provides a view of Mt. Fuji.

from Shibuya Station toward the **Yoyogi National Stadium**, is especially crowded with boutiques, department stores and fashion shops. There are many small, narrow streets like **Spain Dôri** and **Fire Dôri**, with small cafés and boutiques that make for nice walks if you can make it through the crowds of young people. At the top of Kôen Dôri is the **NHK Broadcasting Center**, which is partly open to the public, and where some TV programs can be observed in the making. Almost next to NHK is the Yoyogi National Stadium, one of the modern architectural landmarks of Tokyo.

Throughout Tokyo's history, Shibuya has surely changed. Once a village of Edo, Shibuya has evolved over the years to become one of the city's "hottest" spots, both day and night. Shibuya's main intersection is exemplary of Tokyo urban life – millions of people crammed into a very small space. Shibuya today is a maze of buildings, a combination of business and entertainment. Cinemas, nightclubs and discos, shopping and restaurants attract thousands upon thousands of people to Shibuya. With its famous landmark meeting spot, Hachiko, Shibuya has become a favorite place for the young and old alike, Japanese or foreign.

The Tokyû Group has constructed a facility within the city to promote higher cultural awareness of things both foreign and Japanese. Tokyû Corporation, which has long carved out its niche in Shibuya with its department store complexes – the **109 Building** (One-Oh-Nine), **Tokyû Department Store** – and other Tokyû buildings and enterprises, has embarked on its latest project, **Bunkamura.** The name is a fusion of two Japanese words: *bunka* meaning culture and *mura*, village.

Tokyû has constructed a complex of halls, some for concerts, theater productions, movies, and cultural gatherings, and a museum. The running theme behind the entire complex is Music.

Left, the alleyways of bars on Shinjuku's West side. **Right**, browsing in a local bookstore.

Bunkamura is located adjacent to the main Tokyû Department Store. Its **Orchard Hall**, the largest in the complex seats an audience of 2,150. **The Tokyo Philharmonic** has made the hall its new home.

There is also **Theater Cocoon** with a capacity of 747 seats, and director Kazuyoshi Kushida of **On-Theatre Jiyûgekijô** directs the theater's leading dramas. In addition, there are two cinema's, **Le Cinema 1 and 2.** Both cinemas shows highly artistic works. Lastly, there is a museum located within the complex, which is used for exhibitions and other events.

Harajuku: You will find two very different worlds on either side of Harajuku Station, which in many ways reflects the reality of modern Tokyo and Japan. On one side, an area of fashionable boutiques, fancy restaurants, coffee shops, and many people dressed up as if they were on a fashion parade. This all happens along and around **Omote-Sandô Boulevard**, which is the closest

that Tokyo has to a "Champs Elysées," and the smaller but very famous **Take-shita Dôri**, a very short (200 meters) and narrow street leading down from **Harajuku Station** to **Meiji Dôri**. However short it may be, it seems that every square inch of this street has been packed with shops, stalls and people catering to the throngs of young shoppers.

A contrast to this colorful, ultra-modern and sometimes garish setting, can be found in the **Meiji Shrine,** on the other side of the station. This shrine is dedicated to the Emperor Meiji and the Empress Dowager, Shôken. The shrine, located in the middle of a thickly wooded forest with many large old trees, extends over an area of 72 hectares. Its Japanese garden is noted for its iris blossoms in mid-June. Chiyoda Subway Line, Meiji-Jingûmae Stn.

Jingû Gaien, Outer Garden of Meiji Shrine, is a favorite area for joggers who live in the surrounding areas. It is located in the Aoyama district and con-

Preparing for tonight's performance at a roof-top beer garden.

tains many sports facilities, including the **Jingû Baseball Stadium, National Stadium, Prince Chichibu Rugby Field** and **Jingû Swimming Pool.** Ginza Subway Line, Gaienmae Stn.

Aoyama: Aoyama, with its international appeal, is looming large as one of Tokyo's most fashionable towns. It is one of the upper-class residential areas of Tokyo, and the shops, boutiques and restaurants in this area reflect this. The pace is slower, and in general, everything is quieter, a nice contrast to some of the other areas surrounding it. **Aoyama Bochi** (cemetery) in **Minami Aoyama** is a very pleasant place to take a walk (for the Japanese). Entombed here are quite a few historically famous people, most of them active statesmen and writers during the Meiji Era (1868-1912), but also buried here are two prominent prime ministers of the Shôwa Era: Shigeru Yoshida and Hayato Ikeda.

In the spring, this is one of the nicest places to view cherry blossoms, and to watch the Japanese sitting under the cherry trees drinking *sake* (Japanese rice wine) and singing songs as they enjoy the cherry blossoms and celebrate the end of winter. Hanzômon and Ginza Subway Lines, Aoyama Itchôme Stn.

Otemachi, Marunouchi and Kanda: The areas of Otemachi, Marunouchi and Yaesu, which surround the **JR Tokyo Station**, form the mammoth business center of Tokyo where the headquarters of many of Japan's leading banks and business firms are lined along the moat. Built in 1914 on the model of the Amsterdam Central Station in the Netherlands, Tokyo Station serves as the hub of public transportation to the Marunouchi business center. The **Tôkaidô Shinkansen** ("Bullet Train") super express lines **"Hikari"** and **"Kodama"** originate from here. **Tôzai, Marunouchi** and **Chiyoda Subway Lines, Otemachi Stn.**

Kanda is known everywhere as the biggest bookstore center in the world. The center of Kanda is the **Jimbôchô**

_eft,
'Everything must go, only ¥1,000!"
Right,
electronic goods for sale in Akihabara.

Crossing where there is a conglomeration of over 150 second-hand bookshops. Kanda is one of the other remaining *"shitamachi"* (downtown) areas left in Tokyo, and regardless of whether you need any books or not, you should take a look, as these last remnants of what Tokyo used to be like are quickly disappearing under the bulldozer and greedy developers. Since this is a university district, the area is heavily populated with students to whom the book shops cater. **Oya Shobô** is one of the more well known of such bookstores. Toei Mita Subway Line, Jimbôchô Stn.

Akihabara: Akihabara is now rated as the internationally recognized discount center for electronics and electrical appliances in all of the country. While the surrounding areas like Kanda and **Ochanomizu** still retain some of their old-fashioned *"shitamachi"* atmosphere, Akihabara is literally a different world. With over 600 outlets it's hard to imagine that you wouldn't be able to find what you are looking for. On Sundays, the main street of Akihabara closes down all the way to Ueno.

What is most unique about Akihabara, however, is its contrasts. Some stores have the most state-of-the-art electronic wares, like computers, while others sell nothing the tiny screws and wires. There are mammoth stores with each floor handling one type of appliance, and there are tiny stalls with one person squeezed in amongst the merchandise. Most stores sell only new products, but for sale on some of the side streets are goods which have both been used and abused.

As well as every new item manufacturers have thrust on the market, Akihabara is the mecca for electronic parts and accessories. From telephone jacks to 256k DRAMS, Akihabara is a big kid's dream. If one thinks he or she can build it, Akihabara has the parts. **JR Yamanote**, **Keihin Tôhoku** and **Sôbu Lines**, or **Hibiya Subway Line**, Akihabara Stn.

East Exit of Ikebukuro: The East Exit of Ikebukuro Station has an accumulation of camera discount outlets such as **Bic Camera, Camera-no Sakuraya, Sangô Camera,** etc. Apart from these, this is **Seibu** territory. The main **Seibu Department Store** is located right on top of the station, and it is connected with the large **Parco** building, another Seibu venture. Seibu has a reputation for being the first to change or to set new trends, as opposed to the more traditional Mitsukoshi and Takashimaya Department Stores, so it's a nice place to check out and see what is new in Japan, or for that matter, what will be new in the near future!

A ten-minute walk from the station, past Bic Camera, will get you to what is presently the largest building in Japan, **Sunshine 60.** The name already gives away its height, and there's not much else to say about it except that it is a major landmark and for many Japanese a symbol of Japan's joining the modern world.

DUTY-FREE

For tourists, Akihabara's attraction is its wide selection and large duty-free outlets, offering the newest and widest selection in Japan if not the world. The word "free" is a rather dubious word. First, nothing is free. Secondly, when looking at the price, the item may actually cost less outside of Japan than even duty-free. Akihabara's store managers have moaned about reduced revenue from foreign tourists since the strengthening of the yen. Tourists still flock to Akihabara, but according to one store manager, most are only window-shoppers.

The customer can bargain with the salesman for a reduction; however, the salesman already knows the bottom line pulling out his calculator. Foreigners have an added problem when buying in Japan. An item made for domestic distribution – as opposed to an export model – may have different specifications.

Right, Japanese women – a perceived mix of oriental mystery and beauty.

TAKE ME TO
THE WATERS

As a result of rises in fuel costs and a loss of customers to private baths, the number of bathhouses in Tokyo has declined severely in recent decades – there are around 2,300 today, compared with almost 7,000 forty years ago – and yet their importance as neighborhood centers where friends can meet to exchange news and views, and, consequently, their appeal to the foreign visitor are as strong as ever.

In form and function, many have retained the fundamental features of their Edo-period antecedents, except that they are now segregated by sex. Customers first leave their shoes in lockers in the small entrance hall and undress in a large changing room presided over by the proprietor, or his wife, who collects the entrance fee (around ¥250) and sells soap, shampoo, razors and other necessities to anyone who has forgotten to bring their own. Inside the washroom, patrons take their place in front of one of the faucets, and occasionally shower heads, that are set low along the walls, and wash and rinse themselves thoroughly before settling into the communal pool to soak away the stress of the day. Water temperatures are by law a minimum of 42 degrees C (a considerable drop from times past, when the citizens of Edo took great pride in braving scalding waters) and rarely go much higher.

Several modern-day Tokyo bathhouses (the traditional-style **Asakusa Kannon Onsen** and **Azabu Jûban Onsen** baths are excellent examples) have also preserved the clubhouse atmosphere of the earlier relaxation rooms, built on the second floor, by adding a small stage where the clientele – particularly elderly men and women with more time on their hands – can watch occasional variety shows or entertain themselves with their own songs and dances. Unfortunately, one aspect

The public bath – a place of cleanliness and community.

of old bathhouses that has almost entirely disappeared is their access to natural surroundings. Edo washrooms, even those in the most crowded parts of the city, were usually built to incorporate a carefully manicured garden, which customers could enjoy from a wide veranda as they cooled off from the steam or hot water.

Today, Tokyo's real estate prices have made such decorative use of space an unaffordable luxury. Consciously or unconsciously, however, the connection with nature has been preserved in modern establishments, either with large landscape murals on the rear wall of the washroom – the murals of **Ueno's Tsubame-yu** baths and the **Daikoku-yu** bathhouse in **Kitasenju** are a delight – or with reconstructed rock grottos housing the main pool.

For the majority of Tokyo's inhabitants, the role once played by the bathhouse, the *sentô*, in community life is one they cannot forget in a hurry, and one many of them sorely miss. No wonder, then, that though they no longer have any practical need to go there, more than a few private-bath owners still make the trip on a cold night, towels and washbasins in hand, to take the waters and catch up on a little local gossip.

Addresses: Asakusa Kannon Onsen, 2-7-10 Asakusa, Taitô-ku, mineral spring bath, open daily: 6:30 a.m. to 6:30 p.m; **Daikoku-yu**, 32-6 Kotobukichô, Adachi-ku, a traditional style *sentô* featuring a wall-mural of Mt. Fuji, 15 minutes from Kitasenju Station, on the Chiyoda Subway Line; **Azabu Jûban Onsen**, 1-5 Azabu Jûban, Minato-ku, bicarbonate spring pools, open daily: 11 a.m-9 p.m.; **Onsen Hoyô Center**, 1-41-54 Nishi-Mizue, Edogawa-ku, a sand bath costs around ¥3,000, open daily: 12 p.m.-9 p.m. Five minutes from Mizue Station on the Toei Shinjuku Subway Line; **Tsubame-Yu**, 3-14-5 Ueno, Taitô-ku, main pool set in a re-created mountain grotto, open daily: 6 a.m-9 p.m.

Wall murals set the mood at public a bath.

TOKYO LANDMARKS

For most of its history, Tokyo has been a low-slung city of small houses and shops packed close together in tight neighborhood clusters. This has been true for most of this century as well. While other cities around the world followed the lead of Manhattan and built their downtowns skyward with impressive high-rises, Tokyo stayed low. One reason for this has been the earthquake hazard that imperils the city. Indeed, one of the most enduring images of the Great Kantô Earthquake that destroyed most of Tokyo in 1923 is what happened to the Asakusa Twelve Stories. It was the tallest structure in the city and an exceedingly popular landmark, but it broke off above the eighth floor during the seismic jolt and tumbled to the street below.

However, with the advance of earthquake-proof building techniques in more recent times, and because of sky-high land values, Tokyo has been catching up, with a vengeance, to other cities with construction of tall buildings. The low buildings from the past are now almost all gone from the center of the city, and the new profile is of narrow mid-rise structures (5- to 10-stories high) jammed as close together as possible, punctuated by a growing number of high-rises with 20 or more stories. The proportions are not yet those of Manhattan or Hong Kong, but they are getting there.

The first modern skyscraper in Tokyo was the 147-meter (36 floors) **Kasumigaseki Building**, opened in 1968. It is in the district of national government buildings immediately south of the Imperial Palace and offers a spectacular panorama of central Tokyo from the free observatory at the top. It is Tokyo's best view behind the walls and moats that protect the Imperial Palace. The building was quite a sensation when it opened. Nowadays, it is best known as a measure of large volume – so many Kasumigaseki Buildings of beer were drunk in Japan last year, and so on.

The tallest building in Tokyo is **Sunshine 60** (240 meters, 60 stories, extremely plain and uninspired). It is north of the center in Ikebukuro, in a complex of four new buildings that was put up in 1980 to replace a notorious prison. A bonus of the fine view from the observatory (admission ¥620) is that it is one of the few high places in Tokyo where the building itself cannot be seen. There is also an aquarium and a planetarium (¥1,850 for both and the observatory), as well as many floors of offices. The base of Sunshine 60 has a large, U.S.-suburban-style shopping mall.

The place where Tokyo looks most like a modern skyscraper city is **Nishi Shinjuku**. This is a meticulously planned and super-orderly urban renewal district of high-rise offices and international hotels on the west side of Shinjuku Station. It has the second through seventh tallest buildings in the city, as well as several other high-rises, and is a leading backdrop for big-city detective dramas on TV in Japan and commercial advertising aimed at sophisticated urban tastes.

Highlights of Nishi Shinjuku include the observation window on the 53rd floor of the **Shinjuku Center Building**; the distinctive shape and texture of the **Yasuda Kasai Kaijô Building** (reminiscent of the walls of an ancient Japanese castle); and the massive atrium (30 stories) of the **Shinjuku NS Building**. The Yasuda tower has an art museum on the 42nd floor (the **Tôgô Seiji Museum**) that features the famously expensive ($40 million) *Sunflowers* by Van Gogh. The **Keio Plaza Intercontinental Hotel,** the first of the area's high-rises to be completed (1971), has a fine selection of restaurants and an observation level on the 47th floor.

A giant construction project on the west side of Nishi Shinjuku has given Tokyo a new tallest building – taller than Sunshine 60 by a whole three

Left, Shinjuku rises above the sprawling city.

meters. This is the new city hall for Tokyo. It is a distinctive structure designed by Japan's master architect Kenzô Tange and is certain to become a widely recognized landmark.

Landmarks and Architecture: Some visitors to Tokyo might get a feeling of *deja vu* as they travel around the city. This is because a surprising number of Tokyo's landmarks, both major and minor, are to one degree or another copies of famous places in other cities abroad.

Europe-in-Tokyo starts at the city's main passenger rail station, **Tokyo Station**. It is a good facsimile of the central station in Amsterdam. A few blocks away is the famous **Nihombashi Bridge**. It is the symbolic, historic starting point for roads leading from Japan's capital to the provinces, but its Renaissance style makes it look like it belongs in Brussels or Vienna or Prague, or some other European capital. Then it's off to the main intersection of Ginza to see the sculpture of the lion from London's Trafalgar Square. It is a popular rendezvous point at the entrance to the **Mitsukoshi Department Store.** Nearby (three floors below ground in the basement of the Sony Building), you can dine at **Maxim's.** The chef is from the Paris original and so is the decor.

For more of London, we go to see a replica of the Globe Theater. It's a new building designed for performances of Shakespeare's plays and is similar to the original structure that is now being excavated, except that it is pink. You can find this building in, of all things, a subsidized high-rise housing project (**Nishi Toyama Tower Garden**) located south of Takadanobaba Station.

To see Moscow, we visit **Nikolai-dô**, a Russian Orthodox cathedral near Ochanomizu Station that was designed by an architect brought over from the czar's capital. After that, we can go stand outside the gates of **Akasaka Palace,** once the home of Japan's Crown Prince but now used as the official state guest house. It's two European capitals

Left, formerly a church, now a love hotel. **Right,** Tokyo Station stands up against a facelift.

in one: Buckingham Palace on the outside and some of Versailles on the inside.

Then, to top things off, it's south along Gaien Higashi Dôri through Roppongi ("High Touch Town" read the signs that welcome you, whatever that means) to Tokyo's number one landmark, the Eiffel, er... **Tokyo Tower**. It's not exactly like the Paris structure, but close enough to have made many a person hold photos of the two side by side for comparison, and ask why the Tokyo designer, Dr. Tachû Naitô (or "Dr. Steel Tower" as he was lovingly called in Japan), did not dream up something more original.

For romance, how about the **Gallery Hotel** (a.k.a. Hotel Meguro Emperor) west of Meguro Station? It's one of the hundreds of "love hotels" in the city (rooms by the hour; fantasy architecture galore), but its turrets and battlements are straight from the Middle Ages. Ludwig, the compulsive castle-builder of Bavaria, would have been immensely satisfied. If you prefer the New World to the Old, you can go west to the suburbs, to **Kichijôji** on the JR Chûo Line, and see the **Hotel New York**. To welcome you, there is a multistory replica of the Statue of Liberty on the roof.

There are no easy explanations for all of this, nor can any one reason apply equally to each of these very diverse structures. What we see, though, is that Tokyo is very self-consciously international, at least on the surface. This is a personality trait of the city that began with the sudden opening of Japan to the West in 1853 with the arrival in Tokyo Bay of Commodore Perry's "black ships" from America, and that has been part of the city ever since. At one time, Tokyo copied the West to show the foreigners that it could; nowadays, it often uses Western themes in buildings because they are good for drumming up business.

Neighborhood Tokyo: To experience the full flavor of Tokyo, it is necessary to venture off the beaten path and spend some time in one or more of Tokyo's dozens of quiet residential neighborhoods. The city is one of the safest in the world for walking and its neighborhoods are fascinating, so don't miss the chance.

Part of the fun is discovery. Just walk away from the crowded commercial streets, turn off on any small lane that catches your eye, and – voila!, enter the Tokyo that is behind the scenes. Every neighborhood is different, so go to several places if you can, but there are also enough similarities to permit some generalizations.

The neighborhoods present a dramatic contrast to the bustle of the city. They are amazingly quiet, intimate, and private social worlds that are hidden just out of sight behind the tall buildings that line busy streets.

Warren-like street patterns discourage through traffic, so there are often few cars despite horrendous traffic jams just a short distance away. Privacy is further enhanced by walls and fences

Tokyo Tower behind Zôjôji Temple.

around individual houses, and by barriers of greenery. People live shoulder to shoulder in this crowded city, but property lines are clearly marked, and landscaping is used in clever ways to reduce noise and provide seclusion from passersby and neighbors.

There is also a strong feeling of community. Every neighborhood has a local shopping street where residents take care of daily needs at the stores, and where neighbors greet one another as they pass and stop for conversation and gossip. More and more, the action is at the supermarket or in front of the new 7-11 or other convenience store, but every neighborhood also has its established small shops: fishmongers, rice sellers, noodle makers, etc. At certain times of the year, these streets are given over to boisterous neighborhood festivals.

Many shopping streets are identified by a prominent gate or arch at the entrance that gives the name of the street, and by architectural devices such as distinctive lampposts and decorative

pavements. In some neighborhoods, the principal shopping street is an arcade that provides cover from bad weather. There is also a lot of plastic foliage affixed to utility poles. It is changed with the seasons (cherry blossoms, lush greenery, autumn colors, giant snowflakes) by the beautification committees of local civic associations.

An important institution in many neighborhoods has been the *sentô*, or public bath. There are still quite a few left in the city, especially in the older districts, where houses lack facilities for washing, or in areas where there are tiny apartments. However, their number has been getting smaller as housing conditions improve.

You are welcome to go in and use the facilities provided that you adhere to norms about what to do, how to do it, and what not to do. A good first rule to remember is that men's and women's facilities are separate. You can find a *sentô* by looking for the characteristic tall smokestack, or by its entrance with elaborately carved wood doorway and banks of lockers just inside. Often there is a coin laundry as part of the building because of the facilities to heat water.

Another landmark is the neighborhood Shinto shrine. This is often to the side of the shopping street and can sometimes be spotted from a distance by a tall stand of trees – usually the only large trees in the area. The entranceways are marked by distinctive gates called *torii*. They consist of two upright pillars that support two horizontal lintels above, the top one of which curves upwards. The *torii* separate the holy world inside from the secular world outside. You are usually welcome to explore the grounds of a shrine, or to sit and relax in the garden and enjoy the serenity.

Even though you are in one of the world's largest cities, you may never feel overwhelmed. Cultural reminders, polite smiles, and landmarks around the city allow you to feel reasonably secure in an unfamiliar city.

Left, Red *torii* gate leads to a neighborhood shrine. **Right**, on what to do when a quake hits.

EARTHQUAKES

Tokyo is highly prone to earthquakes. There are minor shakes recorded on seismological instruments almost every day, and bigger ones that startle people from their sleep, rattle dishes, and knock objects off shelves several times a year. From time to time, a major quake hits the Tokyo area, causing heavy damage to property and leading to huge loss of life.

The reason for the earthquakes is that Tokyo, and indeed all of Japan, is at a place where three moving segments of the earth's crust – the Pacific Plate, the Philippine Plate, and the Eurasian Plate – come into violent contact. This also explains why there is so much volcanic activity in the mountains of the Izu Peninsula near Tokyo and in various off-shore islands. In Tokyo, the danger from earthquakes is made worse because much of the city is on unconsolidated alluvial soil and on landfill. This is a very poor foundation that makes buildings tremble more than they would on solid ground.

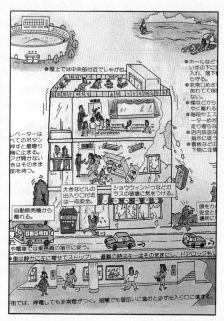

A major tremor whiplashes the Tokyo area every 60 years on the average, and the last one, the Great Kantô Earthquake – a 7.9 magnitude jolt on the Richter scale – took place in 1923.

Most of the central part of the city was levelled and totally destroyed by fire, and over 100,000 people were killed. There is a haunting memorial to this disaster near the new *sumo* stadium close to Ryogoku Station. Called Cenotaph Hall, it is on the spot where 40,000 people were burned to death when a fire tornado swept across the open area where they had sought safety.

Here is some really bad news: experts agree that another killer quake of the same magnitude or greater will strike the city again. It's just that no one knows when. However, there seems to be a pattern of major earthquakes in Tokyo every 69 or 70 years, so it could be that the next one will strike soon.

When it does happen, what will it be like? Some experts say that Tokyo is now much safer than it was in 1923. Buildings, bridges, elevated highways, etc., are all reinforced and built according to the latest techniques. In addition, much of the city is made to be fireproof. There are also shelters and other emergency facilities, and elaborate plans to provide food, water, and medical help should the worst happen. Chronic traffic jams can block emergency vehicles even in the best of times.

A highly conservative 1983 report by the Metropolitan Research Center estimates that an earthquake of the same magnitude as the 1923 quake will result in thousands of fires – 300 of them major – destroy around one million homes and leave some 3.5 million Tokyo residents homeless.

What should you do if while you are in Tokyo everything around you starts to shake violently? Two things are most important: seek shelter from falling objects by ducking into a doorway or under some furniture; and help to prevent fire by extinguishing any open flames such as on gas stoves or heating units. Whatever you do, don't panic and don't run out into the street where you can be hit by falling glass or other debris. Many hotels have information available in English about shelters and other procedures to help you be prepared in advance.

TEMPLES
AND SHRINES

Tokyo is a city of shrines and temples. From awesome Buddhist temples to the local neighborhood Shinto shrines, these revered places remind today's Japanese of their ancient historical past and culture. When asking a Japanese about his/her religion, nearly all will respond: "I am Buddhist" without giving much thought to its meaning.

Shinto is the natural indigenous religion that grew out of everyday life. Shinto gods, or *kami*, are worshipped at shrines *(jinja)*. All natural objects or phenomena were considered to have *kami*. The gods of Shinto were understandably numerous. In Japanese mythology there is the phrase *"yaoyorozu no kami"* or "eight million gods."

There is no God in Buddhism. Ridding oneself of hate and jealousy through infinite love, tolerance and equality is emphasized. The ultimate state is one of self-enlightenment by awaking to the truth.

Buddhism reached Japan in the 6th century via China and Korea. In the early 7th century, Prince Shôtoku used his influence to spread the belief. Initially a religion of the aristocracy, by the 13th century it had filtered down and was popular among the common folk. About the same time Zen, one denomination of Buddhism, became widespread among the *samurai* class.

Today, major festivals held throughout the year are most often connected to a temple or shrine. Festival processions usually begin or end on its grounds. There are special ceremonies for newborn children, coming of age (20 years old), marriage, the dead, and prayers for one's ancestors.

Shrines and temples are also places of good luck; students go and offer a prayer (or make a wish) before examinations, and if one is ill one may pay a visit for a speedy recovery. There is a shrine or temple within a few minutes' walk – whether a little neighborhood shrine or a large Buddhist temple.

Following is a list and brief description of main temples and shrines in Tokyo that are worth visiting for their beauty, history and cultural interest.

Sensôji Temple: Located in the heart of the Asakusa district of Tokyo, Sensôji is the oldest temple in the Tokyo Metropolitan area. Legend has it that it was founded in the year A.D. 628, when three local fishermen enshrined a small statue of *Kannon*, the Goddess of Mercy, which they had caught up in their fishing net.

According to the legend, at the time the statue first appeared, a great golden dragon danced its way down to earth from the heavens. For this reason, a Golden Dragon Dance is held on the temple grounds on the 18th of March each year.

The statue still lies preserved in the inner sanctum of the large facade of the **Main Hall** (*Hondô*), though it has never

Preceding pages, finding the real Japan in Tokyo's numerous temples and shrines. Left, prayers and wishes hung outside a temple. Below, Flower beauty at Honganji temple.

been shown to the public.

The temple compound includes such well-known structures as the **Kaminarimon** (Thunder Gate), the five-story pagoda (*Gojûnotô*), and the **Hôzômon Gate.**

On the west side of the Hondô, a small temple dedicated to the guardian deity of women (*Awashima Myôjin*) can be found. On the other side of the Hondô, to the back of the compound, lies **Asakusa Shrine** (the construction of which began around 1649 and is considered very representative of Edo period architecture), which is dedicated to the three fishermen who fished up the golden statue of *Kannon*. It is the site of the Sanja Festival held in May. Ginza Subway Line, Asakusa Stn.

Kan-eiji Temple: The Kan-eiji Temple was established in 1625 by the Buddhist high priest, Tenkai, who performed certain purification rites meant to protect Edo Castle from the ravages of fire – it subsequently burned down.

Besides the present main temple

which was brought from the **Kawagoe Kitain Temple** in 1879, the compound includes the **Kiyomizudô Temple** (patterned after the famous **Kiyomizu Temple** in **Kyôto**), a five-story pagoda, and the **Jômeiin**, an ancillary temple, where you can see the 30cm-high stone image of *Jizô* and invoke the image to foretell your chances of being granted a divine wish. It is believed that if you can easily raise the little statue, you will be assured of good luck. JR Yamanote Line, Uguisudani Stn.

Tôshôgû Shrine: Established in 1627, the Tôshôgû Shrine is dedicated to the first generation of the Tokugawa Shogunate, Tokugawa Ieyasu. The present structure was remodeled in 1651 by the third-generation *shogun*, Tokugawa Iemitsu.

Though not as luxuriously decorated as it was in the Edo period, the main shrine building, **Konjikiden**, or Golden Hall, is still a magnificent, ornate building. The **Haiden**, or Outer Hall, features murals painted by the famed Edo artist, Kanô Tanyû.

Also interesting to see is the Chinese-style **Karamon Gate**, decorated with dragons that are meant to be ascending and descending to and from heaven. The legend says that these dragons go to the nearby **Shinobazu Pond** to drink their fill when night falls. JR Yamanote Line, Ueno Stn.

Zôjôji Temple: After the Kan-eiji Temple, Zôjôji is the second largest temple in Tokyo. Belonging to the *Jôdo* Buddhist sect, it was originally built in 1393 and moved to its present location in 1590. It grew in importance to become the patron temple of the Tokugawa family.

Among the important structures are the **San-gedatsumon Gate** (erected in 1605) and what remains of the Tokugawa Mausoleums. The tomb of the 6th generation *shogun*, Tokugawa Ienobu, still remains intact and available for viewing. JR Yamanote, Line, Hamamatsuchô Stn.

Sannô Hie Shrine: This shrine was the

Adhering to the teachings of Confucius.

site of worship of the *Ubusuna* god, protector of the birthplace of the Tokugawa family. It was originally built in 830 and later enjoyed the auspicious position of being the largest of all the shrines in old Edo (Tokyo's former name). Chiyoda Subway Line, Akasaka Stn.

Sengakuji Temple: This is the famous site, known to most Japanese, where the 47 Akô *samurai* (Chûshingura), who avenged the death of their master before committing harakiri, are buried.

In the **Hall of the Loyal Retainers**, there is a large number of personal effects and historical artifacts related to this celebrated event. Toei Asakusa Subway Line, Sengakuji Stn.

Meiji Jingû Shrine: This shrine is consecrated to the Emperor Meiji and the Empress Dowager Shôken. It is located amidst a forest of beautiful trees (donated from all over Japan), ponds and the **Meiji Garden**.

In fact, apart from the Imperial Palace grounds, most of which are closed to the public, it is the only spacious area of its kind left in the center of Tokyo. It receives most visitors at New Year's when over two million people reportedly come to make wishes for the new year on January 1st. JR Yamanote Line, Harajuku Stn. or Chiyoda Subway Line, Meiji Jingûmae Stn.

Oji Inari Shrine: This shrine dates from the 10th century and is dedicated to the guardian deity *Inari*, who takes the form of a fox. The Shogunal family would come here to make their supplications. The present main sanctuary (*Honden*) was built in 1808. (**JR Keihin Tôhoku Line, Oji Stn.**)

Zôshigaya Kishibojin: The guardian deity of children, called *Kishibojin*, is enshrined here. The present structure was built in 1666. There is a massive gingko tree in front of the shrine that is over 500 years old and has long been famous for having powers affecting birth and the raising of children. JR Yamanote Line, Otsuka Stn. Then a 6-minute ride on the streetcar to Kishi-

Yasukuni Shrine – a shrine dedicated to the war dead.

bojin-mae Stn. 4th stop.

Yushima Seidô: This Confucian temple was established in 1690. The images of Confucius and his main disciples are enshrined here. The present Chinese Ming-style building was rebuilt in 1935 due to damage caused by the 1923 earthquake. JR Chûo Line, Ochanomizu Stn.

Otori Shrine: This is an old shrine famous for the *Torinoichi* (Cock Fair) which is held in November. People come to buy ornamental bamboo rakes, known as *kumade*, which are then hung up in the home and are said to rake in good fortune during the year. But even if they don't help you too much in that regard, they do make nice decorations. Hibiya Subway Line, Iriya or Minowa stations.

Sumiyoshi Shrine: This shrine is dedicated to the god of safety at sea. A large festival is held here every three years (for three days before or after August 7th). Yûrakuchô Subway Line, Shintomichô Stn.

Yasukuni Shrine: This Shinto shrine is controversial because of its military connotations. Built on **Kudan Hill** in 1869, it is dedicated to war and deifies as gods all those who have died fighting for their country.

It was traditional for servicemen embarking on mortal missions to pledge to their comrades, "We shall meet at Yasukuni." Tôzai Subway Line, Kudanshita Stn.

Koganji Temple (Togenuki Jizô): Established in 1598, this temple contains the image of *Emmei Jizô*, known as *Togenuki (tweezer) Jizô* since the Edo period. Worshippers flock here on the 4th, 14th and 24th of each month (meant to be lucky days). Little and not so little old ladies are in abundance on these days. Many of them come to a particular *jizô* that is believed to have healing powers. It is said that if you rub any part of your body that may be afflicted with some pain or illness on that *jizô*, you will be restored to perfect health. JR Yamanote Line, Sugamo Stn.

Left, an old remedy: touching the *jizo*. **Right**, New Year archery ritual in Meiji Shrine's Outer Garden.

MEIJI SHRINE

No visit to Tokyo can be complete without seeing the Meiji Shrine. This is one of the most sacred of Japanese landmarks, an outstanding example of Shinto architecture, and a beautiful preserve of nature in the midst of a crowded city.

The main entrance is close to Harajuku Station (JR Yamanote Line) near the end of Omote-sandô Boulevard. It is marked by a 40-foot (13 meters) *torii* the largest wooden gate in Japan – made from cypress trees that are said to be over 1,500 years old. It prepares the visitor symbolically for the spiritual presence of a Shinto god, Emperor Meiji, who ruled the country between 1868 and 1912 and set it on its path of modernization. Also enshrined is the Emperor's wife, the Empress Dowager Shôken.

The Meiji Shrine was opened in 1920 on imperial land that once belonged to the Ii family. It covers 180 acres (72 hectares) and is heavily forested with 120,000 trees (365 species) that were collected from all over Japan. There is also an iris garden, a water-lily pond, and a beautiful open field. The landscaping adds to a contemplative mood and reflects Shinto beliefs about the sanctity of nature.

The main complex of buildings of the **Meiji Shrine** hidden among the trees at the end of a long gravel pathway is in a style called *"Nagare-zukuri"* and was crafted in Japanese cedar by the country's leading traditional architects. The original building was destroyed in an air raid in 1945, so the present structure is a reconstruction finished in 1958. The rebuilding is a source of great national pride, because it was financed largely by donations from the citizens of Japan during a time of considerable hardship and economic poverty. Another part of this **Inner Garden** section of the Meiji Shrine is the **Hômotsuden**, or the Treasure Museum. Inside are

numerous items that were used by the Emperor and Empress in their daily lives. A beautiful six-horse carriage that was used by the Emperor during the 1889 ceremony that promulgated Japan's Constitution is a favorite attraction.

On several festival days each year the Meiji Shrine is especially crowded. On November 3, Japanese celebrate Emperor Meiji's birthday. April 29 – May 3 is the coming of spring. This is celebrated with competitions of archery on horseback (*yabusame*) and performances of traditional music. January 15, Adults Day, brings thousands of 20-year-old women in gorgeous *kimono* for a ritual blessing. December 31 is *Omisoka*, the Grand Last Day, when huge crowds descend on the shrine (and other places of worship) to hear 108 peals of a ceremonial bell heralding the start of a new year. Meiji Shrine is also an extremely popular place for traditional weddings and for family portraits on any occasion.

PARKS
AND GARDENS

There are over 60 metropolitan urban parks covering over 1,000 hectares of land in Tokyo. There are also many other urban parks and playgrounds that are administered by wards and municipalities, plus **Marine Park** constructed on reclaimed land along **Tokyo Bay**. Putting all the green together, that amounts to about 6,700 parks in Tokyo.

In addition, there are two natural national parks located within the metropolitan area in the **Tama** and island areas.

The long-term planning department for metropolitan Tokyo is steadily looking for space – and ways to make the city greener – with a goal of having six square meters of park per city resident.

Various gardens are located through-

out Tokyo. The meticulous care of the gardens – the precise placement of a stone, or the careful cutting of a branch – displays the Japanese love for beauty and tradition.

Chidorigafuchi Park: This is the moat area of the ancient Edo Castle in **Kudanshita**. Part of the fun is renting a boat and sipping your *sake* while on the water. Tôzai Subway Line, one minute from Kudanshita Stn.

Hibiya Park: This park is situated on land that once belonged to the feudal lord Matsudaira Bizennokami, up until the end of the Edo era. Later, the land served as a military parade ground during the Meiji era. Located nearby Tokyo's business center, it provides an oasis amidst the high-rise concrete office buildings. Located in the park is a four-hundred-year-old ginkgo biloba, 635 cm around. Seasonal flowers bloom all year round. JR Yamanote Line, a 5-minute walk from Yûrakuchô Stn., or Hibiya Subway Line, Hibiya Stn., or Chiyoda or Mita Subway Lines, Kasumigaseki Stn.

Hamarikyû Garden: A typical feudal-lord garden of the Edo era. It is the only garden where seawater actually flows in and out. There are two duck-hunting fields that are presently fenced off as a natural preservation area. The **Otsutaibashi Bridge**, modeled after the **Yatsuhashi Bridge** in **Kyôto**, and a 300-year-old pine add to the the park's beauty. JR Yamanote Line, a 15-minute walk from Shimbashi Stn., or Ginza and Asakusa Subway Lines, Shimbashi Stn., or you can get to it on the Takeshiba-Asakusa water bus.

Hamarikyû Teien: An elegant place to catch the blossoms, this was one of the Showa Emperor's favorite viewing spots. JR Yamanote Line, a 7-minute walk from Shimbashi Stn.

Imperial Palace East Garden: Higashi Gyoen or **East Gardens** of the Imperial Palace. Enter through the **Otemon Gate** to a garden area measuring over 210,000 square meters. The garden contains the beautifully landscaped

Preceding pages, Hibiya Park, surrounded by modern office buildings. Below, ducks take refuge at Shinobazu Pond in Ueno.

Ninomaru Gardens, **Dôshin-bansho**, **Hyakuninbansho** (100-men guard-house), **Tenshudai** (Donjon Base), **Tôkagakudô** (Music Hall), **Fuji-mitamon** (armory) and **Suwano-Chaya Teahouse**. Tozai, Chiyoda and Marunouchi Subway Lines, a 5-minute walk from Otemachi Stn.

Inokashira Park: Cherry trees surround the large pond in the park, where you can also rent a boat and view the blossoms from the water. Great at night. A 5-minute walk from JR Chûo or Sôbu Lines, or Inokashira Line, Kichijôji Stn.

Koganei Park: There are 1,300 cherry trees here, and the park and surroundings are worth going a bit out of your way for. (A short distance from **Koganei Kôenmae** stop on the **Kantô** (Seibu) bus. (Take any bus for **Mitaka Stn**. from **Chûo Line**, **Musashi Koganei Stn.**)

Koishikawa Kôrakuen Garden: A landscaped garden in the go-round style built in the 17th century. The garden includes many Chinese features as well as a lake in the center. Also an iris pond. JR Chûo Line, or Marunouchi Subway Line, a 7-minute walk from Kôrakuen Stn.

Meiji Park: A park surrounded by **Jingûnomori**, a sports mecca containing the **National Stadium** and the **Jingû Baseball Stadium**. The National Stadium was the main site for the Tokyo Olympics. JR Sôbu Line, a 3-minute walk from Sendagaya Stn.

Rikugien Garden: Rikugien is a famous garden representing the Edo Era. It contains views copying famous scenic spots in Japan extolled in "Man-yô-shû" (A Collection of Myriad Leaves) and "Kokin Waka-shû" (A Collection of Ancient and Modern Poetry). A 5-minute walk from Mita Subway Line, Sengoku Stn.

Shiba Park: **Zôjôji Temple** resides within this park. There are also many camphor, Chinese black pines, and ginkgos. Mita Subway Line, Shibakôen Stn. or a 10-minute walk from JR Yamanote Line, Hamamatsuchô Stn.

Springtime at the Imperial Palace moat.

CHERRY BLOSSOM FEVER

Spring fever in Tokyo takes its cue not from the sight of maddened March hares or recordings of the first cuckoo, but from the intense and short-lived beauty of the city's cherry trees when they burst into bloom sometime around the beginning of April. The event is a highly anticipated one: newspapers and television stations vie with each other to give the most accurate opening date predictions and report daily on the progress of the buds. Traditional confectionery stores begin to fill their shelves with cherry-based sweets and dumplings, and hundreds of flower-viewing (*ohanami*) parties are planned and prepared for.

The capital's near-infatuation with the color, odor, and potent natural symbolism of its cherry blossoms is as old as the city itself. To its rustics and

rustics-at-heart of four centuries ago, cherry trees were more than just a pleasant addition to the landscape, they were also the favored resting places of rice paddy spirits who traditionally took up residence in the trees' branches when the flowers first appeared. Since the blooms' arrival coincided with the start of the rice planting season, the city's rice growers decided to pay their respects and ensure a good harvest, which they did by drinking *sake* under the tree. After food, making *sake* was the whole point of growing rice anyway, and the more they drank, the greater the homage they paid. It was a perfect formula, and one that would be taken to the height of refinement by shogunates of the 16th and 17th centuries before returning to the defiantly popular status that it holds today.

Modern *ohanami* parties are a time for mixing outward boisterousness with a little private sentimentality. (Once used by poets to symbolize the nobly abbreviated fighting lives of young samurai, the cherry blossom is after all the country's national flower.) Some partygoers prefer the early buds, others the pathos of the last few clinging flowers, and many come to drink at night, either under the moonlight or illuminating the trees with torches. Traditional festive ingredients are *sake*, singing, *odango* dumplings and straw mats to sit on; non-traditional whiskey, beer and portable *karaoke* machines are optional extras. Competition for a choice picnicking position is intense, particularly if the party is an office affair: staff juniors carrying the company name plaque are often sent to reserve a space up to 24 hours in advance, camping overnight at the foot of the chosen tree.

For first-timers the best places to enjoy the show, botanically or otherwise, are the parks in **Ueno** and **Shinjuku Gyoen** and the banks of the **Imperial Palace** moat. Information concerning exact blossoming dates can be obtained from English-language newspapers and the Japan National Tourist Office (JNTO).

Spring fever affects young and old alike.

Sotobori Park: The moats between **Yotsuya** and **Iidabashi** are the traces of outer moats of the old Edo Castle. JR Chûo Line, Yotsuya, Ichigaya, & Iidabashi Stations, or Marunouchi Subway Line, Yotsuya Stn.

Shinjuku Gyoen Garden: The history of this garden goes back to the 16th century. It contains a Western-style garden and a Japanese garden, as well as a lake. Various flowers are in bloom at different seasons. There is a chrysanthemum exhibit between the 1st and 15th of November. Marunouchi Subway Line, a 2-minute walk from Shinjuku Gyoen Stn.

Sumida Park: This is located right alongside the Sumida River, where there are about 1,400 cherry trees eagerly waiting to be viewed. One-minute walk from Asakusa Station on the Ginza Subway Line.

Yoyogi Park: Tokyo's largest urban park, this park is divided into a forested park area and an open area with athletic facilities and an outdoor stage. The verdant forest borders neighboring **Meiji Shrine**. JR Yamanote Line, a 3-minute walk from Harajuku Stn., or Chiyoda Subway Line, Yoyogikôen Stn.

Ueno Park: One of the oldest parks in Japan the park contains **Tôshôgû Shrine** and **Shinobazu Pond**. The park is a favorite spot for viewing springtime cherry blossoms. Three cherry trees in the park have been designated the official trees for forecasting the blooming of the buds by the weather service. Probably the most famous place in Tokyo for viewing, but frankly, once the buds begin to bloom, the park becomes noisy, littered, and very crowded. A trip here is essential if it's the crazy, rowdy times of *ohanami* you're after. The park borders **Ueno Zoo**. JR Yamanote Line, a 2-minute walk from Ueno Stn., or Ginza and Hibiya Subway Lines, Ueno Stn., or Keisei Subway Line, Ueno or Hakubutsukan-Dôbutsuenmae stations.

Azalea-viewing at Nezu Shrine Garden.

MUSEUMS AND GALLERIES

During the 1980s, the major auction houses of Europe and the U.S. felt the impact of the Japanese desire and ability to invest heavily in works of art.

Some of this was very conspicuous. Many of the highest prices ever paid for Western art came from the coffers of Japanese corporations eager to invest and to impress. Less conspicuously, the Japanese began to buy back all those Japanese art works plundered by foreigners during the 19th century.

There are excellent collections of the world's art on display all over Tokyo, as well as many specialist galleries and museums and touring exhibitions. All major department stores are connected with various kinds of cultural activities and most of them have extensive display areas somewhere at the top of the building. Exhibitions are well covered by the English-language newspapers. They can cost US$10 or more, but are often spectacular. The Japanese are also fond of producing the finest-quality catalogs, often with English included, posters and post cards.

The best area for small galleries is undoubtedly the up-market area of the **Ginza**, in all the little back streets between **Ginza 2-chôme** and **Ginza 7-chôme**. Other galleries around Tokyo have exhibitions of individual artists, foreign and Japanese.

Needless to say, there are many outlets for Japanese art. Some major hotels have well-stocked shops with English-speaking staff, and the **Oriental Bazaar** near **Harajuku** is a mecca for anyone searching for any type of Japanese product, old ·or new, including wood-block prints. Another good area for wood-block prints is **Jimbôchô**, where many of the bookshops have a print section.

Art Museums: If you have limited time in Tokyo, there are two areas you should certainly visit to fit in a lot of fine art in a short time. The first of these is the **Kitanomaru Park** area, next to the Imperial Palace. Here you can find the **National Museum of Modern Art**, the **Craft Gallery** and the **Museum of Science and Technology**.

The National Museum of Modern Art has a permanent collection of over 4,000 items on display on three floors, and a first-floor exhibition hall for special exhibitions. A good place for Picasso and his Japanese contemporaries. The Craft Gallery next door, the former Imperial guard division headquarters and one of the few Western-style brick buildings still standing in Tokyo, has a huge collection of textiles, lacquerware, ceramics and other handicrafts.

The second area is **Ueno Park**, that vast area of cultural interest with everything from gorillas to Francis Bacon. Here you can visit the **National Museum of Western Art**, the **Tokyo Metropolitan Art Museum**, **Ueno Royal Museum** and other museums men-

An exquisite 12th century silk painting.

tioned later.

The National Museum of Western Art is quite a surprise to many visitors. Not only is it a particularly pleasant place, well air-conditioned and designed by Le Corbusier, but it has an extraordinary collection of works by Rodin and all major 19th and 20th century Western painters, particularly Monet. The basis of the collection is unusual in itself. The collection of Kôjirô Masukata, former president of the Kawasaki Shipbuilding Company, was originally kept in Paris and seized by the French authorities after the war. The surviving items made their way back to Ueno only in 1959.

The more recent Tokyo Metropolitan Art Museum is the site for major exhibitions of contemporary Japanese art as well as regular exhibitions based on its own extensive collection. The interesting little Ueno Royal Museum is primarily used for the exhibitions of various art societies and associations. Other art museums are to be found all over the city. Particularly recommended are the **Idemitsu Art Gallery** in **Marunouchi** (Asian ceramics and Zen calligraphy); the **Iwasaki Chihiro Art Museum of Picture Books** in **Nerima-ku** (the private collection of the late children's book illustrator, including many of her own works); the **Ukiyoe Ota Memorial Museum of Art** in **Harajuku** (the massive print collection of another businessman, Seizo Ota); the **Okura Shûkokan Museum of Art** in **Akasaka** (a beautiful 11th-floor gallery which specializes in artistic items for daily life); the **Sôgetsu Art Museum** in **Akasaka** (the collection of the founder of the Sôgetsu School of Flower Arranging); the **Nezu Institute of Fine Arts** in **Minami-Aoyama** (especially famous for its collection of tea ceremony utensils and an extensive garden); the **Bridgestone Museum of Art** in **Kyôbashi** (based on the collection of the founder of the Bridgestone Tire Company, especially strong on modern French paintings); the **Riccar**

Hokusai's famous wave woodblock print.

Art Museum in the Ginza (a superb collection of wood-block prints). There are many, many more. Admission is about US$3-4 on average.

Museums: The major museums in Tokyo include two in Ueno Park. The massive **Tokyo National Museum** has a history of over 170 years. It features thousands of major Far Eastern artifacts. The **National Science Museum** boasts over one million items, with everything from dinosaurs to space technology and a flight simulator.

Tokyo has a wide-ranging selection of museums to visit, which include a fascinating assortment of specialized collections. These include: the new **Camera Museum**, near the British Embassy; the **Transportation Museum** in **Kanda** (a great place for the family, with many exhibits, including the development of the bullet train); the ship-shaped **Maritime Museum** out in **Tokyo Bay Park** (complete with observatory and the preserved Antarctic survey vessel *Soya*); the **Tsubouchi**

Memorial Theater Museum, inside **Waseda University** (a memorial to the great Japanese translator of Shakespeare, Shôyô Tsubouchi, and dedicated to theater items); the **Meguro Museum of Parasites** in **Shimomeguro**; the **Sword Museum** in **Yoyogi** (where you can even have your sword heirlooms evaluated); the **Japanese Folkcraft Museum** in **Meguro**; the **Tobacco and Salt Museum** in **Shibuya** (a fascinating history of the part played in Japanese cultural history by these two essential items); the **Bicycle Culture Center** in **Akasaka**; the **Paper Museum** in **Kitaku**; the **Shitamachi Museum** in **Ueno** (the whole, vivid history of the traditional downtown areas of Edo and Tokyo); the **Kite Museum** in **Nihombashi**; and the **Sumo Museum** at the **Kokugikan Sumo Tournament Hall** in **Ryôgoku**.

Another popular hands-on museum is the **Museum of Science and Technology** in **Kitanomaru Park**, near the National Museum of Modern Art.

Ueno National Museum is filled with ancient treasures.

HOLIDAYS AND FESTIVALS

Festivals or *matsuri* seem to be happening at any time somewhere in Tokyo. An important part of Japanese life for hundreds of years, many of them have their roots in the long history of Japan's agricultural society. In today's ever modernizing Japan, they are one of the few occasions when Japanese can dress up (or down) and relive a nostalgic past. Below is a short list of the main national holidays and important festivals.

January: (*Shôgatsu*) **New Year's Day** is a national holiday. People don their *kimono* and visit Buddhist temples and Shinto Shrines to make wishes for the new year. Japanese *sake* is the featured drink the first few days of the year. The 15th is *Seijin no Hi* (Coming-of-Age Day), another national holiday. Most girls who have reached the age of 20 put on traditional *kimono* and go to a shrine for a special "adult" ceremony. *Hatsubasho,* first **sumo** tournament of the year, is held for fifteen days at the **Kokugikan** in mid-January.

February: On the 3rd is *Setsubun,* the traditional bean throwing ceremony that is meant to purify the home of evil. Roasted beans are thrown from windows and doors to the outside while people shout, *"Oni wa soto"* (devils, go out!) followed by, *"Fuku wa uchi"* (good luck, come in). Similar, yet more formal ceremonies are held at temples and shrines. Some of the main ceremonial sites are **Kanda Shrine, Zôjôji Temple, Hie Shrine**, and **Nishiarai Daishi Temple.** On the 11th is *Kenkoku Kinen no Hi* (National Foundation Day), a national holiday.

March: On the 3rd of the month is *Hina Matsuri* (Girl's Day). Small *hina* dolls representing imperial court figures are displayed at home and in public places. The 21st is *Shumbun no Hi* (Vernal Equinox Day), a national holiday.

April: From early to mid-April is *Ohanami* (Cherry Blossom viewing), one of the important spring rites. People love to turn out and picnic, drink *sake,* and sing songs under the pink blossoms. Some of the famous spots for cherry blossom viewing are **Aoyama Bochi** (Cemetery), **Chidorigafuchi Park, Kôrakuen, Sumida Park, Ueno Park,** and **Yasukuni Shrine**. On April 8 is *Hana Matsuri* (Birthday of Buddha), when commemorative services are held at various temples such as **Gokokuji Temple, Sensôji Temple, Zôjôji Temple,** and **Hommonji Temple**. The 29th – the late Showa Emperor's birthday – has now become *Hana to Midori no Hi* (Flower and Greenery Day), a national holiday. The Golden Week holiday period also begins on this day.

May: May 3 is the national holiday *Kempô Kinembi* (Constitution Memorial Day). On the 5th is *Kodomo no Hi* (Children's Day), another national holiday. Though the emphasis is on little boys, it is supposed to be for all

The young don traditional wear.

children. Carp banners (*koinobori*) are flown from homes where little boys live. It is hoped that the boys will grow up big and strong like the carp – a symbol of strength and manhood. *Samurai* dolls are also displayed inside the home. In mid-May, the *Natsubasho* (summer *sumo* tournament) is held for fifteen days at the **Kokugikan**. On the 3rd Saturday and Sunday, *Sanja Matsuri* is held. Honoring the three fishermen who found the image of *Kannon* in the river, this is one of the big *Edo* festivals. The **Asakusa Shrine** is a great place to go at this time to see processions of portable shrines, traditional dancing and music. From the end of May to the beginning of June is the iris-viewing time, and the best place by far to see them in bloom is the **Meiji Shôbuen.**

June: On the 2nd Sunday, at the **Torigoe Shrine**, is *Torigoe Jinja Taisai* – a nighttime festival when the biggest and heaviest portable shrine in Tokyo is carried through the streets. From the

10th to the 16th is *Sannô Sai,* another big Edo festival featuring a *gyôretsu* (people parading in traditional costumes) on Saturday at the **Hie Shrine.**

July: From the 6th to 8th is *Asagao Ichi* (Morning Glory Fair) when over one hundred merchants set up stalls selling the morning flower at **Iriya Kishibojin.** On the 7th is the *Tanabata Matsuri,* celebrating the only day of the year when, according to the legend, the Weaver Princess (Vega) and her lover the Cowherd (Altair) cross the Milky Way to meet. People write their wishes on pieces of colored paper, hang them on bamboo branches, and then float them down a river the next day. On the 9th and 10th is *Hôzuki Ichi* (Ground Cherry Fair) at **Sensôji Temple** from early morning to midnight on both days. A visit to this temple on the 10th is equivalent to 46,000 other-day visits. On the last Saturday of July, the *Sumidagawa Hanabi Taikai* (Sumida River Fireworks) – biggest fireworks display in Tokyo is held. The best places to

The white Heron Dance is performed on Culture Day.

watch it are between the **Kototoi** and **Shirahige bridges,** or at the **Komagata Bridge.**

August: Between the 13th and 16th is ***Obon.*** People return to their hometowns to clean up the graves and offer prayers to the souls of departed ancestors. Traditional ***Bon Odori*** folk dances are also held all over Japan.

September: On the 15th is the national holiday ***Keirô no Hi*** (Respect-for-the-Aged Day). In mid-September, the ***Akibasho*** (autumn *sumo* tournament) is held. It is the last tournament of the year held at the **Kokugikan.** The 23rd is ***Shûbun no Hi*** (Autumnal Equinox Day), a national holiday.

October: On the 10th is the national holiday ***Taiiku no Hi*** (Sports Day). From mid- to late-October is chrysanthemum-viewing time. There are gorgeous flowerbeds blossoming around the city. Some of the best viewing places are at **Hibiya Park, Meiji Shrine, Sensôji Temple,** and **Yasukuni Shrine.**

November: On the 3rd is ***Bunka no Hi*** (Culture Day), a national holiday. The 15th is ***Shichi-Go-San*** (Seven-Five-Three) a ceremony for 5-year-old boys and 3- and 7-year-old girls. The children usually dress up in *kimono* and are taken to visit local shrines. The national holiday ***Kinrô Kansha no Hi*** (Labor Thanksgiving Day) is on the 23rd.

December: The 14th is ***Gishi Sai,*** a memorial service for the famous *47 Akô samurai* who, on this day in 1702, avenged the death of their master and later committed suicide. They are buried at the **Sengakuji Temple** where the service is held. From the 17th to the 19th, ***Hagoita Ichi*** (Battledore Fair), is held at **Sensôji Temple.** On the 31st, at the stroke of midnight, every temple bell throughout the country begins to toll. The bells toll 108 times, representing the 108 evil human passions. This is called ***Joya no Kane*** and the general public is allowed to strike the bells at the **Zôjôji Temple** and the **Kan-eiji Temple.**

"Miss Small Edo" beauty contest in Kawagoe, a Tokyo suburb.

TOKYO DISNEYLAND

Tokyo Disneyland, the first Disney theme park constructed outside the United States, has been a continuous success since its opening in April 1983. Approximately 10 million people were admitted in 1989 alone. On most days, the park is filled to or beyond capacity with enthralled throngs of Japanese of all ages. The park has proven that at least on one level, that of self-serving (and preferably cuddly) cultural myths, Japanese and American culture are entirely compatible.

Walt Disney's original plan for a place where a family could go for a clean, safe, relatively cheap holiday with acceptable food (at Tokyo Disneyland that means curry rice and noodles) perfectly fits the needs of Japanese families looking for an exotic weekend closer and cheaper than that other playground, favored Hawaii.

America's important cultural icons are omnipresent. Cowboys stroll along Westernland's streets. American "know-how" is touted in George Lucas's Star Tours, space being the one obvious area left where American technology has not been surpassed by the Japanese. Small town values are lauded on Main Street. "American Journey," the 360-degree movie of the truly magnificent American continent, is accompanied by a 100-or-so-voice choir singing "God Bless America." Even when dressed in *kimono* and speaking Japanese, (Mickey, Donald and Minnie) are still 100% red-blooded Americans.

Since many of the attractions at Tokyo Disneyland are in Japanese only and are more crowded than the U.S. equivalents, it may seem strange to recommend that Americans go there. There is, however, a great deal to be learned from watching Japanese people at play. Moreover, the crowds are much easier to control than in the U.S. as

Japanese find foreign fantasy at Tokyo Disneyland.

Japanese people are more cooperative and patient in large crowds than Americans. The Japanese are extremely family oriented and the kids are so visibly delighted with everything that they add a substantial glow to the park.

In addition, there is one very interesting attraction which is not in the United States, "Meet the World," presented by Matsushita Electronics. Kônosuke Matsushita, the founder of Matsushita Electronics (Panasonic), had a profound belief in the importance of international cooperation. His position in Japanese history parallels that of Thomas Edison in America as a technological innovator and entrepreneur. Matsushita Electronics' exhibit covers Japanese history up to the Meiji era. The story is told through projected images and robots. Especially interesting is the emphasis on Japan's dependance on the rest of the world. The exhibit avoids complications by stopping short of Japan's twentieth century expansion, but is nonetheless worth visiting.

Tokyo Disneyland is easy to reach from Tokyo on the **Tôzai Subway Line** by getting off at **Urayasu Station**. From there, follow the signs (in Japanese) or Mickey's ears. A short walk down a pedestrian street leads to the Disneyland shuttle bus station. The bus ride is about 10 minutes (¥260). Or, taxis perform a more expensive shuttle alternative, pulling up one after another in front of Urayasu Station. The queue is often long. There is also a Disneyland stop on the new Keiyo Line – Maihama –and the park is a short distance away.

Disneyland can also be reached from Tokyo Station (Yaesu-North Exit) by bus and there is also a shuttle bus service to and from each of the nearby Tokyo Bay hotels. During spring, summer, and fall, Tokyo Disneyland is open every day, but in the winter it generally closes on Tuesdays and Wednesdays. Travel agents and information offices will be able to provide details of opening hours and days. The telephone number for Tokyo Disneyland is 03-366-5600.

Everybody loves Mickey Mouse.

DAYTRIPPING

After spending several days in Tokyo, you may well wish to escape the city and see a bit (or a whole lot) more of Japan. There are a number of destinations nearby Tokyo that let the visitor get more of a feel for Japan. A great many sights can be taken in by traveling only a few hours from Tokyo – you can be back in your Tokyo hotel room that evening after a full day out exploring Japan.

To Tokyo's south is Yokohama, although it's hard to tell exactly where Tokyo ends and Yokohama begins. However, it's history as a port city has contributed to the city's distinctive atmosphere. If it's the exotic Far East you are looking for, Kamakura's giant Buddha and numerous temples offer the opportunity to peer into Japan's past and considerer the various influences that have shaped Japanese society.

Japan for the most part is a moutainous country. Hakone and the Fuji Five Lakes area offer a spectacular sight of majestic Mt. Fuji. as well as the serenity of Japan's mountainous countryside. Yet Japan is an island. Seacoast areas such as Miura and Enoshima offer a glimpse of the more tranquil side of Japan as compared with the hectic pace of Japanese cities.

To the north there is Nikko, famous for its ornate temples along with its beautiful natural surroundings.

For destinations far from Tokyo, such as Osaka or Kyoto, travelers have usually opted for utilizing Japan's extensive train system in order to see the country. JR's *shinkansen* or bullet train travels at speeds of 220 kph. S*hinkansen* fares may seem rather steep; taking the economical local trains are fine if you have a lot more time and don't mind the countless station stops.

You can strike it out on your own, and that experience can truly be most rewarding. For others, though, the energy spent in trying to get things arranged may in the end not equal the rewards received. Japanese companies are good at marketing and when it come to group tour packages, they have done their research into the needs of the foreign tourist market: price, ease of making travel and accommodation arrangements, and flexibility.

Preceding pages: A crisp autumn morning at the foot of Mt. Fuji; the Japanese coastline – historically, a natural barrier to foreign influence. **Left**, the agony and the ecstasy: an outdoor hot spring bath in the wintertime.

YOKOHAMA

To see **Yokohama,** start at the top. Jutting 108 meters into the sky, the **Marine Tower** near **Yamashita Park** offers an exciting panorama of Yokohama's past and future.

Look south for a glimpse of the past. There you can see the tree-studded **Bluff Area** and hear the tombstones in the **Foreign Cemetery** whisper stories about hardy foreign residents who forged a new chapter in Japanese history.

Formerly a tiny seaside village with barely 100 households, Yokohama sprung to life in 1859 as Japan's first international port city.

Yokohama soon carved a niche in Japanese history as a city of firsts. The first to have a railway, a water works, English-language newspapers, gas-lit streets, a beer brewery, a barber shop. The first to watch American circus

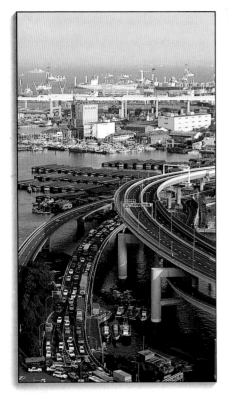

acrobats perform feats of daring, to enjoy the pomp and circumstance of a British marching band, and to hear the plaintiff sounds of jazz.

In 1871, Mary Kidder began teaching a small group of young women. Her concern for women's education gave birth to the first school for girls in Japan, known today as **Ferris Girl's Junior and Senior High School.**

Plan to browse through the shops along Yokohama's **Motomachi Street.** Before 1859, the majority of Yokohama's original inhabitants lived in the Motomachi area. In 1860, they were forcefully relocated to make room for the foreign settlement. Motomachi Street became the thoroughfare for foreign merchants to commute from their homes on the Bluff to their offices in the Kannai district.

Plan to walk around the Bluff. Drop in the **Yamate Museum** opposite the Foreign Cemetery (open every day, 11 a.m. to 4 p.m. except December 30 to January 1) and get a feel for the bygone days in the old foreign settlement.

Then go next door to the **Jûbankan** for a leisurely coffee or beer in a 19th century atmosphere. Let your mind wander back in time. Imagine Dr. James Hepburn struggling over the romanization of the Japanese language. Or imagine Charles Wirgman drawing caricatures of foreigners and Japanese – sometimes witty, sometimes savage – which appeared in the monthly Japan Punch. Or imagine General Douglas MacArthur walking through the corridors of the **New Grand Hotel** on his first day as the "American Shogun."

Then observe the Japanese tourists gazing thoughtfully at the tombstones in the Foreign Cemetery, which exert as much fascination on them as the Giant Buddha in Kamakura does on foreign visitors.

Don't linger too long in the past. From your perch in the tower, follow the graceful lines of the **Bay Bridge.** At night, the bridge with its blue and white lights provides a spectacular memory

Yokohama Port: gateway to internationlism.

for romantic couples. **Sky Promenade**, walkways which line the bridge on both sides, provides a romantic stroll along the bridge and leads to the bridge's **Sky Tower** and **Sky Lounge**. The Sky Lounge is a circular observatory located 320 meters from the end of the tower foundation, suspended under the two highway decks. For a spectacular view of Yokohama at night, the ¥600 charge is well worth it.

The ships sailing under the bridge serve as reminders that the **Port of Yokohama** is still Japan's largest international port. It is ranked first in terms of the number of vessels entering port, total tonnage, and export and import values. The total amount of trade handled at the port accounts for approximately 15% of the total trade transacted in Japan.

Move eastward toward Tokyo and look down at Yamashita Park. The dot-like figures you see sitting on park benches, fishing from piers, or walking hand in hand represent a fairly accurate cross section of the population in Yokohama.

Over 3.1 million residents (nearly 2.6% of the total population of Japan) live in the sixteen ward districts of the city. Since 1984, the city has exhibited the highest rate of population growth (12.6%) among Japan's six major cities.

The historical atmosphere and the ambience of living in a "manageable urban center" are among the features attracting people to Yokohama. Residents here do not feel trapped in a concrete labyrinth.

Now move northward for a view of the 21st century. Bold and futuristic, the *Minato Mirai 21* city project reflects Yokohama's response to the decentralization of the urban functions in the greater Tokyo metropolitan area – and to the demands of an ever increasing international and information-oriented society.

Already opened to the public are the **Yokohama Museum of Art,** the 2nd largest in Japan, and the **Yokohama**

Left, Marine Tower overlooks Yokohama. **Right**, selling oriental goods at a shop in Chinatown.

Maritime Museum. By the year 2000, the construction of the ultra modern convention center, the office buildings, the shopping centers, the apartments, and the spacious parks will also be completed to offer Yokohama residents exciting new vistas of life and living in the 21st century.

By now your stomach must be growling. Move westward in the observation tower and map out the route to **Chinatown.** The hundreds of restaurants lining the streets offer an exciting array of Chinese food – just what you need after a journey that spans 130 years of history. (The major advantage of starting at Marine Tower is that with the price of admission (¥700), you will receive an informative brochure of major attractions in the area).

Historic Chinatown: Yokohama's Chinatown has a long rich history and cultural diversity special to the city. Chinatown's 260 business establishments give that part of Yokohama a distinct oriental atmosphere.

Yokohama Port opened 130 years ago in 1859. Taking that year as Yokohama's yardstick in calling it a city, some Chinese families are now seventh generation. Chinese people came to Japan as interpreters for trade, sailors, laborers, and domestics. Going back to immigration statistics of 1867, some 1,002 Chinese were living in Yokohama. Yokohama's Chinese residents were forced to live in **Yamashitachô** and the **Kannai** area – away from Westerners. Gradually this led to the concentration of businesses and residences in what is now known as Chinatown.

With the opening of Yokohama port, many shopkeepers flocked to the Motomachi area in order to serve the foreign community residing nearby. Situated next to Chinatown, Motomachi today is Yokohama's shopping district with numerous fashionable shops lining both sides of the main boulevard. Particularly popular with the younger set, weekends are always crowded.

An old Western residence on Yokohama's Bluff.

ONCE UPON A TIME IN JAPAN....

Just a short train ride away from the hustle and bustle of busy **Shinjuku**, across the **Tama River**, and tucked away in the hills of **Kawasaki**, you will find the **Nihon Minka-En Open-Air Museum** – a great place to go to spend a few hours getting a feel for the Tokyo and Japan of old.

The site was set aside in 1965 by the City of Kawasaki, and the work of obtaining and relocating several old traditional houses from all over Japan began at once. At present, there is a total of 22 houses, including a shrine, a working water mill and a *kabuki* stage. Much of the furniture, the tools and utensils used in daily life, are mostly left intact and very accessible.

In addition, several folk activities are held here every year, such as tool-making demonstrations, straw craft, bamboo craft and weaving. All the houses bear the names of their original owners, and in one of the larger ones, **Yamashita's house**, is a noodle shop and a small museum upstairs (no extra charge) displaying antique furniture, clothing, tools, etc.

For architecture buffs, or anyone else interested in traditional Japanese homes, or if you just want to see some green and get away from the crowds, this is highly recommended. Just outside the grounds you can also visit the **Youth Science Museum** and **Planetarium**.

Getting There: A 15- to 20-minute train ride out of Shinjuku on the **Odakyû Line** to **Mukôgaokayûen Stn.**, south exit. The Nihon Minka-En is about a 12-minute walk from there. The hours are 9:30 a.m. to 4 p.m. Closed on Mondays. Admission is ¥300 for adults and ¥100 for children aged 6 and over and students. You can contact The Minka-En directly for information on upcoming events at (044) 922-2181.

Minka-En: a visit to the way life used to be in Japan.

KAMAKURA

Kamakura, between the 12th and 14th centuries, was the seat of the first military government in Japanese history, and for 141 years prospered politically, economically and culturally as the new capital of the country after Kyoto. Now both a coastal resort town and an exclusive residential area for Tokyo's more mobile professionals, it is home to some of Japan's most fascinating and best-preserved medieval shrines, temples and historical artifacts. Accessible from Tokyo within an hour by rail, the sights of Kamakura are at once modestly picturesque, impressively grandiose, utterly beguiling and absolutely unmissable.

The Shogun Yoritomo Minamoto established Kamakura as a political base in 1192 after seizing control over the country from the Taira clan, which had been closely connected with the imperial government in Kyoto. After the assassinations of his two successors, political power fell into the hands of the family of Yoritomo's wife, the Hôjôs, where it remained until 1333.

During the reign of Regent Tokimune Hôjô, the Kamakura government was strong enough to defeat two invasion attempts by Mongolian forces (in the pay of China's Yuan Dynasty), but only at great financial expense to itself and its supporters. Weakened and vulnerable to their enemies among the local warlords, the Hôjôs were finally overthrown by the armies of Emperor Godaigo. The town slid slowly and quietly into obscurity as a regional government center and finally lost all special status in 1603.

Getting There: The **JR Yokosuka Line** linking Tokyo and **Kurihama** via **Ofuna**, **Kamakura** and **Yokosuka** is the simplest route to Kamakura. The service leaves the capital approximately every 15 minutes and the ride takes just under an hour. You can pick

The Great Buddha of Kamakura.

up the train at the **Tokyo**, **Shimbashi** or **Shinagawa** stations on the **JR Yamanote (Loop) Line**.

Getting Around: From Kamakura station there are numerous buses as well as the local narrow-gauge **Enoden** railway running between this part of town and the attractions towards the West and **Enoshima** island. Almost all of the temples are signposted in English and are within walking distance of one another.

The following proposed route stretches between **Kita-Kamakura Station** (one stop before Kamakura proper) and the area's three points of interest: the **Tsurugaoka Hachimangû Shrine, Hasedera Temple** and the **Great Buddha** at **Hase**.

Engakuji Temple: Although the temple dates originally from 1282, many of the old buildings have been destroyed either by fire or earthquakes. The reconstructions still carry a dignified atmosphere however, and Engakuji remains one of the town's most celebrated Zen temples.

The original **Shariden** (Holy Relics of Buddha) hall – designated a national treasure, and the oldest Chinese-style structure in Japan – still stands, and entry to the temple precincts is through the impressive **Sanmon Gate**. Another gate intricately carved with lions and dragons stands at the top of the well-worn stone steps leading to the main building. At the rear of the complex is the **Obaiin**, the mausoleum of Tokimune Hojo, set at the foot of the cliff, and in the compound's calm and pretty **Butsunichian Garden,** there is a small tea room where you can try traditional powdered green tea.

Kenchôji Temple: The most important Zen temple in Kamakura, Kenchôji was built in 1253 as a training center for young monks aspiring to the priesthood and at one time numbered over 50 different buildings and minor temples within its precincts. Its elegantly proportioned wings and main hall were rebuilt in the 17th century and are all

Hachimangû
Temple.

based on the original designs. Standing solemnly within their protective screen of ancient cedar trees, they are a good indication of the architectural sophistication of the town's governors when the latter were at the height of their power, and the compound's gardens are a marvelous living illustration of the harmonic principles underlying Zen thought.

Tsurugaoka Hachimangû Shrine: Down the hill from Kenchôji on the left of the main road, the shrine dominates the town from its imperious position overlooking **Sagami Bay** and **Wakamiya-ôji Boulevard**. It is dedicated to Hachiman, the god of war who was an obvious favorite of Kamakura's military founders.

The site was first used in 1180, when the shrine was built at the order of Yoritomo Minamoto, the first Kamakura *shogun*, and is a favorite of the Japanese public, particularly as a place to make resolutions on New Year's Day. The main orange-colored halls at the top of the stone steps were rebuilt in 1828, and include a small museum housing medieval *samurai* armor, swords and festival masks. At the foot of the steps there is a *Noh* stage, still in use, and the long parade leading to the entrance with its curiously impractical **Drum Bridge** (**Taiko Bashi**), that is so steep that only athletes and the ruthlessly determined can cross it (of course, if you succeed you are granted a wish). On the left of the bridge behind the municipal museum there is a modern *kendô* hall which admits small numbers of public visitors during training sessions. A festival of mounted archery, or *yabusame*, is held in the shrine compound in September.

For some, the distance separating **Zeniarai Benten Shrine** and the remainder of the itinerary from Kamakura Station may warrant taking the Enoden railway to Hase and either walking the rest of the way or taking a taxi (there is no bus to this shrine). The route to Zeniarai Benten, the "money-washing"

Japanese gardens surround a Kamakura home.

shrine, is well indicated and well worth the extra effort. Skeptics and believers alike come here to rinse money in the shrine's small cave pool in the hope that it will be returned to them in a greater quantity at a later date, and the ritual presents an extraordinary vision of the way the sacred can so easily blend with simple pagan superstition in Japan.

Part of the shrine is built inside the cave; the rest occupies the space between two rock outcrops and is entered through a narrow tunnel at the top of the hill above **Hase Kannon Temple** nearby.

Hase Kannon Temple is one of the few compounds in Kamakura which allows visitors inside its main (Amida and Kannon) halls rather than just the temple precinct. The temple is famous for its huge golden image of an eleven-faced Kannon, the Goddess of Mercy (and the inspiration behind the Canon camera company), carved in 721 from a single tree. It is the tallest wooden statue in the country. The grounds of the temple are also interesting: as you climb the stone steps leading from the entrance to the main building you will see dozens of small *jizô* figures and offerings made to them by bereaved or expectant mothers. *Jizô* is the patron deity of children, pregnant women and travelers, which is why many of the figures are dressed in bibs and hats and surrounded by children's pinwheels.

The **Daibutsu**, or Great Buddha, just 200 meters from Hase Kannon is perhaps the single most famous sight in the whole of Kamakura and the main object of worship at **Kôtokuin Temple**. Cast in bronze in 1252, the figure was originally housed in a wooden hall, but has been sitting in the open air since 1495 when the building was swept away by a tidal wave.

You can return to Kamakura Station from the Daibutsu either by bus – there is a regular service from immediately in front of the temple grounds – or by the Enoden Line train which leaves from **Hase** at the bottom of the hill.

A bamboo garden.

ENOSHIMA

The wooded islet of **Enoshima** ("Bay Island") is one of those charming spots that few Japanese these days would think of recommending to visitors for a day-trip. But it has many attractions in any weather and is easily reached either from **Shinjuku** in Tokyo on the private **Odaykû Line** (a pleasant 75-minute ride) or from Kamakura on the quaint and rattling **"Enoden"** railway.

In the good old days before the invention of Turbos, 4WDs and windsurfing, Enoshima was one of *the* places to visit from Tokyo. It has gone into something of a decline since the advent of glossier, high-tech, must-go-see places like Disneyland. However, this is a point in its favor for travelers tired of endless queues and high prices, especially in summer when everywhere else seems impossibly packed and sweaty.

Enoshima has a very distinct personality, a kind of faded homeliness, that makes it very attractive. The attractions of Enoshima haven't changed at all since its heyday: fresh sea food (especially shell fish); bracing sea breezes; spectacular views of Sagami Bay and Mount Fuji; and a wealth of greenery.

The island is basically a wooded hill surrounded by rocky beaches and cliffs about two kilometers in circumference. But these days it hardly deserves the name of island: the 600-meter-long **Benten Bridge** which connects it to the bright lights of **Katase Beach** and the adjacent resort town has gradually turned into a causeway. The unbelievably crowded **Shichirigahama** and **Miami beaches** stretch away to east and west. Access on foot or by car is simple, and there is plenty of parking space at the foot of the hill. Just along from the causeway is the yacht harbor constructed for the Olympics in 1964.

The ascent of the hill begins at the end of Benten Bridge with a narrow street crammed with restaurants and souvenir

The beach at Enoshima.

shops. Genuine craft items rub shoulders with plastic octopuses and real shellfish bubbling away ready for instant consumption. This street leads up to the start of a series of user-friendly covered escalators, which make the upward progress very simple. First stop is the charming **Enoshima Shrine,** built in 1182 and dedicated to Benten, the goddess of fortune. Her naked statue used to reside in a cave on the far side, but fears for her safety (from falling rocks) led to her removal to a safe resting place in the shrine itself.

And so on up to the top, a fun place for adults and kids alike. It features tropical plants, greenhouses, a mini-zoo, game machines, miniature trains, a short go-kart track, and restaurants and patios providing views of the ocean. Look out for the machine which will give you ¥10 back for every drink can inserted. An observation tower (177 feet high) accessible by elevator, gives more exposed but uninterrupted views. Having ridden on a giant dog at a speed of 100 yards per hour, bashed toy moles on the head with a mallet, partaken of a bowl of noodles and a hot dog, and watched the surfers far down below vainly searching for surf, you then slowly wend your way back down the hill via several hundred steps.

You can explore the beaches around the island, or cross the causeway again to visit all the noisier attractions of life on the other side, including swimming pools with giant chutes and performing aquatic mammals at **Enoshima Marineland**. Those more spiritually minded might like to visit the famous **Ryûkôji Temple,** near the station. This features a fine pagoda, albeit 20th century. The temple is dedicated to Nichiren, founder of the only genuinely Japanese sect of Buddhism. It was here that he was saved from execution by a timely stroke of lightning which hit the uplifted blade of the executioner's sword. The festival (September 11th-13th) is a spectacular all-night phantasmagoria of lanterns, drums and incense.

Fresh delicacies from the sea.

MT. FUJI

An opening ceremony for the two-month **Mt. Fuji** climbing season is held annually on July 1, where a Shinto ceremony is observed at the **Fuji Segen Shrine** located at the foot of Mt. Fuji in **Fuji Yoshida City** (**Yamanashi Prefecture**).

Traditionally, mountain climbing was considered more of a religious rite than a sport. Shrines which deify the mountains observe a festival of the opening and closing of the mountain to climbers. It used to be forbidden to climb these mountains except during summer periods. In the case of Mt. Fuji, the official climbing period is from July 1 to August 31.

The volcanic mountain, standing 3,776 meters, is perhaps Japan's most revered symbol and a sight that should not be missed first-hand. It's up to the individual to decide the degree of "experiencing" Mt. Fuji.

Mt. Fuji can be seen in the distance on an infrequent clear day from Tokyo. Trains from Tokyo will bring you closer to the mountain for picture-taking. Buses will journey up to Mt. Fuji's 5th station; from there the immensity of Fuji-*san* can be fully appreciated.

The paved road up to the 5th station or about mid-point of the climbing route is the common starting point for the ascent to the top which can be done leisurely in six hours, of course varying according to one's fitness. It takes some four hours to come down. Also, one does not need to be an experienced climber – children and the aged are among the thousands who make the trek up the mountain each year.

The path is not as tranquil as one would hope. First, there is a line of climbers in which you are just another head plunking up the mountain path. Loudspeakers continuously bellow announcements. Various shops along the climb break its natural beauty. Litter strewn on the scenic mountainside is, to say the least, unsightly.

The experience of *goraikô*, or watching the sunrise from the top at daybreak around 4 a.m., is the climax of the climb. However, this means that the climb up the mountain is done at night. Along with the hundreds of other climbers, a lighted, well-trodden trail poses little difficulty. There are lodges and rest areas at each of the climbing stations so one can plan an overnight climb.

For the hearty climbers, however, an assault from the Gotemba side is much the opposite; few climbers dare to attempt the more rigorous climbing path. With few switchbacks the climb is nearly straight to the top, or like climbing stairs for hours.

Getting There: To get to the 5th station of Mt. Fuji, take the express train of the **Main Chûo Line** from **Shinjuku** to **Kawaguchiko Station**, or take a bus via the **Chûo Expressway** to **Kawaguchiko**, and take a a local bus that runs up to the 5th station.

Climbers trek up Mt. Fuji.

HAKONE

If mammoth Tokyo becomes too much, you might want to head off to **Hakone**. Historically, Hakone's fame comes from travelers who had to trek across the area's steep rugged trails.

The **Tôkaidô**, a highway that connected Edo (Tokyo's former name) and Kyoto, passed through the steep mountains. Remnants of the ancient road are still visible around **Moto-Hakone**, but in 1619 a check point, or *sekisho* in Japanese, was built to divide Edo (the seat of the Tokugawa Shogunate) and Kyoto (where the Imperial court resided).

Hakone also has numerous hot springs that go along with its volcanic territory (the volcano **Owakudani** continually puffs smoke into the fresh mountain air).

The hot springs of Hakone have been used by monks, soldiers and travelers for centuries. During the Edo period, many bathers visited Hakone to soak in the healing waters of the seven Hakone hot springs (**Yumoto, Tonosawa, Miyanoshita, Dôgashima, Sokokura, Ashinoyu**, and **Kiga**).

Hakone-Yumoto hot spring resort has the longest history of any in Hakone (since the 8th century). At last count it had over 60 inns, and while the streets are bustling, if you wander off the beaten track you find a bit of Japanese tranquility.

The second largest resort in Hakone is **Gôra** and sits just east of **Mt. Sôunzan**. Gôra is connected to Owakudani and **Lake Ashinoko** by cable car.

Cable cars are available from Gôra to Mt. Sôunzan (a nine-minute ride) and from **Komagatake-nobori-guchi** to **Komagatake Peak**. There are ropeways from Mt. Sôunzan to **Tôgendai** and from **Hakone-en** to Komagatake Peak. The views are spectacular, so have your cameras ready.

To the southwest of Tokyo, Hakone offers a pleasurable escape from the hustle and bustle of megalopolis Tokyo, but is not far enough away to necessitate a long stressful journey. If it's hiking that you are into, the entry point for the higher pleasures of Hakone is at **Sengokuhara**.

Getting There: Hakone is accessible access from Tokyo through **Odawara** on either the **Tôkaidô Line** from **Tokyo Station** or the **Odakyu Line** from **Shinjuku**. The Odakyu line's Romance Car is especially comfortable although the seats are a bit narrow for romance. From Odawara, a bus makes the ascent at regular intervals to Sengokuhara.

For an extended stay, there are several fine *ryokans* in the area, among them the Fuji-Hakone Guest House. Accommodations generally include baths filled with water from local hot sulphur springs. In addition there are several fine restaurants which serve high-quality Japanese cuisine at reasonable prices.

Fantasy cruise on Lake Ashinoko in Hakone.

NIKKO

No visit to Japan would be complete without a trip to the delightful temple town of **Nikkô**, the site of some of the country's most impressive religious art and architecture ever produced during the all-important Tokugawa era, and the starting point for a number of short excursions to the lakes and waterfalls of the **Nikkô National Park.** Just 80 miles and a pleasant two-hour train ride to the north of Tokyo, most of what Nikkô has to offer is closely grouped together and can be seen in one day – if you get an early start.

Nikkô began as a regional center for Shintoism in 782 with the construction of **Shinhonryûji Temple**, precursor of the present-day **Rinnôji** building. The temple prospered over the years – monks from around the country went there to complete their training – and expanded to include almost 300 minor temples and associated buildings before its decline during the civil wars of the 16th century, when its congregation incurred the wrath of the Shogun Hideyoshi by supporting the army of one of his opponents. The center's fortunes improved when it was chosen by the country's most influential rulers, the Tokugawas, in 1617 as the burial place of their first *shogun*. The clan went to enormous trouble and expense to build an astonishingly elaborate memorial in the Shihonryuji clearing – the **Tôshôgû Shrine** – which they completed in 1636. Today, the shrine and the neighboring mausoleums dedicated to Ieyasu Tokugawa and his successors stand as some of the best preserved and most breathtaking examples of the highly refined artistry and craftsmanship that was unique to the Tokugawa era.

Getting There: The simplest and cheapest way to get to Nikkô is by the private **Tôbu Nikkô Line** which runs between **Asakusa Station** in Tokyo and **Tôbu-Nikkô Station.** (The ticket of-fice for this line is on the first floor of the Asakusa building, the platforms are on the second). Asakusa is most easily reached either by the **Ginza** or **Toei Asakusa Subway lines**, and Tôbu Railway's Asakusa Station is a few minutes' walk from the subway station.

The Tôbu Nikkô Line operates two types of service: a Limited Express, which is a deluxe train with reserved seats (reserving is a good idea if you are travelling on a public holiday), and a Rapid Service train, a regular commuter train with only non-reserved seats. The Rapid Service is about half the cost of the Limited Express, and both types of service leave Asakusa every hour. Another solution, although more costly and more complicated, would be to take the **JR Tôhoku Shinkansen** (Bullet Train) from **Ueno** to **Utsunomiya**, and then the **JR Nikkô Line** from **Utsunomiya** to Nikkô – the JR station in Nikkô is about 300 m down the hill from the Tôbu Line station. This route is only worthwhile if you have a Japan

Left, fall foliage provides a colorful tapestry for Nikko. **Below**, Tôshôgû Shrine's five-tiered pagoda.

Rail Pass, or if you are particularly anxious to ride a short section of the world's fastest rail network.

Getting Around: Nikkô's major historical points of interest are in or nearby the Tôshôgû Shrine precincts about 2 km from the train stations and reached by walking up the main street (15 minutes) or by bus. Buses leave from stands 1 and 2 outside the Tôbu Nikkô station. You can get off at **Shinkyô Bridge** or at **Nishi-sandô**; the bus signs are in Japanese and English. To get up to the **Chûzenji Lake** area, take the same route and carry on as far as **Chûzenji-Onsen**; the ride takes about 40 minutes and from there you can walk either to the cruise boat pier on the lake or to the **Kegon Waterfalls**. (If you are considering a trip up to the falls during the summer, first check that they are actually open – the water authority shuts off the flow at the first sign of drought!)

The Tôshôgû Shrine Area: The ideal way to approach the complex is via the steps immediately opposite the vermil-ion Shinkyô, or Sacred Bridge, spanning the Daiya River at the top of the main street: starting at Nishi-sandô feels too much like going in through the servants' entrance. From there, follow the cedar avenue to **Rinnôji Temple** where you can buy a combination ticket for admittance to this and the two other main attractions, the **Futarasan Shrine** and the Tôshôgû Shrine. Rinnôji was the focal point for most religious activity in Nikkô until the 16th century and is still an important regional Buddhist center. The temple's impressive Sanbutsudô hall houses three gigantic images, of Batô Kannon (protective deity of horses), Amida, and the thousand-armed Kannon (Goddess of mercy). The bronze Sorinto pillar decorated with golden bells on the northwest side of the hall contains 10,000 volumes of holy sutras. You will need to pay extra if you want to visit the medieval weaponry and statues kept in the Treasure House and its attached garden.

Up the main **Omote-sandô** path to-

Lake Chûzenji in the morning mist.

wards the Tôshôgû Shrine, you will pass the five-story pagoda, an 1818 reconstruction of the original, before you reach the main entrance to the shrine, the Buddhist-style **Omotemon Gate** guarded by two Diva kings. The adjacent **Sacred Horse Stable** (occasionally inhabited by one of the horses offered to the temple) is carved with scenes illustrating the life cycle of mankind, and features the well-known hear-, speak- and see-no-evil monkey trio. Buildings on the right of the path are used to store equipment used in the Festival of the Warriors – a procession well worth seeing on May 18th or October 17th.

Beyond the *torii* gate at the top of the stone steps is the shrine's most famous feature, the **Yômeimon Gate**. Small as it is (the gate stands just 11m high), this national treasure covered with hundreds of intricate carvings and painted in a riot of brilliant colors is overwhelming. More treasures await inside: the East and West Corridors surrounding

The Kegon Waterfalls.

the main building are also covered with magnificent carvings, among them the celebrated **Sleeping Cat** on the side of the **Sakashitamon Gate**, and beyond the gate is the staircase leading to the mausoleum of one of the most important figures in Japanese history, Ieyasu Tokugawa. In the **Honchido Hall** is a dragon painting recreated from the original which was lost during a fire in 1961. On the way to the Shinto Futarasan Shrine buildings, the **Tôshôgû Treasure House** houses an interesting collection of Tokugawa portraits as well as a selection of *samurai* armor and swords.

Futarasan itself is the oldest of all the buildings in the complex, dating from 1617; it is dedicated to the god of nearby **Mount Nantai** and was donated by the second Tokugawa *shogun*. The latest of the area's mausoleums, **Daiyûinbyô**, was built for the third *shogun* in 1653, to the west of Futarasan. Similar in conception to the Tôshôgû Shrine, it has been less lavishly decorated and built to a more humble scale.

Lake Chûzenji: If you have had enough of temples, *torii* gates and treasure houses and still have time to spare, consider taking the bus ride up the winding mountain road to Chûzenji-Onsen. The journey takes around half an hour. From there you can either savor the altitude's (4,163 feet) clear air and take in the lakeside scenery, or travel still higher, by cablecar, to the **Chanokidaira Observatory** on **Mount Hangetsu** and cast your gaze over the entire valley.

A sightseeing boat leaves the pier just across the road from the bus stop every hour for a one-hour tour of the lake. Five minutes' walk in the opposite direction is the observatory of the Kegon Waterfalls, where an elevator takes you to the bottom of the gorge for a full dramatic effect. The falls, plunging a distance of some 325 feet, are held in great esteem by the Japanese but may prove a less than entrancing vision for European and American water enthusiasts.

MIURA PENINSULA

The woodblock artist Andô Hiroshige (1797-1858) stood on the beach at **Akiya** on the west coast of the **Miura Peninsula** and looked out across the sea. In the foreground were the impressive rocks of **Tateishi** with black-eared kites soaring on the evening breeze, and on the horizon, **Mount Fuji** outlined against a pollution-free sunset. He decided to immortalize the view with his chisel.

That evening, perhaps he strolled along the tideline again, lamp in hand...a dead blowfish, a discarded straw sandal, an empty *sake* flask. Suddenly looking up, he would have seen a fantastic sight – the snow-clad slopes of Mount Fuji, 50 miles away, glowing brilliantly in the moonlight.

Akiya beach has hardly changed: the kites, blowfish and rocks remain, as does Fuji by moonlight. The sandals are now plastic and the flasks have become beer cans, but otherwise it is just as tranquil when the holidaymakers have gone and the night is left to the raccoons and the couples in the car park.

There have been many changes on the peninsula, of course, since the early 19th century, especially during the 1980s when the apartment blocks and holiday homes began to blossom and the newly-affluent youth of Tokyo and Yokohama discovered that a day-trip round the peninsula was a perfect way to indulge in their passion for *doraibing* (bumper-to-bumper driving).

And over on the east side, there is the city of **Yokosuka**, centered on the American naval base, home of the U.S. Seventh Fleet and Big Brother to one-third of the world's oceans. Like Yokohama, its history is all bound up with Japan's opening to the world. It has close associations with Will Adams ("Miura Anjin" in Japanese), the English pilot who was advisor to Tokugawa Ieyasu, the *"Shogun"* in the book.

Adams is buried in **Tsukayama Park.** Just to the south is the port of **Uraga,** where Commodore Perry anchored in 1853, and **Kurihama,** where a monument commemorates his delivery of the presidential letter. Yokosuka also features Admiral Tôgô's flagship in the Russo-Japanese War (1904-5), the *Mikasa,* preserved as a floating museum.

But the real attraction of the Miura Peninsula for the Tokyo visitor is that it has so much to offer to anyone interested in clean air, excellent water, fresh fish and vegetables, marine activities or gentle hiking.

The gray volcanic sand beaches may not quite be Big Sur or Maui, but the many little inlets all down the west coast from **Zushi – Hayama** (site of an Imperial villa), **Chojagasaki, Kuruwa,** Akiya – provide safe bathing with refreshment stands and changing facilities throughout the summer. Most beaches have windsurfing rental and lesson facilities and there are several yachting harbors and marinas, includ-

A sunset on Akiya Beach.

ing Zushi, Hayama, Sajima, Seabornia and Aburatsubo.

The Japanese have a peculiar attitude to seasonal activities. They regard September 1st as the start of autumn and the end of sea swimming, regardless of the temperature (hot). Jellyfish and typhoons are minor hazards in September, but the beaches are virtually empty from September to May. Hardy *gaijin* have been known to swim until November, when the water is still warmer than the North Sea in August.

Farther down the coast, there are rocky coasts with walking courses and a view towards **Oshima Island,** with its active volcano, and **Itô** on **Izu Peninsula,** where an underwater eruption in 1989 gave hope of extending Japan's land area – it didn't. Also of interest are several lighthouses, in particular the one at **Kannonzaki Point** on the southeast tip, where the entrance to **Tokyo Bay** is at its narrowest – less than 10 kilometers. A perfect place to picnic and watch Japan's trade imbalance come and go.

But to get a taste of unspoilt Japan, it is well worth investigating some of the excellent hill trails inland. These are a delight for botanists, ornithologists and entomologists alike and traverse stretches of natural broad-leaved evergreen forest. Many trees along the trails are labelled: take along a Japanese friend to read them and a dictionary to explain them. Other attractions include the chance to see small rural temples, farmers at work, terraced fields, and from the top of **Mount Ogusa** (794 feet or 242 meters), a wonderful 360-degree view: Yokohama and Tokyo Bay to the north; the **Bôsô Peninsula** to the east; the Izu Peninsula to the southwest; and Mount Fuji to the west.

The Miura Peninsula is just over an hour from Tokyo on the **JR Yokosuka Line**, via Yokohama and **Kamakura,** or on the private **Keihin Kyûkô Line** from **Shinagawa**, which winds all the way along the eastern coast to **Misakiguchi.**

Fisherman sets off for his daily catch.

TRAVEL TIPS

GETTING THERE

BY AIR

Being made up of four main islands, and considering the time and distance involved in getting here by boat, the most practical way of entering Japan is by air. All international flights come into the **New Tokyo International Airport** at Narita except China Airlines flights which come into the very convenient **Haneda Airport,** located in between Tokyo and Yokohama. Narita is quite a distance from the center of Tokyo. You have to allow at least an hour and a half to two hours, sometimes more depending on the time of day, to get into town. Three major domestic airlines maintain air routes throughout Japan. They are Japan Air Lines (JAL), All Nippon Airways (ANA), and Japan Air Systems (JAS).

There is a ¥2,000 airport tax for all passengers departing on international flights.

TRAVEL ESSENTIALS

VISAS & PASSPORTS

Visitors must have a visa prior to entering Japan. A proper visa is necessary for foreigners living in Japan and engaged in business or study. Passengers with confirmed departure reservations can obtain a stopover pass for up to 72 hours.

Visitors from the following countries are not required to obtain a visa prior to arrival in Japan, provided they do not intend to stay for more than 90 days nor receive remuneration in Japan: Argentina, Bahamas, Bangladesh, Barbados, Belgium, Canada, Chile, Colombia, Costa Rica, Cyprus, Denmark, Dominican Republic, El Salvador, Finland, Greece, Guatemala, Holland, Honduras, Iceland, Iran, Israel, Italy, Lesotho, Luxembourg, Malaysia, Malta, Mauritius, Norway, Pakistan, Peru, Portugal, San Marino, Singapore, Spain, Surinam, Sweden, Tunisia, Turkey, Uruguay, and Yugoslavia.

Visitors from the following countries may reside in Japan for up to six months providing they are not earning an income: Austria, West Germany, Ireland, Liechtenstein, Mexico, Switzerland, and the United Kingdom. New Zealanders may visit Japan for 30 days without a visa.

MONEY MATTERS

The unit of currency is the yen (indicated as ¥), and the coins are ¥1, ¥5, ¥10, ¥50, ¥100 and ¥500. Bills are ¥1,000, ¥5,000 and ¥10,000. Foreign currencies are accepted at a very limited number of hotels, restaurants and souvenir shops. You can buy yen at foreign exchange banks and other authorized money changers on presentation of your passport. At the international airport at Narita, the bank is open 24 hours.

Major credit cards, such as American Express, Diner's Club, Master Card and Visa, are accepted at most establishments in and around Tokyo, and there is no surcharge for their use.

No tipping remains the rule in Japan, except for unusual or exceptional services. Though you will be very lucky to find one, porters at large stations and airports charge around ¥300 per piece of luggage, depending on the distance, and the size of the luggage in question.

BANKS

Despite the wide use of computers and on-line systems, Japanese banks are often slow and inefficient in many fields. Especially when transferring money in or out of the country, you can expect the process to take a long time and to be costly. Also, small neighborhood branches are often not able to process any international transactions. In order to send money out of the country, or cash foreign checks, you will find it much easier to go to a major branch, where someone will be able to speak English and usually understand what you want to do. The bank charges for remitting money out of the country are ¥2,500 to ¥5,000 depending on how fast you want the money to be sent. Banks are open Monday to Friday between 9 a.m. and 3 p.m. for normal banking. Cash dispensers are open from 9 a.m. to 6 p.m. on weekdays, and 9 a.m. to 2 p.m. on Saturdays. Below is a list of some of the major Japanese and foreign bank offices in Tokyo.

JAPANESE BANKS

Bank of Tokyo
1-3-2 Nihombashi, Hongokucho, Chuo-ku
Tel: (03) 245-1111

Dai-Ichi Kangyo Bank
1-1-5 Uchisaiwaicho, Chiyoda-ku
Tel: (03) 596-1111

Daiwa Bank
2-1-1 Otemachi, Chiyoda-ku
Tel: (03) 231-1231

Fuji Bank
1-5-5 Otemachi, Chiyoda-ku
Tel: (03) 216-2211

Mitsubishi Bank
2-7-1 Marunouchi, Chiyoda-ku
Tel: (03) 240-1111

Mitsui Bank
1-1-2 Yurakucho, Chiyoda-ku
Tel: (03) 501-1111

Sumitomo Bank
1-3-2 Marunouchi, Chiyoda-ku
Tel: (03) 282-5111

FOREIGN BANKS

Bank of America
1-12-32 Akasaka, Minato-ku
Tel: (03) 587-3111

Bank of Korea
Hibiya Park Bldg.,
1-8-1 Yurakucho, Chiyoda-ku
Tel: (03) 213-6961

Banque Indosuez
French Bank Bldg.,
1-1-2 Akasaka, Minato-ku
Tel: (03) 582-0271

Barclays Bank
Mitsubishi Bldg.,
2-5-2 Marunouchi, Chiyoda-ku
Tel: (03) 214-3611

Chase Manhattan Bank
1-2-1 Marunouchi, Chiyoda-ku
Tel: (03) 287-4000

Citibank
Shin Otemachi Bldg., 1st Fl.,
2-2-1 Otemachi, Chiyoda-ku
Tel: (0120) 322-522 (toll-free)

Commerzbank A.G.
Nippon Press Center Bldg.,
2-2-1 Uchisaiwaicho, Chiyoda-ku
Tel: (03) 502-4371

Commonwealth Bank of Australia
1-1-3 Marunouchi, Chiyoda-ku
Tel: (03) 213-7311

Credit Lyonnais
Hibiya Park Bldg.,
1-8-1 Yurakucho, Chiyoda-ku
Tel: (03) 214-4561

Credit Suisse
Yurakucho Denki Bldg.,
1-7-1 Yurakucho, Chiyoda-ku
Tel: (03) 214-0035

Standard Chartered Bank
3-2-3 Marunouchi, Chiyoda-ku
Tel: (03) 213-6541

Union Bank of Switzerland
Yurakucho Bldg.,
1-10-1 Yurakucho, Chiyoda-ku
Tel: (03) 214-7471

CREDIT CARD COMPANIES

American Express
Toranomon Mitsui Bldg.,
3-8-1 Kasumigaseki, Chiyoda-ku
Tel: (03) 504-3348
Cardmember Services:
0120-020222 (toll-free)

INSIGHT GUIDES

East asia
special

**Available at all
leading
bookshops.**

APA PUBLICATIONS

THE PROBLEMS OF A

HEAVY TRAFFIC.

You'll come across massive Thai jumbos at work and play in their natural habitat. In Thailand, elephants are part of everyday rural life.

FALLING MASONRY.

A visit to the ruined cities of Sukhothai or Ayutthaya will remind you of the country's long and event-filled history.

EYESTRAIN.

A problem everyone seems to enjoy. The beauty of our exotic land is only matched by the beauty and gentle nature of the Thai people.

GETTING LOST.

From the palm-fringed beaches of Phuket to the highlands of Chiang Mai there are numerous places to get away from it all.

MNC&H/THA/8652P

OLIDAY IN THAILAND.

GETTING TRAPPED.

In bunkers mostly. The fairways, superb club houses and helpful caddies make a golf trap for players of all standards.

HIGH DRAMA.

A performance of the 'Khon' drama, with gods and demons acting out a never-ending battle between good and evil, should not be missed.

EXCESS BAGGAGE.

Thai food is so delicious you'll want to eat more and more of it. Of course, on Thai there's no charge for extra kilos in this area.

MISSING YOUR FLIGHT.

In Thailand, this isn't a problem. Talk to us or your local travel agent about Royal Orchid Holidays in Thailand.

Thai
We reach for the sky.

Lost or Stolen card:
0120-376100 (toll-free)

Carte Blanche International
Tel: (03) 508-7838

Diner's Club (Japan)
Senshu Bldg.,
1-13-7 Shibuya, Shibuya-ku
Tel: (03) 499-1311

Master Charge Card
Tel: (03) 254-6751

Visa Card (Sumitomo)
Tel: (03) 350-6646

HEALTH

In general, levels of hygiene are very high, and it is very unlikely that you will become ill as a result of eating or drinking something. The tap water, though heavily chlorinated, can be drunk. Most food is of a high standard, however, because the Japanese place so much emphasis on presentation and how food looks, there is wide use of chemical fertilizers in Japan, and therefore it is not recommended to eat the peels of fruits and some vegetables.

Toilets: Apart from major hotels and some train stations, most toilets in Japan are of the Asian squatting type, which takes some getting used to, but are supposed to be the most hygienic (no part of your body actually touches them) and physiologically best. In Tokyo, they are slowly being replaced with Western-style toilets in many establishments. By law, every coffee shop/ restaurant etc. must have its own toilet, or access to one in the same building.

CUSTOMS

Japan strictly bans the import and use of narcotic drugs, firearms and ammunition. If caught in possession of any of the above, you will not face the death penalty, but you can expect no leniency. Many a foreigner is still sitting in a Japanese prison, long forgotten by everyone but himself. Pornographic magazines and videos showing any pubic hair are also forbidden in Japan. You can bring in any currency, personal ornaments and other valuables into Japan, but there is

an official limit of ¥5 million that can be taken out. You are allowed, when entering into Japan to bring with you, free of tax, three 760 ml bottles of spirits, 400 cigarettes and 100 cigars or a total of 500 grams of tobacco, and two ounces of perfume.

EXTENSION OF STAY

Foreigners wishing to extend their stay in Japan must report, in person, to the Immigration Bureau within two weeks before their visa expiration. Present your passport, a statement with the reasons why you want an extension to stay, and documents certifying the reasons. Fee: ¥4,000.

Foreigners living in Japan must obtain a re-entry permit from the Immigration Bureau if they leave Japan and plan to return. Present, in person, your passport and certificate of alien registration (held by foreign residents in Japan) along with the appropriate re-entry form to the Immigration Office. The fee for a single re-entry is ¥3,000 and for a multiple re-entry ¥6,000.

Those wishing to transfer visas to new passports must report to the Immigration Bureau. Present both old and new passports and certificate of alien registration. There is no fee for a transfer.

To the rejoice of many "old-timers" in Tokyo, a new immigration branch office has opened in the Tokyo City Air Terminal Building (**TCAT**). The branch office provides basic services to include the following: extension of period of stay, issuance of re-entry permits, application to acquire or change status of residence, and consultation for residence procedures.

Hakozaki Immigration Branch Office
Tokyo City Air Terminal
42-1 Nihombashihakozaki, Chuo-ku
Tel: (03) 664-3046.
Hours: 9 a.m. to 12 p.m., 1 p.m. to 5 p.m., until noon on 2nd and 4th Saturdays; closed on Sundays.

Convenience has never been one of the Immigration Bureau's strong points. TCAT is a 15-minute bus ride from Tokyo Station, a 7-minute walk from Ningyocho subway station on the Hibiya and Asakusa lines, or a 10-minute walk from Kayabacho on the Hibiya and Tozai lines. If you prefer to stand in long queues to walking, try your luck at Tokyo's main immigration office:

Tokyo Regional Immigration Bureau
1st Otemachi Common Government Office
2nd Fl., 1-3-1 Otemachi,
Chiyoda-ku, Tokyo.
Tel: (03) 213-8111.
Hours: 9 a.m. to 12 p.m., 1 p.m. to 5 p.m.,
until noon on 2nd and 4th Saturdays; closed
on Sundays.

ALIEN REGISTRATION

Foreigners planning to stay in Japan for more than three months are required to register at the ward office in their residing area. The application must be made in person within 90 days. The applicant must have his/her passport containing the proper visa and two photographs (3cm x 4cm).

If the alien registration card is lost or defaced, report to the ward office within 14 days. Take your passport and two new photographs and you will be issued a new one.

For visitors under 16 years of age, applications may be made by a parent or legal guardian by producing the applicant's passport. No photograph is necessary.

Ward office hours are from 8:45 a.m. to 5 p.m. Monday through Friday, and 8:45 a.m. to 12:30 p.m. on Saturdays.

Minato Ward Office
1-5-25 Shibakoen, Minato-ku, Tokyo
Tel: (03) 578-2111
English service is available on Monday, Wednesday, and Friday from 9:00 a.m. to 4:00 p.m. at its public affairs department.

Tokyo Metropolitan Government
Tokyo Daisan Chosha
3-5-1 Marunouchi, Chiyoda-ku, Tokyo
Tel: (03) 211-4433
English service is available on Monday and Thursday from 1:00 p.m. to 4 p.m.

Information regarding alien status and visas presented above is general and subject to change. For further information contact your appropriate embassy, consulate or the Japan Immigration Bureau.

GETTING ACQUAINTED

GEOGRAPHY & POPULATION

Japan is made up of four main islands, Honshu, Hokkaido, Kyushu and Shikoku, and several hundred smaller ones that stretch nearly 3,000 km in the temperate and sub-tropical zones, between 20 and 45 degrees latitude. The total land area is 377,435 square kilometers, 85% of which is mountainous. The country is divided into four different climatic and cultural zones by mountain ranges: the Japan Sea and Pacific Ocean on the north-east half, and the Japan Sea and Inland Sea on the south-west half. The famed Mount Fuji, seen on clear days from many places in and around Tokyo, is the highest mountain in Japan at 3,776 meters. The population of Tokyo is around 12 million. Tokyo is +9 hours GMT, as is the rest of Japan.

CLIMATE

"Japan has four seasons" is a phrase you will hear often, though it is still not clear why the Japanese feel that it is a feature unique to their country. The climate in Tokyo can be a bit of everything, and in recent years, the manifestation of the "four seasons" has not been all that clear, but generally in spring it is pleasant until May. In June begins the rainy season which should last about a month, but often lasts longer. The summers are hot and sticky through to September. The typhoons usually come through in August and September. Autumn begins in late September and lasts through mid-November and is cool and pleasant. The winter lasts from sometime in mid-November to the end of February or beginning of March. Though usually not too harsh, it is known to snow in Tokyo, sometimes heavily.

CULTURE & CUSTOMS

At work and in most formal situations, the Japanese may seem a very reticent and reserved people, lacking in spontaneity or personality. There are books and theories explaining this behavior, but it only provides one side of the picture. Japanese (especially men) can become extremely raucous when drinking, and often let out their real opinions and feelings after a few drinks.

On the crowded trains you will find yourself being pushed and bumped around. You do not need to be polite here; just push along with everyone else. It is often said that "the Japanese are only polite with their shoes off," which means that they are polite and courteous with people they know well and would be indoors with (where shoes are almost always removed).

Japanese distinguish between inside and outside the home. Inside the entrance to all homes (and some restaurants) is an area for removing shoes. You then step up into the living area, wearing slippers or in your stockinged feet. (Slippers are never worn on *tatami* mats, however.) Taking shoes off keeps the house clean, besides being more relaxing, and it also increases the amount of usable space, since you can sit on the floor without worrying about getting dirty. The toilet, however, is one area of the house that is considered "dirty," so separate slippers are provided there.

The custom of bowing has, in many cases, become somewhat a conditioned reflex. Foreigners, in general, are not expected to bow, and this is especially evident if a Japanese person first extends his hand to shake yours.

As to punctuality and keeping appointments, the Japanese have a reputation for not being very punctual. This can be seen very often at several of the famous "meeting places" where you can observe people waiting, often for an hour or more for someone. After several apologies and explanations, everything is usually forgotten and forgiven. The way the Japanese usually speak and express themselves gives a very good picture of their culture. Direct statements of fact are most often avoided as this implies that the speaker has a superior knowledge, and this is considered impolite. Therefore, much "beating around the bush" is done which often leads to misunderstandings and seems like a waste of time to foreigners, but is something that must be understood when dealing with most Japanese.

When eating with Japanese people, if you don't know what to do, the best policy is to just watch what the people around you are doing and do as they do. Below are a few helpful tips:

•Do not rest your chopsticks vertically in your rice as this is associated with death.

•Do not pass food from chopstick to chopstick as this is only done with the cremated bones of the dead at funeral services.

•When drinking beer or *sake*, one person will pour for the other, who will hold up his glass while it is being filled. Each person takes turns at pouring until enough is drunk and people will often begin to pour their own.

In any case, whatever happens, foreigners are usually forgiven any breach of etiquette, so you don't have to spend a lot of time worrying about what is right and wrong. Japanese behavior in general is situational, and the Japanese themselves often do not know the right thing to do in any given situation. "It all depends on the situation," but it's often fun for everyone involved when one of "us" makes a slip. Sometimes it can help to break the ice and put everyone in a more relaxed mood.

ELECTRICITY

The power supply is 100 volts AC and Tokyo runs on 50 cycles. Most hotels have adaptors for shavers and hair dryers.

BUSINESS HOURS

Officially, business is done on a 9 a.m. to 5 p.m. basis, but this is in theory only. The Japanese will often do overtime till 8 p.m. or 9 p.m. In general **Government** offices are open from 8:30 a.m. or 9 a.m. to 4 p.m. or 5 p.m. Monday to Friday, and from 9 a.m. to noon on the 1st and 3rd Saturdays of the month. **Main post offices** are open 9 a.m. to 7 p.m. Monday to Friday, 9 a.m. to 5 p.m. on Saturday, and 9 a.m. to noon on Sunday and holidays. **Branch post offices** are open 9 a.m. to 5 p.m. Monday to Friday **Department Stores** are open daily from 10 a.m. to 6 p.m., except for one day during the week which varies with each store. **Restaurants** are open for lunch from 11:30 a.m. to 2 p.m. and for dinner from 5 p.m. to 9 or 10 p.m. **Major companies and offices** are open from 9 a.m. to 5 p.m. Monday to Friday. Some are also open on Saturday mornings. **Most shops** open between 9 and 11 a.m. and close between 6 and 8 p.m.

HOLIDAYS & FESTIVALS

Festivals, or *matsuri* seem to be happening at any given time somewhere in Tokyo, and indeed have been an important part of Japanese life for hundreds of years. Many of the festivals have their roots in the long history of Japan's agricultural society. In today's ever modernizing Japan, they are one of the few occasions when the Japanese can dress up and live a nostalgic past. Below is a short list of the main national holidays and the most important festivals. For information on upcoming events going on during any particular week or month, please consult TIC or any of the tourist publications.

JANUARY

(*Shogatsu*) **New Year's Day** is a national holiday, and a time for people to put on their *kimono* and visit Buddhist temples and Shinto shrines to make their wishes for the new year. A lot of *sake* is drunk during the first few days of the year.

The 15th is *Seijin no Hi* (Coming-of-Age Day), another national holiday, on which most girls who have reached the age of 20 put on a traditional *kimono* and go to a shrine for a special ceremony.

The first *sumo* tournament of the year, *Hatsubasho,* is held for fifteen days at the **Kokugikan** in mid January.

FEBRUARY

On the 3rd is *Setsubun,* the traditional bean throwing ceremony that is meant to purify the home of evil. Roasted beans are scattered from the inside of the house to the outside while people shout, *"Oni wa soto"* (Devils, go out!), and from the outside of the home to the inside while *"Fuku wa uchi"* (good luck, come in) is shouted. The same ceremony is also held at temples and shrines. Some of the main ones are **Kanda Shrine, Zojoji Temple, Hie Shrine**, and **Nishiarai Daishi Temple.**

On the 11th is *Kenkoku Kinen no Hi* or the National Foundation Day, a national holiday.

MARCH

On the 3rd of the month is *Hina Matsuri* (Girl's Day), a festival for little girls. Small *Hina* dolls, representing imperial court figures, are displayed at home and in several public places.

The 21st is *Shumbun no Hi* (Vernal Equinox Day) and a national holiday.

APRIL

From early to mid April is *Ohanami* (Cherry Blossom viewing), one of the important spring rites. People love to turn out and picnic, drink *sake* and sing songs under the pink blossoms. Some of the famous spots are **Aoyama Bochi (Cemetery), Chidori-gafuchi Park, Korakuen, Sumida Park, Ueno Park and Yasukuni Shrine.**

On the 8th is *Hana Matsuri* (Birthday of Buddha), when commemorative services are held at various temples such as **Gokokuji Temple, Sensoji Temple, Zojoji Temple and Hommonji Temple.**

The 29th was the late Showa Emperor's birthday, and now has become *Hana to Midori no Hi* (Flower and Greenery Day), a national holiday. The Golden Week holiday period also begins on this day.

MAY

The 3rd of May is *Kempo Kinembi* (Constitution Memorial Day), a national holiday.

On the 5th is *Kodomo no Hi* (Children's Day), another national holiday. Though the emphasis is on little boys, in theory it is for all children. Carp banners (*koinobori*) are flown from homes where little boys live. The carp is a symbol of strength and manhood, and so it is hoped that the boys will grow up big and strong like the carp. *Samurai* dolls are also displayed inside the home.

In mid May, the *Natsubasho* (summer *sumo* tournament) is held for fifteen days at the **Kokugikan**.

On the 3rd Sat. and Sun. the *Sanja Matsuri* is held. This is one of the big *Edo* festivals honoring the three fishermen who found the image of *Kannon* in the river. The **Asakusa Shrine** is a great place to go at this time to see the dancing, music and many portable shrines.

JUNE

On the second Sunday is *Torigoe Jinja Taisai,* a night time festival, when the biggest and heaviest portable shrine in Tokyo is carried through the streets by lantern light. It all happens at the **Torigoe Shrine.**

From the 10th to the 16th is *Sanno Sai,* another big *Edo* festival featuring a *gyoretsu* (people parading in traditional costumes) on Saturday at the **Hie Shrine.**

JULY

From the 6th to the 8th is the *Asagao Ichi* (Morning Glory Fair), when over one hundred merchants set up stalls selling the morning flower at **Iriya Kishibojin.**

On the 7th is the *Tanabata Matsuri,* a festival celebrating the only day of the year when, according to the legend, the Weaver Princess (Vega) and her lover the Cowherder (Altair) can cross the Milky Way to meet. People write their wishes on pieces of colored paper, hang them on bamboo branches, and then float them down a river the next day.

On the 9th and 10th is the *Hozuki Ichi* (Ground Cherry Fair) at **Sensoji Temple** from early morning to midnight. A visit to this temple on the 10th is meant to be equal to 46,000 visits at other times.

On the last Saturday of July, the *Sumidagawa Hanabi Taikai* (Sumida River Fireworks) is held. This is the biggest fireworks display in Tokyo, and the best places to watch the display is between the **Kototoi** and **Shirahige bridges,** or at the **Komagata Bridge.**

AUGUST

Between the 13th and the 16th is the *Obon* festival, when people return to their hometowns to clean up the graves and offer prayers to the souls of departed ancestors. The traditional *Bon Odori* folk dances are held all over around this time.

SEPTEMBER

On the 15th is *Keiro no Hi* (Respect-for-the-Aged Day), a national holiday. In mid September, the *Akibasho* (autumn *sumo* tournament) is held. It is the last tournament of the year held at the **Kokugikan.**

The 23rd is *Shubun no Hi* (Autumnal Equinox Day), a national holiday.

OCTOBER

On the 10th is *Taiiku no Hi* (Sports Day), a national holiday.

From mid to late October is Chrysanthemum viewing time. There are flower displays dotted around the city. Some of the best are seen at **Hibiya Park, Meiji Shrine, Sensoji Temple** and **Yasukuni Shrine**

NOVEMBER

On the 3rd is *Bunka no Hi* (Culture Day), a national holiday.

The 15th is *Shichi-Go-San* (Three-Five-Seven), a ceremony for 5-year-old boys and 3- and 7-year-old girls. The children usually dress up in *kimono* and are taken to visit a shrine.

The 23rd is *Kinro Kansha no Hi* (Labor Thanksgiving Day), a national Holiday.

DECEMBER

The 14th is *Gishi Sai,* a memorial service for the famous *47 Ronin* who, on this day in 1702, avenged the death of their master and later committed ritual suicide. They are buried at the **Sengakuji Temple** where the service is held.

From the 17th to the 19th, the *Hagoita Ichi* (Battledore Fair) is held at **Sensoji Temple.**

On the 31st at the stroke of midnight, every temple bell throughout the country begins to toll. The bells toll 108 times representing the 108 evil human passions. This is called *Joya no Kane,* and the general public is allowed to strike the bells at the **Zojoji Temple** and the **Kan-eiji Temple.**

Protestant:
Ginza Church
4-2-1 Ginza, Chuo-ku
Tel: (03) 561-0236

Tokyo Yamate Church
19-5 Udagawacho, Shibuya-ku
Tel: (03) 463-2971

Catholic:
Azabu Church
3-21-26 Nishi Azabu, Minato-ku
Tel: (03) 405-9027

Franciscan Chapel Center
4-2-37 Roppongi, Minato-ku
Tel: (03) 401-2141

Baptist:
Yodobashi Baptist Church
6-18-6 Nishi Shinjuku, Shinjuku-ku
Tel: (03) 342-4684

Tokyo Baptist Church
9-2 Hachiyamacho, Shibuya-ku
Tel: (03) 461-8425

Lutheran:
Tokyo Luther Center Church
2-1 Fujimicho, Chiyoda-ku
Tel: (03) 264-1989

Tokyo Lutheran Center
1-2-32 Fujimi, Chiyoda-ku
Tel: (03) 261-3740

Anglican Episcopal:
Saint Alban's Church
3-6-25 Shibakoen, Minato-ku
Tel: (03) 431-8534

Jewish Community of Japan (Community Center)
3-8-8 Hiro-o, Shibuya-ku
Tel: (03) 400-2559

Islamic Center
1-16-11 Ohara, Setagaya-ku
Tel: (03) 460-6169

COMMUNICATIONS

TELEPHONE & POSTAL SERVICES

Note: It is now necessary to dial an additional 3 for all telephone numbers in the Tokyo area. Thus what used to be (03) 571-2236 is now (03) 3571-2236.

To use the public telephones, which are colored either green, red, pink, blue or yellow, just insert a ¥10 coin and dial the number desired. ¥10 for three minutes. Yellow and green phones accept ¥100 coins, which make them more convenient for long-distance calls (for more information, call 0051), but no change is returned for unused portions thereof. Some phones require a telephone card, which can be obtained at any Nippon Telegraph and Telephone (NTT) office, KDD office, other stores, or through special vending machines. For telegram inquiries, call: Tokyo, (03) 346-2521; Yokohama, (045) 671-4347.

EMERGENCIES

MEDICAL SERVICES

Try to remember that you are in Japan, and must be prepared to adapt to the Japanese system. Although some doctors may speak English, the receptionist and nursing staff may not, so it is advisable to bring along a Japanese friend or someone else who can speak both languages. Most hospitals and clinics do not have appointment systems, so you have to be prepared to wait your turn, however frustrating that may be. Here is a list of hospitals and clinics in Tokyo where you would have no problem in being understood or treated. They all have different hours and systems, so be sure to phone before going. The ambulance and fire services can be reached at this number, 119; and the police at 110.

HOSPITALS

International Catholic Hospital
2-5-1 Nakaochiai, Shinjuku-ku
Tel: (03) 951-1111

Ishikawa Clinic
Azabu Sakurada Heights #201,
3-2-7 Nishi Azabu, Minato-ku
Tel: (03) 479-0081 (401-6340 at night)

Red Cross Medical Center (Nisseki)
4-1-22 Hiro-o, Shibuya-ku
Tel: (03) 400-1311

St. Luke's International Hospital (Seiroka)
10-1 Akashicho, Chuo-ku
Tel: (03) 541-5151

International Clinic
1-5-9 Azabudai, Minato-ku
Tel: (03) 582-2646

Toho Fujin Women's Clinic
5-3-10 Kiba, Koto-ku
Tel: (03) 630-0303

DENTISTS

Harry K. Okamoto, D.D.S.
7-9-7 Akasaka, Minato-ku
Tel: (03) 505-5647
UCLA trained American dentist.

Royal Dental Office
Komuro Bldg., 2nd Fl.,
4-10-11 Roppongi, Minato-ku
Tel: (03) 404-0819

Besford Dental Office
32 Mori Bldg., 2nd Fl.,
3-4-30 Shibakoen, Minato-ku
Tel: (03) 431-4225

OPTICAL CARE

Tokyo Optical Center
Sone Bldg., 3rd Fl.,
6-4-8 Ginza, Chuo-ku
Tel: (03) 571-7216

International Vision Center
Kyowa Gobankan Bldg.,
3-3-13 Kita Aoyama, Minato-ku
Tel: (03) 497-1491

CHIROPRACTIC (*SEITAI*)

Tokyo Chiropractic Center
3-5-9 Kita Aoyama, Minato-ku
Tel: (03) 478-2713

PHARMACIES

American Pharmacy
Hibiya Park Bldg.,
1-8-1 Yurakucho, Chiyoda-ku
Tel: (03) 271-4034

The Medical Dispensary
32 Mori Bldg., 1st Fl.,
3-4-30 Shibakoen, Minato-ku
Tel: (03) 434-5817

National Azabu Supermarket Pharmacy
4-5-2 Minami Azabu, Minato-ku
Tel: (03) 442-3181

LOSS

East Japan Railway Co. (Tokyo Station)
Tel: (03) 231-1880

East Japan Railway Co. (Ueno Station)
Tel: (03) 841-8069

Metropolitan Subways
Tel: (03) 818-5760

Subways of Rapid Transit System
Tel: (03) 834-5577

Tokyo Metropolitan Police
Tel: (03) 814-4151

Tokyo Taxi Kindaika Center
Tel: (03) 648-0300

GETTING AROUND

FROM THE AIRPORT

There is a regular limousine bus service between Narita and **TCAT (Tokyo City Air Terminal)** at Hakozaki and most of the major hotels in Tokyo. The price is ¥2,500 and a bus leaves every 10 to 15 minutes. This is by far the best way to get into town, especially if you have some heavy baggage. There are also special buses to Yokohama and Haneda Airport. Check at the limousine bus counter for the schedules as the departure times are irregular. If you are not carrying too much luggage, then you can take the **Keisei Skyliner Express Train** to **Ueno Station**, and then get onto the subway or the JR, or take a taxi from there. However, this requires a bus ride from the airport to the train station. The price is ¥1,680 and the trip takes 60 minutes. There are departures every 30 minutes. A **taxi** to downtown Tokyo from Narita will cost about ¥20,000. A **hired car** and driver to central Tokyo will cost around ¥29,000. This service is operated by the limousine bus company, and you can order a car at the bus counter or call (03) 747-0305 in Tokyo. If you are coming into Haneda Airport, then a taxi to the center of town will cost about ¥5,000 to ¥6,000 and takes only about 30 to 40 minutes. If you are not carrying too much luggage, then you can take the **Monorail** to **Hamamatsucho Station** on the **JR Yamanote Line**. The price is ¥270 and the trip takes about 17 minutes. There are departures every 10 to 15 minutes.

RAIL TRANSPORT

Japan has one of the most efficient and extensive rail networks in the world.

Rail service is provided by **Japan Railways (JR)** and several regional private lines. The trains on important routes run every few minutes. Trains, such as JR's **Shinkansen** (sometimes called the Bullet Train) which travels at speeds of up to 136 mph (220 kph), offer alternatives to air and long distance bus travel.

The subway system in Tokyo is clean, safe, and convenient. Often it is faster than congested road transportation. However, Japanese trains are notorious for being crowded, especially during morning and evening rush hours. Trains and subways are sometimes packed to more than three times their specified capacity, though it actually feels like a lot more than that!

All subway stations post a timetable. Regular service is Monday through Saturday. The Sunday and holiday schedule has slightly fewer runs. Trains run until around after midnight, so be sure to check the time of the last train.

All subway and train stations have a route map with fares for each stop near the ticket machines. However, it is not always in English. Your present location is indicated with a red mark. The fares are regulated on a station-to-station basis, so if you cannot determine the fare required, just purchase the cheapest ticket available. You can pay the difference, if needed, upon arrival at your destination.

The ticket machine will dispense the ticket and give the correct change. A child's ticket is half fare; a transparent plastic shield is in front of the red buttons for children's tickets. Most ticket machines accept coins only, although some will take ¥1,000 notes. There is usually a machine that gives change nearby. Several types of pre-paid train cards are also available.

Transportation cost savings can be made by buying a *teiki* (train pass), valid for one, three or six months. Major subway and train stations issue passes. Fill out the appropriate form with the names of the two destination points and where transfers will be made. Another way to save on train fares is to buy a *kaisuken,* a series of 11 tickets between two destinations for the price of 10. Lastly, one-day tickets good on either subway lines or JR trains are available. Station arrivals are announced in Japanese inside the trains but are often difficult to understand. There is usually a map of the stops on the line and connecting lines above the train doors. The names of the stations are most often written in both Japanese and English.

Why knowledgeable travelers go by rail in Japan.

Japan's railway network connects you faster to more cities in greater comfort and with unparalleled punctuality than any other kind of transportation. Every hour, frequent Shinkansen (Bullet) trains speed travelers along up to 275 km/hr. These world-famous trains combine with an extensive intra and inter city network running so accurately you can virtually set your watch by arrival and departure times.

The newest example of Japan Railway's (JR) dedication to improved quality services is the Narita Express, NEX. This modern express speeds travelers directly from the Narita air terminal to Tokyo Station within 53 minutes. Riding NEX is the right way to begin your visit to Japan. Whatever your interest, if it's a small mountain spa or a major city for a major deal, traveling by JR assures you of more relaxation and pure pleasure.

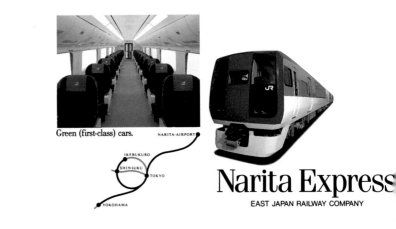

Green (first-class) cars.

NARITA-AIRPORT
IKEBUKURO
SHINJUKU
TOKYO
YOKOHAMA

Narita Express

EAST JAPAN RAILWAY COMPANY

SINGAPORE

Available at all leading bookshops.

INSIGHT *City* GUIDES

Timetables and subway maps in Japanese can be obtained at most stations. Subway maps in English are available in various English-language publications and at some major train and subway stations.

BUSES

Buses are plentiful in Tokyo, and during the commuting hours, like the trains, are often packed beyond capacity. They are not as easy to use as the trains, as their routes and destinations are written in Chinese characters (*kanji*) only. So until you are familiar with where a particular bus goes, it is best to ride them when you are with someone who knows the system.

TAXIS

Taxis are the most convenient way of getting around, but unfortunately, also the most expensive. The basic fare in Tokyo is ¥480 for the first 2 kilometers, and ¥80 for each 370 meters thereafter. Once again, no tipping is expected or required. Taxis are readily available on almost every street corner, and can certainly be found at every major hotel and railway station. There is a red light on in the front window if the taxi is free and available. The doors on taxis are opened and closed by the driver, who has a lever in the front, so when you've hailed a taxi and it stops, just wait for the door to open, and after arriving at your destination and paying, again the door will open by itself. You can get out and just walk away without trying to close the door, because you can't! Most taxi drivers do not speak any language other than Japanese, so it can be helpful to have your destination written in Japanese.

PRIVATE TRANSPORT

Driving in Tokyo can be dangerous. As the city seems to be in a perpetual stage of renovation, there is always construction work going on somewhere, and road divisions are often not easy to see. Most streets are narrow, crowded and often confusing. Most street signs are in Japanese. You will need an international driving license or a Japanese one. Remember that in Japan, driving is on the left-hand side of the road. Renting a car will cost from about ¥4,500 for

6 hours, or from ¥6,800 for 24 hours.

Nippon Rent-a-Car
5-5 Kamiyamacho, Shibuya-ku
Tel: (03) 469-0919

Toyota Rent-a-Car
1-1-8 Fujimi, Chiyoda-ku
Tel: (03) 264-0100

Nissan Rent-a-Car
1-5-7 Azabudai, Minato-ku
Tel: (03) 587-4123

You can obtain the "Driver's Map of Japan" issued by the JAF Publishing Co. 9-3, Shiba Sakaecho, Minato-ku, Tokyo. Tel. (03) 433-8731

WHERE TO STAY

HOTELS

In Tokyo there are hotels everywhere, but unfortunately few of them are up to international standards. Those that are reflect it in their price. However, convenience is a very dear commodity here, so often you are paying for the location more than the service or luxury. Below is a brief listing of major hotels in alphabetical order. Please note that the rankings are according to prices of single or twin rooms. In most hotels and all *ryokan*, you are provided with a *yukata* robe, toothbrush, razor, shower cap etc.

FIRST CLASS (¥17,000 & UP)

Akasaka Prince Hotel
1-2 Kioicho, Chiyoda-ku
Tel: (03) 234-1111
One of the Prince chain. Very modern and efficient, and great views from every room.

IN THE HEART OF TOKYO
NEAR IMPERIAL PALACE

◆ LOCATION ◆

Easy access to the major business district,
government offices, shopping and
entertainment centers. You will also
love our quiet culture-rich location.
· To and from the Airport Direct Bus Service
· To underground station . . . . . 1 min. on foot

◆ ACCOMMODATION ◆

500 comfortable guest rooms.
And the Palace Garden
add to the spacious
feeling inside.

◆ RESTAURANTS & SERVICES ◆

Our five fine restaurants and two pleasant bars
are extremely popular.
Room Service, Laundry, Gift shop,
Florist, Travel Agency and Secretary Service,

◆ RESERVATIONS ◆

Your Travel Agency
or
Utell UK
(01)-995-8211

Hotel Grand Palace

1-1-1 Iidabashi, Chiyoda-ku, Tokyo Japan 102
Tel. 03-3264-1111, Telex. 232-2981 GRAPA J, Fax. 03-3230-4985

In Japan, each season is special.
Especially at Chinzan-So.
──── Experience the heart of Japanese taste. ────

Some 70,000 square meters of greenery, spreading over the high ground of Mejiro. Enjoy the beauty of the Japanese garden, its springs, stones, ponds and tranquillity, while sampling a variety of skillfully prepared Japanese cuisine. Chinzan-So. In its taste, its tradition and its hospitable service, the Japanese spirit lives.

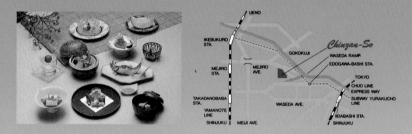

椿 山 荘
Chinzan-So

10-8, SEKIGUCHI 2-CHOME, BUNKYO-KU, TOKYO, 112, JAPAN
Phone 03(3943)1111
FUJITA TOURIST ENTERPRISES CO.,LTD.

In America too, you can find Japan.
Chinzan-So in New Jersey.

On the Hudson River,
opposite Upper Manhattan: Chinzan-So.
While enjoying the Japanese garden,
enhance your pleasure with
Japanese high cuisine.

椿 山 荘
Chinzan-So

595 River Road, Edgewater, New Jersey 07020, U.S.
phone 201-945-9450, 212-213-213

Akasaka Tokyu Hotel

2-14-3 Nagatacho, Chiyoda-ku
Tel: (03) 580-2311
One of the most conveniently located hotels
in Akasaka; it is just minutes away from all
the action.

ANA Hotel Tokyo

1-12-33 Akasaka, Minato-ku
Tel: (03) 505-1111
A very new hotel in the heart of a very new
Tokyo development. Convenient for busi-
ness and fun.

Capitol Tokyu Hotel

2-10-3 Nagatacho, Chiyoda-ku
Tel: (03) 581-4511
Formerly the Tokyo Hilton. A very comfortable and relaxing setting, blending Japanese
and Western design. Excellent restaurants
and pool (summer only).

Century Hyatt Tokyo

2-7-2 Nishi Shinjuku, Shinjuku-ku
Tel: (03) 349-0111
One of the buildings amidst all the skyscrapers of Shinjuku. Japanese-style Hyatt service and accommodation. Health facilities
and disco.

Hotel Okura

2-10-4 Toranomon, Minato-ku
Tel: (03) 582-0111
Officially rated the 2nd best hotel in the
world. Health facilities, excellent restaurants and executive salon.

Hotel New Otani

4-1 Kioicho, Chiyoda-ku
Tel: (03) 265-1111
The largest hotel in Asia. Health facilities, a
400-year-old Japanese garden, and very
good location.

Imperial Hotel

1-1-1 Uchisaiwaicho, Chiyoda-ku
Tel: (03) 504-1111
First built in 1890, with a new tower com-
pleted in 1983. Pool, executive salon, shop-
ping arcade, several excellent restaurants.
Convenient to Government offices and
Ginza shopping.

Keio Plaza Hotel

2-2-1 Nishi Shinjuku, Shinjuku-ku
Tel: (03) 344-0111
A 45-story skyscraper on the west side of
Shinjuku. Health facilities and executive
salon

Miyako Hotel

1-1-50 Shiroganedai, Minato-ku
Tel: (03) 447-3111
Affiliated with the famous Miyako Hotel in
Kyoto. Health facilities and quiet, though
not too convenient.

New Takanawa Prince Hotel

3-13-1 Takanawa, Minato-ku
Tel: (03) 442-1111
Addition to the Takanawa Prince. All of the
rooms have private balconies. Pool (summer
only).

Roppongi Prince Hotel

3-2-7 Roppongi, Minato-ku
Tel: (03) 587-1111
A few minutes from Roppongi Station.
Outdoor heated pool.

Palace Hotel

1-1-1 Marunouchi, Chiyoda-ku
Tel: (03) 211-5211
Old but quiet and peaceful surroundings
overlooking the Imperial Palace moats and
gardens.

Takanawa Prince Hotel

3-13-1 Takanawa, Minato-ku
Tel: (03) 447-1111
Convenient to Shinagawa and the southwest
part of Tokyo. Traditional Japanese garden.
Pool (summer only).

Tokyo Hilton International

6-6-2 Nishi Shinjuku, Shinjuku-ku
Tel: (03) 344-5111
Completed in 1984 and follows in the tradition of the former Hilton. Health facilities
and executive salon.

Tokyo Prince Hotel

3-3-1 Shibakoen, Minato-ku
Tel: (03) 432-1111
Another of the Prince chain. Located next to
Zojoji temple. Pleasant outdoor garden res-
taurant which is very popular in summer.
Pool (summer only).

MODERATE (¥7,000 & UP)

Aoyama Shampia Hotel
2-14-15 Shibuya, Shibuya-ku
Tel: (03) 407-2111
Conveniently located for Akasaka, Harajuku and Roppongi.

Asakusa View Hotel
3-17-1 Nishiasakusa, Taito-ku
Tel: (03) 842-2111
Good location for sightseeing and shopping in downtown Asakusa. There is always something happening in the area.

Diamond Hotel
25 Ichibancho, Chiyoda-ku
Tel: (03) 263-2211
Just a few minutes from Hanzomon Station. Nice quiet area.

Fairmont Hotel
2-1-17 Kudan Minami, Chiyoda-ku
Tel: (03) 262-1151
Old British style. About six minutes from Kudanshita Station, right in front of the Imperial Palace moat.

Ginza Dai-Ichi Hotel
8-13-1 Ginza, Chuo-ku
Tel: (03) 542-5311
Coveniently located, less than five minutes from Shimbashi Station.

Ginza Kokusai Hotel
8-7-13 Ginza, Chuo-ku
Tel: (03) 574-1121

Ginza Nikko Hotel
8-4-21 Ginza, Chuo-ku
Tel: (03) 571-4911
About four minutes from Shimbashi Station.

Ginza Tokyu Hotel
5-15-9 Ginza, Chuo-ku
Tel: (03) 541-2411
Reasonably priced hotel located close to the Kabukiza Theater in Ginza.

Grand Central Hotel
2-2-2 Kanda Tsukasacho, Chiyoda-ku
Tel: (03) 256-3211
Central location and convenient to Kanda and Tokyo Station.

Haneda Tokyu Hotel
2-8-6 Haneda Kuko, Ota-ku
Tel: (03) 747-0311
Right next to Haneda Airport. Shuttle service between the hotel and the airport.

Hillport Hotel
23-19 Sakuragaokacho, Shibuya-ku
Tel: (03) 462-5171
A three-minute walk from Shibuya Station. Excellent access to restaurants, department stores and theaters.

Hilltop (Yamanoue) Hotel
1-1 Surugadai, Kanda, Chiyoda-ku
Tel: (03) 293-2311
Five minutes from Ochanomizu Station. An and very pleasant hotel. This is an old favorite of writers and artists. Excellent food and service.

Holiday Inn Metropolitan Tokyo
1-6-1 Nishi-Ikebukuro, Toshima-ku
Tel: (03) 980-1111
Three minutes from Ikebukuro Station's west exit.

Hotel Atamiso
4-14-3 Ginza, Chuo-ku
Tel: (03) 541-3621
Convenient to the Kabukiza (*Kabuki* Theater) and to all Ginza shopping. Two minutes from Higashi Ginza on the Hibiya line. Formerly a *ryokan,* it opened as a Western-style hotel in 1984.

Hotel Grand Palace
1-1-1 Iidabashi, Chiyoda-ku
Tel: (03) 264-1111
Downtown location. Ten minutes by car to Tokyo Station and Tokyo City Terminal.

Hotel Ibis
7-14-4 Roppongi, Minato-ku
Tel: (03) 403-4411
200 rooms located where a lot of the action can be found.

Hotel New Kanda
2-10 Kanda, Awajicho, Chiyoda-ku
Tel: (03) 258-3911
Quiet and yet only a 5-minute walk to noisy Akihabara electronic quarter.

Hotel Park Side
2-11-18 Ueno, Taito-ku
Tel: (03) 836-5711
Overlooking Ueno Park. Very delightful atmosphere. Easy access to public transport.

Hotel Sunroute Tokyo
2-3-1 Yoyogi, Shibuya-ku
Tel: (03) 375-3211
Old standard. Nothing special, but located minutes from Shinjuku Station.

Mitsui Urban Hotel
8-6-15 Ginza, Chuo-ku
Tel: (03) 572-4131
Great location.

Royal Park Hotel
2-1-1 Nihombashi, Kakigaracho, Chuo-ku
Tel: (03) 667-1111
Next door to the City Terminal. Indoor swimming pool, fitness club, Japanese garden and executive floors.

Satellite Hotel Korakuen
1-3-3 Kasuga, Bunkyo-ku
Tel: (03) 814-0202
Near the famous Koishikawa Korakuen garden, and convenient to Ginza, Asakusa, Shinjuku and Akihabara.

Shiba Park Hotel
1-5-10 Shibakoen, Minato-ku
Tel: (03) 433-4141
Quiet and cozy, away from all the noise and bustle.

Shibuya Tobu Hotel
3-1 Udagawachô, Shibuya-ku
Tel: (03) 476-4891
Good location.

Shibuya Tokyu Inn
1-24-10 Shibuya, Shibuya-ku
Tel: (03) 498-0109
Good location.

Shimbashi Dai-Ichi Hotel
1-2-6 Shimbashi, Minato-ku
Tel: (03) 501-4411
Very central location. Convenient for business, shopping and sightseeing.

Shinagawa Prince Hotel
4-10-30 Takanawa, Minato-ku
Tel: (03) 440-1111
Good year-round sports facilities.

Shinjuku Prince Hotel
1-30-1 Kabukicho, Shinjuku-ku
Tel: (03) 205-1111
Right in the heart of exciting Shinjuku.

Star Hotel
7-10-5 Nishi Shinjuku, Shinjuku-ku
Tel: (03) 361-1111
A popular hotel in a convenient location.

Sunshine City Prince Hotel
3-1-5 Higashi-Ikebukuro, Toshima-ku
Tel: (03) 988-1111
A modern hotel located in the Sunshine City complex.

Tokyo Marunouchi Hotel
1-6-3 Marunouchi, Chiyoda-ku
Tel: (03) 215-2151
A five-minute walk from Tokyo Station and a short walk to the Imperial Palace grounds.

The President Hotel
2-2-3 Minami Aoyama, Minato-ku
Tel: (03) 497-0111
Located near the Crown Prince's residence and the Roppongi and Aoyama areas.

Washington Hotel
3-2-9 Nishi Shinjuku, Shinjuku-ku
Tel: (03) 343-3111
Very modern, very reasonable and very convenient, though the rooms are rather small.

Yaesu Fujiya Hotel
2-9-1 Yaesu, Chuo-ku
Tel: (03) 273-2111
One minute from Tokyo Station.

BUDGET (BELOW ¥7,000)

Taisho Central Hotel
1-27-7 Takadanobaba, Shinjuku-ku
Tel: (03) 232-0101
Just one minute from Takadanobaba Station on the JR Yamanote Line.

Daiichi Inn Ikebukuro
1-42-8 Higashi Ikebukuro, Toshima-ku
Tel: (03) 986-1221
Good for shopping and business.

Hotel Sunroute Ikebukuro
1-39-4 Higashi-Ikebukuro, Toshima-ku
Tel: (03) 980-1911
Convenient location. Minutes away from
Ikebukuro Station on the JR Yamanote line.

Ryogoku River Hotel
2-13-8 Ryogoku, Sumida-ku
Tel: (03) 634-1711
One-minute from Ryôgoku Station. Good
for *sumo* watching if a tournament is on.

Tourist Hotel
3-18-11 Higashi Ueno, Taito-ku
Tel: (03) 831-0237
Minutes away from Ueno Station.

RYOKAN

Ryokan (Japanese-style inns) will give you a
feeling of what traditional Japanese living
was like. You will sleep in rooms covered
with *tatami mats* (straw mats), on *futon*. The
baths are all Japanese style and communal,
though there are usually separate baths for
men and women. Morning and evening
meals are served in your room and your *futon*
will be laid out at night.

Inabaso
5-6-13 Shinjuku, Shinjuku-ku
Tel: (03) 341-9581
Three minutes from Shinjuku Sanchôme
Station. ¥3,900 to ¥4,400 per person. Japa-
nese- or Western-style rooms, and all have
baths. Meals not included.

Katsutaro
4-16-8 Ikenohata, Taito-ku
Tel: (03) 821-9808
Ten-minute walk from Keisei Ueno Station.
Single room from ¥3,900.

Meguro Gajoen
1-8-1 Shimo Meguro, Meguro-ku
Tel: (03) 491-0074
Three minutes from Meguro Station. From
¥14,000 per person inclusive of morning and
evening meals, tax and service. A very old
but beautiful *ryokan*.

Mikawaya Bekkan
1-31-11 Asakusa, Taito-ku
Tel: (03) 843-2345
Five minutes from Asakusa Station on the
Ginza line. Single room from ¥4,500. Japanese-style rooms only, communal bath and
showers. Meals not included.

Sansuiso
2-9-5 Higashi-Gotanda, Shinagawa-ku
Tel: (03) 441-7475
Five-minute walk from Gotanda Station.
Single room from ¥4,000.

Sawanoya
2-3-11 Yanaka, Taito-ku
Tel: (03) 822-2251
Seven-minute walk from Nezu Station on
the Chiyoda Subway line, or 10 min. by taxi
from Ueno Station. Single room from
¥3,800.

Yashima Ryokan
1-15-5 Hyakunincho, Shinjuku-ku
Tel: (03) 364-2534
One minute from Okubo Station. Single
room from ¥3,000, and double from ¥4,600.
Both Western- and Japanese-style rooms,
communal bath and showers. Meals not
included.

YOUTH HOSTELS

Okubo House
1-11-32 Hyakunincho, Shinjuku-ku
Tel: (03) 361-2348
Dorm rooms ¥1,600 per person; single
rooms from ¥2,800.

Tokyo International Youth Hostel
Central Plaza, 18th Fl.,
21-1 Kagurakashi, Shinjuku-ku
Tel: (03) 235-1107
About ¥2,000 per person.

YMCA Asia Youth Center
2-5-5 Sarugakucho,
Chiyoda-ku
Tel: (03) 233-0611
Single room from ¥6,000.

FOOD DIGEST

WHERE TO EAT

It would take a whole book to make a comprehensive list of places to eat in Tokyo. Below is a very short selection of well-known and well-liked restaurants. If you have the time, and feel a little adventurous, you can probably find those special places hidden in little back streets whose sole claim to fame is the food they serve. The list below is roughly divided into sections. The first section lists restaurants that do not easily fit into any one category. Please note that unless otherwise stated, the prices quoted below are for dinner and do not include drinks. However, most restaurants in Tokyo, regardless of their dinner prices, have special lunch menus with prices beginning at around ¥800. The closing times stated are, in most cases, for last orders and not the time the restaurant actually closes.

JAPANESE

Daigo (Shojin)
2-4-2 Atago, Minato-ku
Tel: (03) 431-0811
12 p.m. to 3 p.m. for lunch and 5 p.m. to 9 p.m. for dinner. Closed Thur. From ¥13,000.

Hidano Takayama
1-20-16 Jinnan, Shibuya-ku
Tel: (03) 463-5959
11:30 a.m. to 2:30 p.m. for lunch and 5 p.m. to 11 p.m. for dinner daily. From ¥3,000.

Kocho
Shin Yurakucho Bldg.,
1-12 Yurakucho, Chiyoda-ku
Tel: (03) 214-4741
11 a.m. to 2 p.m. for lunch and 5 p.m. to 9:30 p.m. for dinner. Closed Sun. and holidays. From ¥40,000. Reservation required.

Kogetsu (kyo)
5-50-10 Jingumae, Shibuya-ku
Tel: (03) 407-3033
6 p.m. to 11 p.m. Closed Sun. and holidays. From ¥13,000.

08 (Maru Hachi)
Shopping Caminito 1st Fl.,
1-3-1 Higashi, Shibuya-ku
Tel: (03) 409-8369
5 p.m. to 12:30 a.m. Closed Sun. and holidays. From ¥5,000.

Miyagawa Honten
1-4-6 Tsukiji, Chuo-ku
Tel: (03) 541-1293
11:30 a.m. to 2 p.m. for lunch and 5 p.m. to 8:30 p.m. for dinner. Closed Sat. From ¥1,500. They specialize in eel.

Ryorijaya Hashimoto
4-4-11 Roppongi, Minato-ku
Tel: (03) 408-8388
5:30 p.m. to 10 p.m. for dinner. Closed Sun. and holidays. Dinner from ¥4,000.

Shin Hinomoto
Yurakucho Denki Birumae (below the Shinkansen),
2-4-4 Yurakucho, Chiyoda-ku
Tel: (03) 214-8021
Open seven days a week until at least midnight. Noisy, friendly atmosphere, very reasonable prices and featuring possibly Tokyo's only British "*nomiya*" waiter.

Shirakawago
2-29-10 Kabukicho, Shinjuku-ku
Tel: (03) 200-5255
1 p.m. to 10 p.m. daily. From ¥4,000.

Suzume No Yado
1-11-20 Hyakunincho, Shinjuku-ku
Tel: (03) 361-1991
5 p.m. to 1 a.m. daily. Excellent country-style dishes and wooden slabs to bang to call the waiter. Next to Shin Okubo Station (JR). From ¥2,000.

Tatsumiya
1-33-5 Asakusa, Taito-ku
Tel: (03) 842-7373
12 p.m. to 2 p.m. for lunch and 5 p.m. to 9 p.m. for dinner. Closed Mon. From ¥2,500.

Tengu

A famous chain of cheap food and good drinking spots. Just look for the black and red picture of the long nosed goblin, or just ask for the nearest **Tengu.**

Ukai Toriyama

3426 Minami-Asakawacho, Hachioji-shi
Tel: (0426) 61-0739
11 a.m. to 9:30 p.m. (last orders at 8 p.m.)
This restaurant is like a small village completely surrounded by tree-covered mountains. It is more like a nature park with ponds and rivers. There are twelve dining rooms in separate traditional wooden houses, each with a charcoal *robata* grill. It is definitely worth while taking a trip out to this beautiful place. Take the Keio line from Shinjuku Station to Takao Station (50 min.), then take a taxi from Takao Station north exit (10 min.). On Sun. and holidays there is a free shuttle service from Takao San-guchi Station. From ¥4,000.

Yagurajaya

3-8-15 Roppongi, Minato-ku
Tel: (03) 405-7261
5 p.m. to 1 a.m. Mon. to Fri. and to 5 a.m. on Sat., Sun. and holidays. Space for groups of all sizes, decor changes with the seasons, and colorful waitresses do the serving. From ¥3,000.

Yamamura

2-7-18 Nihombashi, Chuo-ku
Tel: (03) 271-5345
11 a.m. to 2 p.m. for lunch and 5 p.m. to 9:30 p.m. for dinner. Closed Sun. and holidays. Dinner from ¥6,000.

SUSHI

Thin slices of only the choicest parts of the freshest fish, served on a bed of specially prepared vinegared rice, with a dab of *wasabi* (green horse radish) spread in between.

Hamato

787 Bldg., 2nd Fl.,
7-14-18 Roppongi, Minato-ku
Tel: (03) 479-2143
12 a.m. to 10 p.m. Closed Sun. and holidays. From ¥10,000. This shop specializes in *fugu* (blowfish).

Fukuzushi

5-7-8 Roppongi, Minato-ku
Tel: (03) 402-4116
5:30 p.m. to 11 p.m. (5 p.m. to 10 p.m. on holidays.) Closed Sun. Some say this is the best. Between ¥8,000 and ¥15,000.

Ichikan

10-5 Daikanyamacho, Shibuya-ku
Tel: (03) 461-2002
11 a.m. to 2 p.m. for lunch and 5 p.m. to 11 p.m. for dinner. From ¥5,000.

Iseto

4-2 Kagurazaka, Shinjuku-ku
Tel: (03) 260-6363
5 p.m. to 8:30 p.m. for dinner. Closed Sun. and holidays. ¥2,000 to ¥3,000.

Kiyota

6-3-15 Ginza, Chuo-ku
Tel: (03) 572-4854
11:30 a.m. to 9 p.m. Closed Sun. and holidays. Reservations required. From ¥10,000.

Ki-Zushi

2-7-13 Ningyocho, Chuo-ku
Tel: (03) 666-1682
11:45 a.m. to 2:30 p.m. for lunch and 4:30 p.m. to 8 p.m. for dinner. Closed Sun. Dinner from ¥8,000.

Shimbashi Tsuruhachi

New Shimbashi Bldg., 2nd Fl.,
2-16-1 Shimbashi, Minato-ku
Tel: (03) 591-1551
12 p.m. to 2 p.m. for lunch and 5 p.m. to 10 p.m. for dinner. Closed Sun. and holidays. Dinner from ¥5,000.

Sharaku

6-3-11 Ginza, Chuo-ku
Tel: (03) 573-7071
Open from 6 p.m. to 2 a.m. *Sushi* set from ¥1,500.

Sushi Sei

Kanai Bldg., 1st Fl.,
8-2-13 Ginza, Chuo-ku
Tel: (03) 572-4770
12 p.m. to 1:30 p.m. for lunch and 5 p.m. to 10:40 p.m. for dinner. Closed Sun. From ¥3,000.

Tsukiji Fish Market

Tsukiji Station on the Ginza line.

Try to go early in the morning and you'll get the freshest fish at one of the many *sushi* shops in the area.

STEAK, SUKIYAKI, SHABU-SAHBU

Sukiyaki is thinly sliced beef, sauteed for just a few seconds in a hot pan in front of you. A broth is added, and the beef is lightly simmered. Vegetables are added after the beef is cooked. *Shabu-shabu* is prepared in a similar way, but the broth is different. For *sukiyaki*, the broth is soy-based, thick and slightly sweet, while for *shabu-shabu* the broth is a clear stock, only lightly seasoned.

Chaco

1-7-12 Sendagaya, Shibuya-ku
Tel: (03) 402-6066
11:30 a.m. to 10:30 p.m. daily. and 4 p.m. to 9 p.m. on Sun. and holidays. Great steak dinners from ¥1,700.

Ginza Shabu Tei

M1 Bldg., 2nd Fl.,
2-12-23 Ueno, Taito-ku
Tel: (03) 832-1096
4 p.m. to 10:45 p.m. daily. Closed Sun. and holidays. Dinner course from ¥4,000.

Ginza Suehiro

6-11-2 Ginza, Chuo-ku
Tel: (03) 542-2411
The most famous Japanese steak house serving steak, *shabu-shabu*, and *sukiyaki*. Presently under renovation. Due to re-open in Nov. 1990.

Ginza Suehiro (Tsukiji branch)

4-1-15 Tsukiji, Chuo-ku
Tel: (03) 542-3951
11 a.m. to 9 p.m. for lunch and dinner. Lunches and dinners from ¥1,000.

Imaasa

Imaasa Bldg., 2nd Fl.,
1-1-21 Higashi Shimbashi, Minato-ku
Tel: (03) 572-5286
11:30 a.m. to 2 p.m. for lunch and 5 p.m. to 9:30 p.m. for dinner. Closed Sun. and holidays. Lunch from ¥2,500 and dinner from ¥6,000.

Naruse

JBP Bldg., B1,
6-8-17 Roppongi, Minato-ku
Tel: (03) 403-7666
5 p.m. to 10:30 p.m. daily. All the *shabu-shabu* or *sukiyaki* you can eat for ¥3,900 per person.

Serina Roppongi

3-12-2 Roppongi, Minato-ku
Tel: (03) 403-6211
Open from 5 p.m. to 10:30 p.m. daily

Shinjuku

Sumitomo Bldg., 52nd Fl.,
2-6-1 Nishi Shinjuku, Shinjuku-ku.
Tel: (03) 344-6761
Open from 11:30 a.m. to 9:30 p.m. daily. A favorite with tourists. *Shabu-shabu* course from ¥8,000 and *sukiyaki* from ¥7,500.

Shabusen

Ginza Core Bldg., B2 and 2nd Fl.,
5-8-20 Ginza, Chuo-ku
Tel: (03) 572-3806
Open from 11 a.m. to 9:30 p.m. One of the inexpensive *shabu-shabu* restaurants in town. From ¥2,300.

TEMPURA

Mostly fish and vegetables dipped in batter and then deep fried for a short time. It should be eaten hot. *Tempura* is dipped into a soy-based sauce mixed with ginger and radish.

Daikokuya

1-38-10 Asakusa, Taito-ku
Tel: (03) 844-1111
11 a.m. to 8 p.m. daily. Closed Mon. Real *"shitamachi"* atmosphere and cheap. From ¥1,000.

Hashizen

1-7-11 Shimbashi, Minato-ku
Tel: (03) 571-2700
11:30 a.m. to 8:30 daily. From ¥1,000.

Ten-Ichi

6-6-5 Ginza, Chuo-ku
Tel: (03) 571-1949
11:30 a.m. to 10 p.m. daily. Closed Sun. and holidays. Lunch from ¥4,500 and dinner from ¥5,500. One of the most famous *tempura* restaurants in Tokyo. There are over

ten branches throughout Tokyo.

Tenkuni
8-9-11 Ginza, Chuo-ku
Tel: (03) 571-0686
11:30 a.m. to 9 p.m. Closed 1st and 3rd Wed.
Tendon meal from ¥1,400, and others from
¥2,500.

Ten-mo
4-1-3 Hashimoto, Nihombashi, Chuo-ku
Tel: (03) 241-7035
12 a.m. to 2 p.m. for lunch and 5 p.m. to 8
p.m. for dinner. Closed Sun. and holidays.
From ¥4,500.

Tenshige
Daisan Seiko Bldg., 2nd Fl.,
3-6-10 Akasaka, Minato-ku
Tel: (03) 583-3230
11:40 a.m. to 1:40 p.m. for lunch and 6 p.m.
to 8:30 p.m. for dinner. Closed Sun. and
holidays. Lunch special for ¥1,000. Dinner
from ¥5,000.

YAKITORI

Charcoal-broiled, skewered bits of chicken,
beef, vegetables, etc.

Isehiro
8-5-5 Kyobashi, Chuo-ku
Tel: (03) 571-7295
5 p.m. to 1 a.m. Closed Sun. and holidays.
From ¥1,000

Toricho
7-8-2 Roppongi, Minato-ku
Tel: (03) 401-1827
5 p.m. to 11 p.m. and 5 p.m. to 10 p.m. on
Sun. and holidays. From ¥3,500.

Torigin
4-12-6 Roppongi, Minato-ku
Tel: (03) 403-5829
11:30 a.m. to 2 p.m. for lunch and 5 p.m. to
1 a.m. for dinner, daily. From ¥900.

Yakitoriya-gai
Under the train tracks from Yurakucho Station to Shimbashi there are about 75 little
shops and stalls — good places to start
discovering the traditional food and drink of
the common folk in Tokyo.

TONKATSU

Pork cutlets dipped in flour, egg and bread
crumbs, then deep fried.

Tonki
Nogakudo Bldg., B1,
6-5-15 Ginza, Chuo-ku
Tel: (03) 572-0702
11:30 a.m. to 4 p.m. for lunch and 5 p.m. to
9:30 p.m. for dinner. Closed Sun. From
¥1,500.

Maisen
4-8-5 Jingumae, Shibuya-ku
Tel: (03) 470-0071
11 a.m. to 10 p.m. daily. From ¥650.

Tonton-Tei
3-28-15 Shinjuku, Shinjuku-ku
Tel: (03) 352-2825
11:30 a.m. to 10 p.m. Closed 1st and 3rd
Thur. Between ¥600 and ¥1,600.

Futaba
2-8-11 Ueno Hirokoji, Taito-ku
Tel: (03) 831-6483
11:30 a.m. to 3 p.m. for lunch and 5 p.m. to
8 p.m. for dinner. Closed Mon. and Thur.
From ¥1,000.

KUSHI-AGE

Fish, meat or vegetables skewered, dipped
in batter and bread crumbs and then deep
fried.

Chisen
4-12-5 Roppongi, Minato-ku
Tel: (03) 403-7677
5:30 p.m. to 11 p.m. daily. From ¥4,000.

Gomi-Hatchin
8-2-16 Ginza, Chuo-ku
Tel: (03) 571-2486
4 p.m. to 10 p.m. Closed On Sun. and holidays. From ¥5,000.

Kushino-bo
6-2-6 Ginza, Chuo-ku
Tel: (03) 586-7390
11:30 a.m. to 10 p.m. Closed Sun and holidays. From ¥5,000.

SOBA & UDON

Soba are buckwheat noodles, served in hot or cold soup, often with vegetables and/or meat. *Udon* are thick white noodles served in the same way as *soba*.

Sunaba
4-1-13 Nihombashi, Muromachi, Chuo-ku
Tel: (03) 241-4038
11 a.m. to 7:30 p.m. Closed Sun. and holidays. ¥500 to ¥2,000.

Matsuya
1-12 Kanda, Sudacho, Chiyoda-ku
Tel: (03) 251-1556
11 a.m. to 8 p.m. Closed Sun. and holidays. From ¥1,000.

RAMEN

Very popular Chinese noodles served in a similar way to *soba* and *udon*.

Bannai Yurakucho
2-4-4 Yurakucho, Chiyoda-ku
Tel: (03) 215-4669
11 a.m. to 12 p.m. Closed Sun. From ¥490.

Hope-Ken
2-33-9 Sendagaya, Shibuya-ku
Tel: (03) 405-4249
Open 24 hrs. daily. From ¥500.

Keika
Nakagawa Bldg., 1st Fl.,
3-7-2 Shinjuku, Shinjuku-ku
Tel: (03) 354-4591
11 a.m. to 10:45 p.m. daily. From ¥520 to ¥780.

INTERNATIONAL

The Prime
2-29-5 Dogenzaka, Shibuya-ku
Tel: (03) 770-0111
11 a.m. to 11 p.m. daily. Just in case you can't decide what you want to eat, try this place which serves food from all over the world in an open cafeteria type space on the 2nd floor. About sixteen different counters serve *sushi,* pasta, bagels, salads, stews, tacos, Chinese, Indian, German food and lots more! There are eight individual restaurants in the basement, and **La Meme Paris**

serves Vietnamese food on the 3rd floor. On the 5th floor is the **Performance Restaurant—Shiryo Hiroba**, which serves a lunch and dinner buffet from 11:30 a.m. to 2 p.m. for lunch, and 6:30 p.m. to 11 p.m. for dinner daily. This is one of the new "fashionable eating spots" in town, and it's a good place to watch the "new Japanese." From ¥2,000.

CHINESE

Aoba
1-1-15 Okubo, Shinjuku-ku
Tel: (03) 205-3184
11:30 a.m. to 11 p.m. daily. From ¥400.

Chao
Arisugawa West, B1,
5-14-15 Minami Azabu, Minato-ku
Tel: (03) 444-2255
11 a.m. to 9:30 p.m. daily. From ¥7,000.

Daini's Table
6-3-14 Minami Aoyama, Minato-ku
Tel: (03) 499-2408
5 p.m. to 11 p.m. daily. From ¥7,000.

Peking Hanten
4-4-5 Shimbashi, Minato-ku
Tel: (03) 431-7651
11:30 a.m. to 2 p.m. for lunch and 5 p.m. to 9 p.m. for dinner. Closed Sun. One dish about ¥1,200, and courses from ¥5,000.

Reikyo
2-25-18 Dogenzaka, Shibuya-ku
Tel: (03) 461-4220
12 p.m. to 2 p.m. for lunch, 5 p.m. to 12:30 a.m. for dinner, and 12 p.m. to 12:30 a.m. on Sat., Sun., and holidays. Closed Thur. From ¥2,000.

Sasan
Court Daikanyama, B1,
1-33-18 Ebisu-nishi, Shibuya-ku
Tel: (03) 770-0777
5 p.m. to 12 a.m. Closed Sun. 7-dish course for ¥5,500.

Shinsensancho
1-8-21 Nishi Azabu, Minato-ku
Tel: (03) 404-4230
11:30 a.m. to 11 p.m. Closed Sun. From ¥2,000 for lunch and ¥5,000 for dinner.

Tenzan

Fuji Bldg., B2,
1-5-3 Yaesu, Chuo-ku
Tel: (03) 275-2115
11 a.m. to 2 p.m. for lunch and 5 p.m. to 9 p.m. for dinner. From ¥2,000.

Tokyo Hanten

5-1-10 Ginza, Chuo-ku
Tel: (03) 572-1686
11:30 a.m. to 3 p.m. for lunch and 4 p.m. to 1 a.m. for dinner. Closed Sun. From ¥6,000.

Xing Fu

Harajuku Torim, B1,
6-28-6 Jingumae, Shibuya-ku
Tel: (03) 498-4412
11:30 a.m. to 2 p.m. for lunch and 5:30 p.m. to 10 p.m. for dinner. Closed Sun. and holidays. *Kanpo ryori* (Chinese herbal cooking) from ¥5,000.

Yakuzen

2-3-16 Jiyugaoka, Meguro-ku
Tel: (03) 725-6777
5 p.m. to 10:30 p.m. Closed Mon. From ¥5,500.

Zuien

1-10-6 Shinjuku, Shinjuku-ku
Tel: (03) 351-3511
10 a.m. to 10 p.m. daily. Dishes from ¥650.

KOREAN BARBECUE (*YAKINIKU*)

Daiichi Jingu

3-41-8 Jingûmae, Shibuya-ku
Tel: (03) 401-9146
5 p.m. to 12:30 a.m. daily. From ¥7,000.

Juju

3-24-20 Nishi Azabu, Minato-ku
Tel: (03) 405-9911
11:30 a.m. to 4:30 p.m. and 11:30 a.m. to 2 p.m. on Sun. and holidays. From ¥3,000.

Kusano Ie

4-6-7 Azabu-Juban, Minato-ku
Tel: (03) 455-8356
11:30 a.m. to 2:30 p.m. for lunch, 5 p.m. to 1:40 a.m. for dinner, and 5 p.m. to 10 p.m. on Sun. and holidays. From ¥3,500.

Miracle

Shimbashi Kaikan 4th Fl.,
8-6-3 Ginza, Chuo-ku
Tel: (03) 289-2277
5 p.m. to 4 a.m. daily. From ¥2,500.

Sergeant Pepper's

Twin Bldg., B1
Daikanyama, Sarugakucho, Shibuya-ku
Tel: (03) 464-4189
11 a.m. to 3 a.m. daily. From ¥4,500.

INDIAN

Ajanta

3-11 Nibancho, Chiyoda-ku
Tel: (03) 264-6955
Open 24 hours daily. From ¥1,000.

Maharao

Mitsui Bldg., B1,
1-1-2 Yurakucho, Chiyoda-ku
Tel: (03) 580-6423
11 a.m. to 9 p.m. daily. From ¥2,000.

Moti

6-2-35 Roppongi, Minato-ku
Tel: (03) 479-1939
11:30 a.m. to 10 p.m. Mon. to Fri.; 12 a.m. to 10:30 p.m. Sun. and holidays. From ¥2,000.

The Taj

3-2-7 Akasaka, Minato-ku
Tel: (03) 586-6606
11:30 a.m. to 2 p.m. for lunch and 5:30 p.m. to 10 p.m. for dinner. Closed Sun. From ¥6,000.

INDONESIAN

Bengawan Solo

Kaneko Bldg., B1,
7-18-13 Roppongi, Minato-ku
Tel: (03) 403-3031
11:30 a.m. to 3 p.m. for lunch and 5 p.m. to 9:45 p.m. for dinner daily. From ¥4,500.

Indonesia Raya

Suzuya Bldg.,
1-23-15 Kabukicho, Shinjuku-ku
Tel: (03) 200-4835
12 p.m. to 10 p.m. Closed Sun. and holidays. From ¥2,500.

CAMBODIAN

Ankor Wat
1-38-13 Yoyogi, Shibuya-ku
Tel: (03) 370-3019
11 a.m. to 2 p.m. for lunch and 5 p.m. to 11
p.m. for dinner. Sun. and holidays closed at
lunch time. From ¥2,500.

Phnom Penh
Ebisu Nishi Bldg.,
1-10-14 Nishi Ebisu, Shibuya-ku
Tel: (03) 461-2769
5 p.m. to 11 p.m. Closed 1st and 3rd Sun.
From ¥2,500.

THAI

Chiang Mai
Kaede Bldg., 2nd and 3rd Fl.,
1-6-10 Yurakucho, Chiyoda-ku
Tel: (03) 580-0456
11:30 a.m. to 10 p.m. Closed Sat. From
¥5,000.

Kabara
Pink Dragon Bldg., B1,
1-23-23 Shibuya, Shibuya-ku
Tel: (03) 498-0699
6 p.m. to 11:30 p.m. Closed Sun. Courses
from ¥4,000.

Kay
Spiral Bldg.,
5-6-23 Minami Aoyama, Minato-ku
Tel: (03) 498-5790
6:30 p.m. to 12 a.m. Closed Sun. One dish
from ¥1,000.

VIETNAMESE

Aosai
5-4-14 Akasaka, Minato-ku
Tel: (03) 583-0234
5 p.m. to 10:30 p.m. Closed Sun. From
¥5,000.

SRI LANKAN

Araliya
Kanebo Cygnus Bldg., B1,
3-5-3 Ginza, Chuo-ku
Tel: (03) 564-1279
11 a.m. to 8:20 p.m. Closed 3rd Wed. From
¥950.

FRENCH

Brasserie Bernard
Kajimaya Bldg., 7th Fl.,
7-14-13 Roppongi, Minato-ku
Tel: (03) 405-7877
11:30 a.m. to 2 p.m. for lunch and 5:30 p.m.
to 11 p.m. for dinner. Closed Sun. From
¥3,000.

Chez Ino
Dai Hyaku Seimei Bldg., 1st Fl.,
3-2-11 Kyobashi, Chuo-ku
Tel: (03) 274-2020
11:30 a.m. to 2 p.m. for lunch and 6 p.m. to
9 p.m. for dinner. Closed for lunch on Sun.
From ¥10,000.

Chez Lui
17-22 Daikanyamachio, Shibuya-ku
Tel: (03) 461-9550
11:30 a.m. to 2:30 p.m. for lunch and 6 p.m.
to 9:30 p.m. for dinner. Closed Tue. From
¥1,700 for lunch and from ¥6,000 for dinner.

Cote d'Or
Mita House 1st Fl.,
5-2-18 Mita, Minato-ku
Tel: (03) 455-5145
12 p.m. to 2 p.m. for lunch and 6 p.m. to 9
p.m. Closed Mon. Lunch from ¥4,500.

Dolphin Club
1-43-2 Yoyogi, Shibuya-ku
Tel: (03) 370-0083
11:30 a.m. to 2 p.m. for lunch and 5:30 p.m.
to 11 p.m. for dinner. Closed Sun. Courses
from ¥3,500.

La Vita
Harajuku Vivré 21, 5th Fl.,
5-10-11 Jingumae, Shibuya-ku
Tel: (03) 498-2656
11:30 a.m. to 9:30 p.m. Buffet-style lunch
¥1,500 and dinner from ¥2,500 to ¥6,000.

L'ecrin
Mikimoto Bldg., B1,
4-5-5 Ginza, Chuo-ku
Tel: (03) 561-9706
11:30 a.m. to 2:30 p.m. for lunch and 5:30
p.m. to 10 p.m. Closed Sun. From ¥15,000.

L'orangerie de Paris
Hanae Mori Bldg., 5th Fl.,
3-6-1 Kita Aoyama, Minato-ku
Tel: (03) 407-7461
11:30 a.m. to 2:30 p.m. for lunch and 5:30
p.m. to 9:30 p.m. for dinner daily. Closed
Sun. evening. From ¥8,000.

Madame Toki's
14-7 Hachiyamacho, Shibuya-ku
Tel: (03) 461-2263
12 p.m. to 2:30 p.m. for lunch and 6 p.m. to
10 p.m. Closed Mon. From ¥15,000.

Maxim's de Paris
Ginza Sony Bldg., B3,
5-3-1 Ginza, Chuo-ku
Tel: (03) 572-3621
11:30 a.m. to 2:30 p.m. for lunch and 5:30
p.m. to 11 p.m. Closed Sun. From ¥20,000.

Pas-A-Pas
5 Funamachi, Shinjuku-ku
Tel: (03) 357-7888
6 p.m. to 9:30 p.m. Closed on Sun. From
¥2,500

Selan
2-1-19 Kita Aoyama, Minato-ku
Tel: (03) 478-2200
8 a.m. to 9:30 p.m. daily. From ¥8,000.

Tours d'Argent (Hotel New Otani)
4-1 Kioicho, Chiyoda-ku
Tel: (03) 239-3111
5:30 p.m. to 10:30 p.m. From ¥30,000.

ITALIAN

Antonio (Aoyama)
7-3-6 Minami Aoyama, Minato-ku
Tel: (03) 797-0388
11:30 a.m. to 2:30 p.m. for lunch and 5:30
p.m. to 10 p.m. for dinner. Closed Mon.
From ¥5,000.

Antonio (Daikanyama)
29-9 Sarugakucho, Daikanyama,
Shibuya-ku
Tel: (03) 464-6041
11:30 a.m. to 2:30 p.m. for lunch and 5:30
p.m. to 10 p.m. for dinner daily. From
¥6,000.

Basta-Pasta
Face Bldg., B1,
2-32-5 Jingumae, Shibuya-ku
Tel: (03) 478-3022
12 p.m. to 2 p.m. for lunch and 5:30 p.m. to
10 p.m. for dinner daily. From ¥5,000.

Buono Buono
4-2 Ginza, Chuo-ku
Tel: (03) 566-4031
11:30 a.m. to 10:30 p.m. (11 a.m. to 10 p.m.
on Sun.). From ¥5,000.

Chianti
3-1-7 Azabudai, Minato-ku
Tel: (03) 583-7546
12 p.m. to 2 a.m. daily. From ¥15,000.

La Cometa
1-7 Azabu Juban, Minato-ku
Tel: (03) 470-5105
12 p.m. to 2 p.m. for lunch and 5:30 p.m. to
9:30 p.m. Closed Sun. From ¥5,000.

La Granata
TBS Kaikan Bldg., B1,
5-3-3 Akasaka, Minato-ku
Tel: (03) 582-3241
11 a.m. to 3 p.m. for lunch and 5 p.m. to 9
p.m. for dinner. From ¥6,000.

Mikasa Continental Hiroo
Arisugawa West,
5-14 Minami Azabu, Minato-ku
Tel: (03) 448-8924
11:30 a.m. to 10:30 p.m. From ¥1,200.

Nicolas
1-43 Azabudai, Minato-ku
Tel: (03) 583-4712
12 p.m. to 11:30 p.m. daily and to 10:30 p.m.
on Sun. and holidays. From ¥3,000.

Roma Sabatini
Dogenzaka Center Bldg., 3rd Fl.,
2-29-8 Dogenzaka, Shibuya-ku
Tel: (03) 461-0495
11:30 a.m. to 2 p.m. for lunch and 5:30 p.m.
to 11 p.m. for dinner. Closed 1st and 3rd
Mon. From ¥6,000.

Tapas & Tapas
2-25-5 Kami Osaki, Shinagawa-ku
Tel: (03) 493-8956
11 a.m. to 3 p.m. for lunch and 5 p.m. to

10:30 p.m. for dinner. Closed on Sun. From
¥2,000.

SPANISH

El Castellano
Marusan Bldg., 2nd Fl.,
2-9-12 Shibuya, Shibuya-ku
Tel: (03) 407-7197
5 p.m. to 11 p.m. Closed Sun. and holidays.

El Flamenco
Isetan Kaikan, 6th Fl.,
3-15-17 Shinjuku, Shinjuku-ku
Tel: (03) 356-3816
11:30 a.m. to 2:30 p.m. for lunch and 5 p.m.
to 10:30 p.m. for dinner. Closed Wed. From
¥5,500.

España
Tokyo Plaza Bldg., 3rd and 4th Fl.,
2-2-10 Yoyogi, Shibuya-ku
Tel: (03) 379-1159
11:45 a.m. to 2:30 p.m. for lunch and 5 p.m.
to 10 p.m. for dinner. Closed Sun. On holidays open for dinner only. From ¥3,000.

Los Reyes Magos
5-55-7 Shibuya, Shibuya-ku
Tel: (03) 469-8231
5:30 p.m. to 10:30 p.m. daily. From ¥3,500

Vidrio
5-2-14 Roppongi, Minato-ku
Tel: (03) 405-6665
11 a.m. to 10:30 p.m. Closed 3rd Sun. From
¥2,500.

BRITISH

1066
3-9-5 Kami-Meguro,
Meguro-ku (near naka-Meguro Station)
Tel: (03) 719-9059
Open 11 a.m. to 4 p.m. for English Tea and
cakes and 5:30 p.m. to 10:30 p.m. for traditional authentic British home-cooked meals.
Menu changes constantly. Frequent musical
evenings. Closed on Mon. From ¥4,000.

GERMAN

Hofbrauhaus München
Meiji Seimei Shinjuku Higashi Bldg.,
1-1-17 Kabukicho, Shinjuku-ku

Tel: (03) 207-7591
5:30 p.m. to 11 p.m. daily. From ¥4,000.

Keitel
5-6-4 Shinjuku, Shinjuku-ku
Tel: (03) 354-5057
11:30 a.m. to 4 p.m. for lunch and 6 p.m. to
10:30 p.m. for dinner. Closed on Mon. From
¥4,000.

Ketel Restaurant
5-5-14 Ginza, Chuo-ku
Tel: (03) 571-5056
11:30 a.m. to 10 p.m. daily. From ¥1,600.

Pauke
Nomura Bldg., B1,
4-8 Yonbancho, Chiyoda-ku
Tel: (03) 264-7890
5 p.m. to 2 a.m. Closed Sun. and holidays.
From ¥2,000.

ROMANIAN

Darie
Uematsu Bldg., B1, 7-8-5 Ginza, Chuo-ku
Tel: (03) 571-5462
11:30 a.m. to 9:30 p.m. Closed Sun. From
¥3,000.

MEXICAN

El Pollo Loco
1-13-12 Jingumae, Shibuya-ku
Tel: (03) 408-4024
10 a.m. to 10 p.m. From ¥590.

Mexico Lindo
2-20-7 Akasaka, Minato-ku
Tel: (03) 583-2095
11:30 a.m. to 2 p.m. for lunch and 5:30 p.m.
to 11:30 p.m. for dinner. Closed Sun. From
¥3,000.

Mexico Mura Ventura
Tsubasa Mansion, 2nd Fl.,
2-1-1 Kitazawa, Setagaya-ku
Tel: (03) 414-1001
6 p.m. to 11 p.m. daily and 12 p.m. to 11 p.m.
on Sun. and holidays. Closed on Tue. From
¥1,700.

La Mex
1-15-23 Minami Aoyama, Minato-ku
Tel: (03) 470-1712

11:45 a.m. to 2 p.m. for lunch and 6 p.m. to 11:30 p.m. for dinner. Closed Sun. From ¥5,000.

Zapata
Ebina Bldg., B1,
6-18-10 Jingumae, Shibuya-ku
Tel: (03) 499-5888
11:30 a.m. to 2 p.m. for lunch and 6 p.m. to 11 p.m. for dinner, and till 1 a.m. for drinks. From ¥1,500.

Zest
Yokoshiba Daini Bldg.,
2-13-15 Nishi Azabu, Minato-ku
Tel: (03) 400-3985
11:30 a.m. to 4:45 a.m. daily. Tacos from ¥800 and Sunday brunch from 11:30 a.m. to 3 p.m. for ¥1,500.

BRAZILIAN

Amazon Club
1-10-45 Kaigan, Minato-ku
Tel: (03) 435-0701
5:30 p.m. to 11 p.m. daily. From ¥5,000.

STEAKS & RIBS

Cowboy
2-12-3 Kitazawa, Setagaya-ku
Tel: (03) 419-6929
5 p.m. to 10:30 p.m. Closed on Mon. From ¥1,000

George & Ray
2-6-4 Shibuya, Shibuya-ku
Tel: (03) 409-0677
12 p.m. to 2:30 p.m. for lunch and 6 p.m. to 9:30 p.m. for dinner. Closed Sun. From ¥4,000.

Hard Rock Café
5-4-20 Roppongi, Minato-ku
Tel: (03) 408-7018
11:30 a.m. to 2 a.m. on Mon. to Wed.; 11:30 a.m. to 4 a.m. on Thur. to Sat.; 11:30 a.m. to 11:30 p.m. on Sun. and holidays.

Tony Roma's
Sumitomo Seimei Aoyama Bldg., B1,
3-1-30 Aoyama, Minato-ku
Tel: (03) 479-5214
12 p.m. to 2:30 p.m. for lunch and 5 p.m. to 11 p.m. for dinner daily. From ¥4,000.

Victoria Station Akasaka
3-5-13 Akasaka, Minato-ku
Tel: (03) 586-0711
11 a.m. to 10:30 p.m. daily. From ¥3,000.

Victoria Station Roppongi
Haiyuza Gekijo, B1,
4-9-2 Roppongi, Minato-ku
Tel: (03) 479-4601
11 a.m. to 12 a.m. daily. From ¥3,000.

Victoria Station Shibuya
Chitose Kaikan, 2nd Fl.,
13 Udagawacho, Shibuya-ku
Tel: (03) 463-5288
11 a.m. to 2 a.m. daily. From ¥3,000.

CULTURE PLUS

MUSEUMS

Asakura Sculpture Museum
7-18-10 Yanaka, Taito-ku
Tel: (03) 821-4549

Bridgestone Museum
1-10-1 Kyobashi, Chuo-ku
Tel: (03) 563-0241

Hara Museum
4-7-25 Kita Shinagawa, Shinagawa-ku
Tel: (03) 445-0651

Matsuoka Art Museum
5-22-10 Shimbashi, Minato-ku
Tel: (03) 437-2787

National Museum of Western Art
7-7 Ueno Park, Taito-ku
Tel: (03) 823-6921

National Science Museum
7-20 Ueno Park, Taito-ku
Tel: (03) 833-4191

Nezu Art Museum
6-5-36 Minami Aoyama, Minato-ku
Tel: (03) 400-2536

Seibu Art Museum
1-28-1 Minami Ikebukuro, Toshima-ku
Tel: (03) 981-0111

Suntory Art Museum
Tokyo Suntory Bldg.,
1-2-3 Moto Akasaka, Minato-ku
Tel: (03) 470-2536

Sumo Museum
1-3-28 Yokoami, Sumida-ku
Tel: (03) 622-0366

Tokyo Central Museum
Ginza Boeki Bldg., 5th Fl.,
2-7-18 Ginza, Chuo-ku
Tel: (03) 564-0711

Tokyo Metropolitan Museum
8-36 Ueno Park, Taito-ku
Tel: (03) 823-6921

Tokyo National Museum
13-9 Ueno Park, Taito-ku
Tel: (03) 822-1111

Tokyo National Museum of Modern Art
3 Kitanomaru-koen, Chiyoda-ku
Tel: (03) 214-2561

Ueno No Mori Museum
1-2 Ueno Park, Taito-ku
Tel: (03) 823-0111

GALLERIES

There are art galleries all over the Ginza area and other parts of Tokyo, but below are four well-known ones that almost always hold interesting shows.

Kaneko Art Gallery
Mitsunari Bldg., 3-7-13 Kyobashi, Chuo-ku
Tel: (03) 564-0455
11 a.m. to 6:30 p.m. Closed Sun. and public holidays.

Maruzen Gallery
2-3-10 Nihombashi, Chuo-ku
Tel: (03) 272-7211

10 a.m. to 6:30 p.m. Closed Sun.

Nichido Gallery
7-4-12 Ginza, Chuo-ku
Tel: (03) 571-2553
10 a.m. to 7:30 p.m. daily.

Parco Gallery
Parco Part 1, Udagawacho, Shibuya-ku
Tel: (03) 477-5781
10 a.m. to 8:30 p.m. daily

THEATERS & CONCERTS

ABC Kaikan Hall
2-6-3 Shibakoen, Minato-ku
Tel: (03) 436-0430

Akasaka La Foret *(Avant Garde)*
Akasaka Twin Tower Bldg.,
2-17-22 Akasaka, Minato-ku
Tel: (03) 582-9255

Aoyama Enkei Gekijo *(Avant Garde)*
5-53-1 Jingumae, Shibuya-ku
Tel: (03) 797-5678

Ginza Nogakudo *(No)*
Ginza Nogakudo Bldg., 9th Fl.,
6-5-15 Ginza, Chuo-ku
Tel: (03) 571-0197

Hakuhinkan Gekijo
8-8-11 Ginza, Chuo-ku
Tel: (03) 571-1003

Hayuza Gekijo *(Actor's Theater)*
4-9-2 Roppongi, Minato-ku
Tel: (03) 470-2880

Hibiya Kokaido *(Public Hall)*
1-3 Hibiyakoen, Chiyoda-ku
Tel: (03) 591-6388

Hitomi Memorial Hall
1-5-57 Taishido, Setagaya-ku
Tel: (03) 422-5131

Honda Gekijo *(Contemporary)*
High Town,
2-10-15 Kitazawa, Setagaya-ku
Tel: (03) 460-0005

Jean Jean *(Recitals/intimate)*
Yamate Church, B1,

19-5 Udagawacho, Shibuya-ku
Tel: (03) 462-0641

Kabukiza *(Kabuki)*
4-12-15 Ginza, Chuo-ku
Tel: (03) 541-3131

Kanze Nogakudo *(No)*
1-16-4 Shoto, Shibuya-ku
Tel: (03) 469-4843

Kinokuniya Hall *(Japanese Drama)*
3-17-7 Shinjuku, Shinjuku-ku
Tel: (03) 354-0141

Kokuritsu Gekijo *(Contemporary Japanese Drama)*
4-1 Hayatocho, Chiyoda-ku
Tel: (03) 265-7411

Kosei Nenkin Hall
5-3-1 Shinjuku, Shinjuku-ku
Tel: (03) 356-1111

Meijiza *(Historical Japanese Drama)*
2-31-1 Hamacho, Nihombashi, Chuo-ku
Tel: (03) 660-3939

Nakano Sun Plaza
4-1-1 Nakano, Nakano-ku
Tel: (03) 388-1151

National Theater Nogakudo *(No)*
4-18-1 Sendagaya, Shibuya-ku
Tel: (03) 423-1331

NHK Hall *(Classical events)*
2-1 Jinan, Shibuya-ku
Tel: (03) 465-1111

Nihon Budokan
2-3 Kitanomaru Koen, Chiyoda-ku
Tel: (03) 216-0781

Nissei Gekijo
1-1-1 Yurakucho, Chiyoda-ku
Tel: (03) 503-3111

Shibuya Kokaido
1-1 Udagawacho, Shibuya-ku
Tel: (03) 463-5001

Shinjuku Koma Gekijo *(Musicals)*
1-19-1 Kabukicho, Shinjuku-ku
Tel: (03) 202-0131

Studio 200 *(Avant Garde)*
Ikebukuro Seibu Dept. Store,
1-28-1 Minami-Ikebukuro, Toshima-ku
Tel: (03) 981-0111

Suehirotei *(Rakugo)*
3-6-12 Shinjuku, Shinjuku-ku
Tel: (03) 351-2974

Sunshine Gekijo *(Japanese versions of Western box-office hits)*
Sunshine City Bunka Kaikan,
3-1-4 Higashi-Ikebukuro, Toshima-ku
Tel: (03) 987-5281

Suntory Hall *(Mostly classical events)*
1-13-1 Akasaka, Minato-ku
Tel: (03) 505-1001

Teikoku Gekijo *(Imperial Theater)*
3-1-1 Marunouchi, Chiyoda-ku
Tel: (03) 213-7221

Theater Apple *(Modern drama)*
1-19-1 Kabukicho, Shinjuku-ku
Tel: (03) 209-0222

The Tokyo Globe *(Shakespeare/Opera/Visiting troupes)*
3-1-2 Hyakunincho, Shinjuku-ku
Tel: (03) 360-1151

Tokyo Bunka Kaikan *(Two halls, Classical/Opera)*
5-45 Ueno Park, Taito-ku
Tel: (03) 828-2111

Tokyo Dome (Big Egg)
1-3 Kôraku, Bunkyo-ku
Tel: (03) 811-2111

Tokyo Takarazuka Gekijo *(All-female revue)*
1-1-3 Yurakucho, Chiyoda-ku
Tel: (03) 591-1711

Yubinchokin Hall
2-5-20 Shibakoen, Minato-ku
Tel: (03) 433-7211

Apart from the listings above, there are three groups that perform in English regularly in and around Tokyo. Performances are advertised in most of the English publications. The groups are: **Don Kenny's Kyo-**

gen Troupe, Tokyo International Players, and **Za Gaijin,** who can be contacted at the following number: Tel: (03) 711-4848.

LIBRARIES

National Diet Library
1-10-1 Nagatacho, Chiyoda-ku
Tel: (03) 581-2331
Open 9:30 a.m. to 5 p.m. Closed Sun., holidays and 4th Wed. You must be over 20 to request a book.

Metropolitan Center Library
5-7-13 Minami Azabu, Minato-ku
Tel: (03) 442-8451
Open from 9:30 a.m. to 8 p.m., Tue. to Fri.; until 5 p.m. on Sat., Sun. and holidays; from 1 p.m. to 8 p.m. on Mon.

World Magazine Gallery
Magazine House Bldg.,
3-13-10 Ginza, Chuo-ku
Tel: (03) 545-7227
Open from 10 a.m. to 7 p.m. Closed Mon. They have a selection of magazines from around the world, and a large video screen showing news and promotional videos.

BOOKSTORES

There are bookstores all over Tokyo, and it is quite acceptable to browse through the books and magazines in the shop without having to buy them, so don't feel guilty. In spite of the large number of bookstores, there are relatively few that specialize in English books. Below is a list of the major stores that stock foreign books and books on Japan. They are usually helpful when phoning about information on books in stock. Besides these places, you can also get foreign newspapers and magazines in most hotels.

Kinokuniya
3-17-7 Shinjuku, Shinjuku-ku
Tel: (03) 354-0131
10 a.m. to 7 p.m. Closed 1st and 3rd Wed. of each month. Foreign books on the 6th floor.

Maruzen
2-3-10 Nihombashi, Chuo-ku
Tel: (03) 272-7211
10 a.m. to 6 p.m. Closed Sun. Foreign books on the 3rd floor.

Jena (pronounced "yena")
5-6-1 Ginza, Chuo-ku
Tel: (03) 571-2980
10:30 a.m. to 7:50 p.m. and 12:30 p.m. to 6:45 p.m. on Sun. Closed holidays. Foreign books on the 3rd floor.

Sanseido
1-1 Kanda Jimbocho, Chiyoda-ku
Tel: (03) 233-3312
From Dec. to May open from 10 a.m. to 6:30 p.m. daily. From June to Nov., closed on Tue. Foreign books on 5th floor.

Kitazawa Shoten
2-5-3 Kanda Jimbocho, Chiyoda-ku
Tel: (03) 263-0001
10 a.m. to 6 p.m. Closed Sun. Secondhand books on the 2nd floor, and English and American literature on the 1st floor.

Biblos
F1 Bldg., 4th Fl.,
1-26-5 Takadanobaba, Shinjuku-ku
Tel: (03) 200-4531
10:30 a.m. to 7:30 p.m. daily, and 11 a.m. to 6:30 p.m. on Sun. and holidays. Closed 3rd Sun. of each month. This shop has a very large Penguin Book selection.

National Book Store
National Azabu Supermarket 2nd Fl.,
4-5-2 Minami Azabu, Minato-ku
Tel: (03) 442-3181
9:30 a.m. to 6:30 p.m. Open daily.

NIGHTLIFE

BARS & LIVE HOUSES

Amante
7-108 Corridor St., Ginza, Chuo-ku
Tel: (03) 572-5029
11 a.m. to 11:30 p.m. Closed Sun. and holidays. A great place to practice your *karaoke* singing without losing your wallet.

Berni Inn
Daisan Goto Bldg., 2nd Fl.,
3-13-14 Roppongi, Minato-ku
Tel: (03) 405-4928
4 p.m. to 10:30 p.m. Closed Sun. and public holidays.

Cavern Club
Roppongi Hosho Bldg.,
7-14-1 Roppongi, Minato-ku
Tel: (03) 405-5207
One of several Beatles impersonation spots.

Charleston
3-8-11 Roppongi, Minato-ku
Tel: (03) 402-0372
6 p.m. to 5 a.m. daily.

Crocodile
New Sekiguchi Bldg.,
6-18-8 Jingumae, Shibuya-ku
Tel: (03) 499-52-05
Live music daily, open until 6 a.m. daily.

Henry Africa's
Hanatsubaki Bldg., 2nd Fl.,
3-15-23 Roppongi, Minato-ku
Tel: (03) 403-9751
6 p.m. to 2 a.m. daily; and till 4 a.m. on Fri. and Sat.

Ink Stick
Casa Grande Miwa Bldg.,
7-5-11 Roppongi, Minato-ku
Tel: (03) 401-0429

Maggie's Revenge
Takano Bldg., 3-8-12 Roppongi, Minato-ku
Tel: (03) 479-1096
6:30 p.m. to 3 a.m. Closed Sun.

Mr. Stamp's
4-4-2 Roppongi, Minato-ku
Tel: (03) 479-1390
5 p.m. to 11 p.m. Closed Sun. and holidays.

Pilsen
6-8-7 Ginza, Chuo-ku
Tel: (03) 571-2236
12 p.m. to 10 p.m. and till 9 p.m. on Sun. and holidays.

Praca 11
Daini Seiho Bldg., B1,
3-5-2 Kita Aoyama, Minato-ku
Tel: (03) 405-8015
6:30 p.m. to 12 a.m. and till 2 a.m. on Fri. and Sat. Closed Sun. and holidays. Live Brazilian band playing every night.

The Bärren
4-11-12 Roppongi, Minato-ku
Tel: (03) 408-6123
6 p.m. to 3 a.m. daily.

JAZZ CAFES

In recent years jazz spots have been popping up everywhere, though they really had their heyday in the 1950s and 1960s when live music was still scarce. Many of the old places have disappeared, but some are still at it, and the music they play there is some of the best.

After Six
Zonan Bldg.,
3-13-8 Roppongi, Minato-ku
Tel: (03) 405-7233
8 p.m. to 2 a.m. daily. Closed on Sun. Intimate live jazz.

Blue Note Tokyo
5-13-3 Minami-Aoyama, Minato-ku
Tel: (03) 407-5781
6 p.m. to 2 a.m. daily. Closed on Sun.

Body & Soul
7-14-12 Roppongi, Minato-ku
Tel: (03) 408-2094
6:45 p.m. to 2 a.m. daily. Closed on Sun.

Dug
3-17-15 Shinjuku, Shinjuku-ku
Tel: (03) 354-7776
12 p.m. to 12 a.m. daily.

New Dug
3-15-12 Shinjuku, Shinjuku-ku
Tel: (03) 341-9339
10 a.m. to 2 a.m. daily.

Romanisches Café
Court Annex Roppongi, B1,
3-2-13 Nishi-Azabu, Minato-ku
Tel: (03) 405-6122
7 p.m. to 3 a.m. Closed Sun.

Eagle
1-8 Yotsuya, Shinjuku-ku
Tel: (03) 357-9857
11:30 a.m. to 11:30 p.m. daily.

Genius
3-2-10 Honcho, Nakano-ku
Tel: (03) 372-3471
11 a.m. to 11 p.m. daily.

Lady Jane
5-31-14 Daizawa, Setagaya-ku
Tel: (03) 412-3947
7 p.m. to 3 a.m. daily.

DISCOS

Buzz
Roppongi Square Bldg.,
3-10-3 Roppongi, Minato-ku
Tel: (03) 470-6391
6 p.m. to 5 a.m. daily.

Lexington Queen
Daisan Goto Bldg., B1,
3-13-14 Roppongi, Minato-ku
Tel: (03) 401-1661
6 p.m. to 12 a.m. daily.

Mugen
3-8-17 Akasaka, Minato-ku
Tel: (03) 584-4481
6:30 p.m. to 1 a.m. daily.

Radio City
Toho Twin Tower Bldg., B2,
1-5-2 Yurakucho, Chiyoda-ku
Tel: (03) 503-3675
5 p.m. to 12 a.m. daily.

Samba Club
Hotel Century Hyatt 1st Fl.,
2-7-2 Nishi Shinjuku, Shinjuku-ku
Tel: (03) 342-8877
5:30 p.m. to 2 a.m. daily.

SHOPPING

SHOPPING AREAS

Japan is a very expensive place, but there are still bargains to be had if you can hunt them out. The quality of Japanese products is well known around the world, and there are still things which can only be bought in Japan. Certain areas have become specialized in certain kinds of merchandise, and this means that a little bit of travel is involved for the serious shopper, but this is a good way to see the city. Following is a list of the main shopping areas and what they have to offer:

Akihabara: The electronic jungle of the world featuring hundreds of discount stores.

Aoyama: Mostly high-class fashion and designer boutiques.

Asakusa: Traditional Japanese toys, souvenirs, workmen's clothes, etc.

Ginza: The most expensive shopping center. Several major department stores are located here, such as **Hankyu, Matsuya, Matsuzakaya, Mitsukoshi, Printemps, Seibu** and **Wako**, besides a few "fashion buildings," and many exclusive boutiques. Also some traditional Japanese goods stores scattered around the area.

Harajuku: Another fashion area, though mostly geared to the young, which makes shopping relatively cheap. Several antique shops, and **Kiddyland** for the kids.

Hibiya: Mostly antique shops, jewelry shops, and art galleries.

Kanda Jimbocho: A lot of books in the many second-hand bookstores.

Nihombashi: A good place to pick up traditional craft work. Two of Japan's oldest department stores, **Mitsukoshi** and

Takashimaya are located here.

Roppongi: Several antique shops in the area, the **Axis** design building which features interior design as its main theme, and Seibu's **Wave** building which specializes in audio-visual equipment.

Shibuya: A good place to start, Shibuya has a little bit of everything. **Tokyu Hands** is a must to visit; probably the most complete do-it-yourself department store in the world. Also the **Seibu, Tokyu** and **Marui** departments stores, the **Parco** "fashion" buildings besides the hundreds of little boutiques geared to young shoppers.

Shinjuku: Several big camera and electronic discount stores such as **Yodobashi** and **Sakuraya**. Also, **Isetan** and **Marui** department stores.

Ueno: Ameyoko is good for cheap food, cosmetics, clothing and toys. One of the only open markets in Tokyo. The back streets have numerous shops selling traditional Japanese goods.

CAMERAS

Bic Camera
1-11-7 Higashi Ikebukuro, Toshima-ku
Tel: (03) 988-0002
10 a.m. to 8 p.m. daily.

Camera No Alps Do
3-23-1 Shinjuku, Shinjuku-ku
Tel: (03) 352-6336
10:30 a.m. to 8 p.m. daily.

Camera No Doi
1-18-27 Nishi Shinjuku, Shinjuku-ku
Tel: (03) 348-2241
10 a.m. to 9 p.m. daily.

Camera No Kimura
1-18-8 Nishi Ikebukuro, Toshima-ku
Tel: (03) 981-8437
8 a.m. to 8 p.m. daily.

Camera No Sakuraya
3-17-2 Shinjuku, Shinjuku-ku
Tel: (03) 354-3636
10 a.m. to 8 p.m. daily.

Lucky Camera
3-36-16 Shinjuku, Shinjuku-ku
Tel: (03) 354-7898
10 a.m. to 9 p.m. daily.

Miyama Shokai
3-32-8 Shinjuku, Shinjuku-ku
Tel: (03) 356-1841
10:30 a.m. to 8 p.m. daily.

Shimizu Camera
4-3-2 Ginza, Chuo-ku
Tel: (03) 564-1008
9:30 a.m. to 6:30 p.m. daily.

Yodobashi Camera
1-11-1 Nishi Shinjuku, Shinjuku-ku
Tel: (03) 346-1010
9:30 a.m. to 8:30 p.m. daily.

ELECTRONICS & COMPUTERS

Below is a list of just a few well-known shops in the vicinity of Akihabara Station.

F. Shokai
Radio Kaikan, 7th Fl.,
1-15-16 Soto Kanda, Chiyoda-ku
Tel: (03) 251-2310
10 a.m. to 7 p.m.

Fujimoto "Maikon" Center Ram
Radio Kaikan, 7th Fl.,
1-15-16 Soto Kanda, Chiyoda-ku
Tel: (03) 255-7846
10 a.m. to 7 p.m.

Hirose Musen Audio Center
1-12-1 Soto Kanda, Chiyoda-ku
Tel: (03) 255-5931
10 a.m. to 6:50 p.m. Closed Thur.

Kimura Musen
Radio Kaikan, 4th Fl.,
1-15-16 Soto Kanda, Chiyoda-ku
Tel: (03) 251-7391
10 a.m. to 7 p.m. daily.

Rocket Honten
1-14-1 Sakumacho, Kanda, Chiyoda-ku
Tel: (03) 257-0606
10 a.m. to 8 p.m. daily.

Sato Musen
1-11-11 Soto Kanda, Chiyoda-ku
Tel: (03) 253-5871
10 a.m. to 7 p.m. daily.

Shojin Shokai
Radio Kaikan, 4th Fl.,

1-15-16 Soto Kanda, Chiyoda-ku
Tel: (03) 251-0797
11 a.m. to 7 p.m. daily.

Computerland
Nihonseimei Takanawadai Bldg., 3rd Fl.,
3-5-23 Takanawa, Minato-ku
Tel: (03) 447-0211
They have numerous branches throughout
the city, so it's a good idea to phone first and
ask for the nearest one to you.

FASHION BOUTIQUES

Bigi (By Inaba Yoshie)
The **Shibuya Parco Part 2**, 5th Fl.,
3-7 Udagawacho, Shibuya-ku
Tel: (03) 476-2077

Hanae Mori
Hanae Mori Bldg.,
3-6-1 Kita Aoyama, Minato-ku
Tel: (03) 400-3301
10:30 a.m. to 7 p.m.

Hiroko Koshino
Tokyo Creator Bldg.,
3-51-10 Sendagaya, Shibuya-ku
Tel: (03) 475-5311
10 a.m. to 7 p.m. Closed Sun.

Issey Miyake
Shibuya Parco Part 1, 1st Fl.,
Tel: (03) 464-6626 and
Shibuya Parco Part 2, 6th Fl.,
Tel: (03) 496-0438
La Foret Harajuku, 1st Fl.,
Tel: (03) 478-7698

The Shirts (Hamilton Shirts)
3-2-5 Kita Aoyama, Minato-ku
Tel: (03) 475-1971
11 a.m. to 7:30 p.m. Closed Mon.

Junko Koshino
6-5-36 Minami Aoyama, Minato-ku
Tel: (03) 406-7370
11 a.m. to 7 p.m. Closed Sat.

Junko Shimada
Aobadai Terrace,
1-1-4 Aobadai, Meguro-ku
Tel: (03) 463-2346
11 a.m. to 8 p.m. Closed Mon.

Kansai Yamamoto
3-28-7 Jingumae, Shibuya-ku
Tel: (03) 478-1958
11 a.m. to 8 p.m. daily.

Madame Hanai (By Hanai Yukiko)
Roi Bldg., 2nd Fl.,
5-5-1 Roppongi, Minato-ku
Tel: (03) 404-5791
11 a.m. to 8 p.m. Closed 3rd Thur.

Madame Nicole (By Mitsuhiro Matsuda)
Nicole Bldg., 1st Fl.,
3-1-25 Jingumae, Shibuya-ku
Tel: (03) 478-0998
11 a.m. to 8 p.m. daily. In the same building
is **Monsieur Nicole** by Kobayashi Yukio

Persons
3-28-8 Jingumae, Shibuya-ku
Tel: (03) 401-5524
11 a.m. to 8 p.m. daily.

Takeo Kikuchi
Vivre 21, 1st and 2nd Fl.,
5-10-1 Jingumae, Shibuya-ku
Tel: (03) 498-2221
11 a.m. to 8 p.m. daily.

Tokio Kumagai
Cedarstone Villa, B1,
15-5 Hachiyamacho, Shibuya-ku
Tel: (03) 477-2613
11 a.m. to 8 p.m. Closed Wed.

Yuki Torii
5-7-16 Ginza, Chuo-ku
Tel: (03) 574-8701
11:30 a.m. to 7:30 p.m. daily

JEWELRY

Mikimoto
4-5-5 Ginza, Chuo-ku
Tel: (03) 535-4611
10:30 a.m. to 6 p.m. Closed Wed.

Uyeda Jeweler
Imperial Hotel, B1,
1-1-1 Uchisaiwaicho, Chiyoda-ku
Tel: (03) 503-2587
9:45 a.m. to 7 p.m. daily.

Wako
4-5-11 Ginza, Chuo-ku
Tel: (03) 562-2111
10 a.m. to 5:30 p.m. Closed Wed.

Yamazaki
1-7-7 Ginza, Chuo-ku
Tel: (03) 561-0491
10:30 a.m. to 6:30 p.m. Closed Wed. and holidays.

CUSTOM JEWELRY

Ginza Olfe
7-108 Corridor St., Ginza, Chuo-ku
Tel: (03) 572-6752
Alterations, repairs and custom designing.

DEPARTMENT STORES

Daimaru
1-9-1 Marunouchi, Chiyoda-ku
Tel: (03) 212-8011
10 a.m. to 6 p.m. Closed Thur.

Isetan
3-14-1 Shinjuku, Shinjuku-ku
Tel: (03) 352-1111
10 a.m. to 6 p.m. Closed Wed.

Marui
3-30-16 Shinjuku, Shinjuku-ku
Tel: (03) 354-0101
10:30 a.m. to 7:30 p.m. Closed 2nd or 3rd Wed.

Matsuya
1-4-1 Hanakawado, Taito-ku
Tel: (03) 842-1111
10 a.m. to 6 p.m. Closed Thur.

Matsuzakaya
3-29-5 Ueno, Taito-ku
Tel: (03) 832-1111

Mitsukoshi
1-7-4 Muromachi,
Nihombashi, Chuo-ku
Tel: (03) 241-3311
10 a.m. to 6 p.m. Closed Mon.

Printemps
3-2-1 Ginza, Chuo-ku
Tel: (03) 567-0077
10 a.m. to 7 p.m. Closed Wed.

Seibu (Main Store)
1-28-1 Minami Ikebukuro, Toshima-ku
Tel: (03) 981-0111
10 a.m. to 6 p.m. Closed Thur.
Shibuya Branch
23-1 Udagawacho, Shibuya-ku
Tel: (03) 462-0111
10 a.m. to 6 p.m. Closed Wed.
Yurakucho Branch
2-5-1 Yurakucho, Chiyoda-ku
Tel: (03) 286-0111
10 a.m. to 6 p.m. Closed Thur.

Sogo
1-11-1 Yurakucho, Chiyoda-ku
Tel: (03) 284-6711
10 a.m. to 7 p.m. Closed Tue.

Takashimaya
2-4-1 Nihombashi, Chuo-ku
Tel: (03) 211-4111
10 a.m. to 6 p.m. Closed Wed.

Tokyu
2-24-1 Dogenzaka, Shibuya-ku
Tel: (03) 477-3111
10 a.m. to 6 p.m. Closed Thur.

FASHION BUILDINGS

Not department stores, but not arcades either, "fashion buildings" are uniquely Japanese. Mostly occupied by boutiques, many of them are very similar, so you don't want to spend much time visiting them all.

Axis
5-17-1 Roppongi, Minato-ku
Tel: (03) 587-2781
Hours vary from shop to shop, but most close on Mon.

Bell Commons
2-14-6 Kita Aoyama, Minato-ku
Tel: (03) 475-8111
11 a.m. to 8 p.m. daily.

From 1st
5-3-10 Minami Aoyama, Minato-ku
Tel: (03)
Hours vary with each shop.

International Arcade
1-7-23 Uchisaiwaicho, Chiyoda-ku
Tel: (03) 591-2764

10 a.m. to 7 p.m. Mon. to Sat. 10 a.m. to 6 p.m. Sun and holidays. Many of the shop-keepers speak some foreign language.

La Foret Harajuku
1-11-6 Jingumae, Shibuya-ku
Tel: (03) 475-0411
11 a.m. to 8 p.m. daily.

Lumine
Shinjuku Station South Exit
Tel: (03) 348-5211

Parco
15-1 Udagawacho, Shibuya-ku
Tel: (03) 464-5150
10 a.m. to 8:30 p.m. daily.

Shimbashi Ginza 9
This shopping center stretches along away from Shimbashi Station under the train tracks. 9 a.m. to 9 p.m. daily.

Spiral
5-6-23 Minami Aoyama, Minato-ku
Tel: (03) 498-1171
11 a.m. to 8 p.m. daily.

Seed
21-1 Udagawacho, Shibuya-ku
Tel: (03) 462-0111
10 a.m. to 6 p.m. Closed Wed.

Sukiyabashi Shopping Center
5-1 Ginza, Chuo-ku
Tel: (03) 571-0487
9 a.m. to 9 p.m. daily.

Wave
6-2-27 Roppongi, Minato-ku
Tel: (03) 408-0111
11 a.m. to 9 p.m. daily.

Wing Takanawa
4-10-18 Takanawa, Shinagawa-ku
Next to the Shinagawa Prince Hotel, in front of Shinagawa Station.

ANTIQUE SHOPS

Below follows a list of antique shops in different areas of Tokyo. In most of them English is spoken, and people will be very helpful. If you are looking for collector's pieces, it is a good idea to read up on the sub-ject of Japanese antiques before you start looking, because there are a lot of badly restored pieces that have been given a quick coat of glossy lacquer and sold as something special.

Edo Antiques
2-21-12 Akasaka, Minato-ku
Tel: (03) 584-5280
A large selection of *tansu* and *hibachi*. Mr. Murakawa, the owner, is willing to bargain.

Hasabe-ya Antiques
1-5-24 Azabu Juban, Minato-ku
Tel: (03) 401-9998

Japan Old Folkcraft and Antique Center (Tokyo Komingu Kotto-kan)
3-9-5 Minami Ikebukuro, Toshima-ku
Tel: (03) 980-8228
·35 dealers covering 600 square meters. If you know what you are looking for, you can find a bargain here, but you should know about antiques. Not much English is spoken.

Antique Gallery Meguro
Stork Bldg., 2nd Fl.,
2-24-18 Kamiosaki, Shinagawa-ku
Tel: (03) 493-1971
An antique market of sorts covering 740 square meters that houses several small an-tique shops. They all handle a bit of every-thing and are willing to bargain on expensive items. English is spoken in several of them.

Harumi Antiques
9-6-14 Akasaka, Minato-ku
Tel: (03) 403-1043
David and Harumi Rose are the owners of this shop. No problem with English here. Mostly *tansu* that have been restored, but some unrestored pieces can be purchased.

Oriental Bazaar
5-9-13 Jingumae, Shibuya-ku
Tel: (03) 400-3933
Not really an antique store, but they some-times do have interesting pieces at very reasonable prices. They do not bargain, but will provide a certificate as to the approxi-mate age of the piece. Apart from antiques, it is also a nice place to browse and pick up traditional Japanese toys, paper (*washi*), *kimono*, etc.

Antique Gallery Kikori
Hanae Mori Bldg., B1,
3-6-1 Kita Aoyama, Minato-ku
Tel: (03) 4079363
Warehouse: 1-9-1 Hibarigaoka, Hoya-shi,
Tokyo, tel: (0424) 21-7373
Small but interesting selection of *tansu* and
other items. The owner Mr. Saito also maintains a large warehouse of largely unrestored
pieces. Mr. Saito speaks English and is willing to bargain.

ANTIQUE KIMONO

At most of the flea markets listed below, you
can usually pick up very beautiful old *kimono* and *obi* in good condition. Apart from
them, below are a few shops specializing in
antique *kimono*, *obi*, traditional blue and
white textiles, *furoshiki*, *hanten*, etc. Prices
are anything from ¥1,000 and up.

Ayahata
2-21-2 Akasaka, Minato-ku
Tel: (03) 582-9969
11:30 a.m. to 8 p.m. Closed Sun. and public
holidays.

Hayashi Kimono
International Arcade,
1-7 Uchisaiwaicho, Chiyoda-ku
Tel: (03) 581-9826
9:30 a.m. to 7 p.m. daily.

Ikeda
5-22-11 Shiroganedai, Minato-ku
Tel: (03) 445-1269
11:30 a.m. to 7 p.m. Closed Sun.

Konjaku Nishimura
Hanae Mori Bldg., B1,
3-6-1 Kita Aoyama, Minato-ku
Tel: (03) 498-1759
11 a.m. to 8 p.m. Closed Thur.

GENERAL ARTS & CRAFTS

Bingoya
69 Wakamatsucho, Shinjuku-ku
Tel: (03) 202-8778

LACQUERWARE (*SHIKKI*)

Bushi
Axis Bldg.,
B1 5-17-1 Roppongi, Minato-ku
Tel: (03) 587-0317
11 a.m. to 8 p.m. Closed Mon.

Heiando
3-10-11 Nihombashi, Chuo-ku
Tel: (03) 272-2871
9 a.m. to 6 p.m. Closed Sun. and holidays.

Inachu Japan
1-5-2 Akasaka, Minato-ku
Tel: (03) 582-4451
10 a.m. to 7 p.m. daily.

Kuroeya
Kuroeya Kokubu Bldg., 2nd Fl.,
1-2-6 Nihombashi, Chuo-ku
Tel: (03) 271-3356
9 a.m. to 5 p.m. Closed Sat., Sun. and public
holidays.

CERAMICS

Unless you actually visit the towns where
the ceramics are made, department stores are
good places to see a wide selection of Japanese ceramics, and the prices are not too bad.
On little back streets all over Tokyo, you will
find small shops selling ceramics. At these
places, however, prices tend to be a little
more expensive.

Iseryu Shoten
3-8-2 Ningyocho,
Nihombashi, Chuo-ku
Tel: (03) 661-4820
8:30 a.m. to 6 p.m. Closed Sun. and holidays.

Saga Toen
2-13-13 Nishi Azabu, Minato-ku
Tel: (03) 400-3682
10 a.m. to 8:30 p.m. daily and 11 a.m. to 7:30
p.m. on Sun. and holidays.

Tachikichi & Co., Ltd.
6-13 Ginza, Chuo-ku
Tel: (03) 571-2924
11 a.m. to 7 p.m. Closed Sun.

WOODBLOCK PRINTS (*UKIYOE*)

Asakusa Okuramae Shobo
3-10-12 Kuramae, Taito-ku
Tel: (03) 866-5894
9 a.m. to 7 p.m. Closed on Sun., but will stay open if you make an appointment. Specialist on books and prints on *Edo* and *sumo*.

Hara Shobo
2-3 Jimbocho, Kanda, Chiyoda-ku
Tel: (03) 261-7444
Every type of print old and new, from the highest quality to a "bargain drawer". English spoken.

Matsushita Associates, Inc.
6-3-12 Minami Aoyama, Shibuya-ku
Tel: (03) 407-4966
10 a.m. to 5:30 p.m. Closed Sun. and public holidays.

Oya Shobo
1-1 Kanda, Jimbocho, Chiyoda-ku
Tel: (03) 291-0062
10 a.m. to 6:30 p.m. Closed Sun.

Sakai Kokodo Gallery
1-2-14 Yurakucho, Chiyoda-ku
Tel: (03) 591-4678
10 a.m. to 7 p.m. daily.

MUSICAL INSTRUMENTS

Bachi Ei Gakkiten *(Shamisen)*
2-10-11 Ningyocho, Nihombashi, Chuo-ku
Tel: (03) 666-7263
9 a.m. to 8:30 p.m. Closed Sun. and holidays.

Kikuya Shamisen Ten *(Shamisen)*
3-45-11 Yushima, Bunkyo-ku
Tel: (03) 831-4733
9 a.m. to 7:30 p.m. Closed Sun. and holidays.

Tsurukawa Gakki Honten *(Koto)*
1-12-11 Kyobashi, Chuo-ku
Tel: (03) 561-1872
9:30 a.m. to 6 p.m. Closed Sun. and holidays.

Ishida Biwa Ten *(Biwa)*
3-8-4 Toranomon, Minato-ku
Tel: (03) 431-6548
9 a.m. to 7 p.m. Closed Sun. and holidays.

Chikuyusha *(Shakuhachi)*
3 San-eicho, Shinjuku-ku
Tel: (03) 351-1270
10 a.m. to 5 p.m. Closed Sun. and holidays.

Miyamoto Unosuke Shoten (Drums)
6-1-15 Asakusa, Taito-ku
Tel: (03) 874-4131
8 a.m. to 5 p.m. Closed Sun. and holidays.

PAPER LANTERNS (*CHOCHIN*)

Hanato
2-25-6 Asakusa, Taito-ku
Tel: (03) 841-6411
10 a.m. to 9 p.m. Closed 2nd and 4th Tue.

Kashiwaya
2-3-13 Shintomi, Chuo-ku
Tel: (03) 551-1362
10 a.m. to 5 p.m. Closed Sun.

UMBRELLAS (*KASA*)

Hasegawa Hakimonoten
2-4-4 Ueno, Taito-ku
Tel: (03) 831-3933
8:30 a.m. to 8 p.m. Closed Sun.

Iidaya
1-31-1 Asakusa, Taito-ku
Tel: (03) 841-3644
9 a.m. to 8 p.m. daily.

SWORDS

Japan Sword
3-8-1 Toranomon, Minato-ku
Tel: (03) 434-4321
9:30 a.m. to 6 p.m. Closed Sun.

JAPANESE PAPER (*WASHI*)

Haibara
2-7-6 Nihombashi, Chuo-ku
Tel: (03) 272-3801
9:30 a.m. to 5:30 p.m. Closed Sun. and holidays.

Isetasu
2-18-9 Yanaka, Taito-ku
Tel: (03) 823-1453
10 a.m. to 6 p.m. daily.

Kurodaya
1-2-11 Asakusa, Taito-ku
Tel: (03) 845-3830
11 a.m. to 8 p.m. Closed Mon.

Kyukyodo
5-7-4 Ginza, Chuo-ku
Tel: (03) 571-4429
10 a.m. to 8 p.m. daily.

Ozu Shoten
2-6-3 Nihombashi Honcho, Chuo-ku
Tel: (03) 663-8788
10 a.m. to 6 p.m. Closed Sun.

Washikobo
1-8-10 Nishi Azabu, Minato-ku
Tel: (03) 405-1841
10 a.m. to 6 p.m. Closed Sun. and holidays.

TAILORS

Ricky Sarani
3-3-12 Azabudai, Minato-ku
Tel: (03) 582-9741
Open from 10 a.m. to 7 p.m. Closed Sun, and holidays. Men and women.

Koda Yofuku Kobo
3-24-1 Shimbashi, Minato-ku
Tel: (03) 433-4074
Open from 10 a.m. to 7 p.m. Closed Sun, and holidays. Alterations and mending.

FLEA MARKETS

Nomi no ichi are held almost every week somewhere in or around Tokyo. This is one of the few occasions when bargaining is the rule. Normally held early in the morning till dusk, weather permitting. If you are looking for some nice souvenirs, or something unique to decorate your home with, this is the place to look. However, if you are looking for real antiques, you should be careful. Most of the dealers are rather old-fashioned junk dealers than true antique dealers. The major fairs are listed below:

Togo Shrine (Harajuku)
Every first and fourth Sunday. Nearest station: **Meiji Jingumae** on the Chiyoda subway line.
Tel: (03) 403-3591.

Arai Yakushi Temple (Nakano)
Every first Sunday. Nearest station: **Arai Yakushi-mae** on the Seibu Shinjuku line.
Tel: (03) 386-1355.

Nogi Shrine (Roppongi)
Every second Sunday. Nearest station: **Nogizaka** on the Chiyoda subway line.
Tel: (03) 402-2181.

Roppongi (On the steps of the Roi Bldg.)
Every fourth Thursday and Friday. 8 a.m. to 8 p.m., rain or shine. Nearest station: **Roppongi** on the Hibiya subway line.
Tel: (03) 583-2081.

Hanazono Shrine (Shinjuku-Sanchome)
Every second and third Sunday. 7 a.m. to 5 p.m. Suspended in case of rain. Nearest station: **Shinjuku Sanchome** on the Marunouchi subway line.
Tel: (03) 200-3093.

You can also obtain Flea market information after 5 p.m. at tel: (03) 226-6800 (taped in Japanese at Recycle *Undo Shimin-kai*.)

LANGUAGE

Although more and more foreigners are making the effort to learn Japanese, and learn it to a high degree of fluency, few Japanese expect foreigners to be able to speak their language. Unfortunately, this lack of confidence in the ability of others to speak their language is not matched by a high level of proficiency in foreign languages on the part of the Japanese people. The number who can communicate effectively in any foreign language is very small, in spite of the fact that the majority of them have studied English for at least six years. However, it is rare for the foreign visitor to Japan to find himself in a situation where absolutely nobody can be found to help out. Indeed, some Japanese will go to extraordinary lengths to help the bewildered tourist, using a curious blend of smiles, gestures and Japanese together with the odd recognizable word of English as a fairly effective means of communication. Simply looking helpless will often be enough to attract assistance.

The visitor will have few language problems within the confines of airports and the major Western-style hotels, but outside these the going can get tough for those who are unescorted. Quite apart from finding himself unable to communicate verbally, the hapless visitor will also have the disconcerting experience of being almost totally illiterate. The written language is made up of three different sets of characters: two simple homegrown syllabaries, *hiragana* and *katakana,* consisting of forty-six characters each; and the much more formidable Chinese ideograms, *kanji,* which the Japanese started importing in A.D. fourth century. Knowledge of just under two thousand of these is necessary to read a daily newspaper. While the expenditure of the enormous effort required to memorize this number of *kanji* (it takes the Japanese most of their school career to do so) is clearly unjustifiable for those with only a passing interest in the language, a few hours spent learning the two syllabaries (on the plane trip to Japan!) would not be time completely wasted for those who can afford it. *Hiragana* can be useful for identifying which station your train has stopped at; the platforms are plastered with *hiragana* versions of the station name so that children who have not yet learned *kanji* can see where they are. Station names are usually (but not always) posted in Roman script as well, but not always as obviously. *Katakana* is useful in that it is used to transliterate foreign words. Western-style restaurants often simply list the foreign names for the dishes on their menus in *katakana.* Listed in the table below are the two syllabaries.

With its small number of simple and unvarying vowel sounds, the pronunciation of Japanese should be easy for those who speak Western languages, which are rich in vowel sounds. The consonants should also present few problems (with the possible exception of l/r, ts and f — the only way to learn these is to have someone demonstrate them for you), and Japanese has nothing like the dreaded tonal system of Chinese to frustrate the student. To give you a rough idea of the vowel sounds:

a - halfway between the a in fat and the u in but
e - like the e in egg
i - like the i in ink *
o - like th o in orange
u - like the u in butcher *

* When they occur in the middle of words, i and u are often almost silent. For example, *Takeshita* is really pronounced *Takesh'ta* while *sukiyaki* sounds more like *s'kiyaki.*

In spite of the seemingly simple pronunciation of Japanese, a lot of foreigners manage to mangle the language into a form

---

(H = *hiragana*, K = *katakana*).

	H	K														
a	あ	ア	i	い	イ	u	う	ウ	e	え	エ	o	お	オ
ka	か	カ	ki	き	キ	ku	く	ク	ke	け	ケ	ko	こ	コ
sa	さ	サ	shi	し	シ	su	す	ス	se	せ	セ	so	そ	ソ
ta	た	タ	chi	ち	チ	tsu	つ	ツ	te	て	テ	to	と	ト
na	な	ナ	ni	に	ニ	nu	ぬ	ヌ	ne	ね	ネ	no	の	ノ
ha	は	ハ	hi	ひ	ヒ	fu	ふ	フ	he	へ	ヘ	ho	ほ	ホ
ma	ま	マ	mi	み	ミ	mu	む	ム	me	め	メ	mo	も	モ
ya	や	ヤ				yu	ゆ	ユ				yo	よ	ヨ
ra	ら	ラ	ri	り	リ	ru	る	ル				ro	ろ	ロ
wa	わ	ワ							re	れ	レ	wo	を	ヲ
n	ん	ン												

which is almost impossible for the native speaker to understand. It is mainly intonation that is responsible for this. It would be fallacious to claim that the Japanese language has no rise and fall in pitch — just listen to a group of schoolgirls conversing on the train to confirm this — but it is certainly "flatter" in character than Western languages. It is important to avoid stressing syllables within words; whereas an English speaker would naturally stress either the second or third syllable of *Hiroshima,* for example, in Japanese the four syllables should be stressed equally. Another problem lies in long (actually double) vowel sounds. These are often indicated by a line above the vowel, e.g. Tokyo Station, or simply by a double vowel, e.g. *Iidabashi.* To pronounce these long vowels properly, it is simply necessary to give the vowel sound double length. However, many publishers, including the Japan Times ignore these long double vowels.

The following list is designed simply to start you off in Japanese. Several courses and lengthy phrase books are available for those who wish to study the language more deeply.

GREETINGS

Good morning	*Ohayo gozaimasu* (usually only until about 10 a.m.)
Hello	*Konnichiwa*
Good evening	*Kombanwa*
Good night	*Oyasuminasai*
Goodbye	*Sayonara (Shitsure shimasu* for formal occasions)
How do you do?	*Hajime mashite?*
How are you?	*Ogenki desuka?*
It's good to see you again	*Shibaraku desu* (Informally, *"Domo"* is enough.)
My name is.....	*.....to moshīmasu*
I'm American	*Amerikajin desu*
I'm British	*Igirisujin desu*
I'm Australian	*Osturaraiajin desu*
I'm Canadian	*Kanadajin desu*

ASKING FOR DIRECTIONS

Excuse me, where is the toilet?	*Sumimasen. Toire wa doko desuka?*
Excuse me, is there a post office near here?	*Sumimasen. Kono is chikaku ni, yubinkyoku wa arimasuka?*
Bakery	*Pan-ya*
Meat shop	*Niku-ya*
Fish market	*Sakana-ya*
Greengrocer's	*Yao-ya*
Florist	*Hana-ya*
Stationary store	*Bumbogu-ya*
Pharmacy	*Kusuri-ya*
Shoe shop	*Kutsu-ya*
Barber shop	*Toko-ya*
Bookshop	*Hon-ya*
Electric shop	*Denki-ya*
Cake shop	*Okashi-ya*
Toy shop	*Omocha-ya*
Supermarket	*Supa-Maketto*
Department store	*Depato*
Restaurant	*Restoran*
Hotel	*Hoteru*
Station	*Eki*
Taxi stand	*Takushii noriba*
Bank	*Ginko*
Hospital	*Byoin*
Police Station	*Koban*

SHOPPING

This one	*Kore*
That one (near the other person)	*Sore*
That one (near neither of you)	*Are*
Do you have.......?	*......(wa) arimasuka?*
Could you show me that one please?	*Sore o misete kudasai.*
How much is it?	*Ikura desuka?*
Don't you have anything cheaper?	*Mo sukoshi yasui no arimasenka?*
Can I try it on?	*Shichaku shite mo ii desuka?*
Do you accept (credit) cards?	*(Kurjitto) kado tsukaemasuka?*
I'll take this.	*Kore o kudasai.*
Three of these, please.	*Kore o mittsu kudasai.*

TRAINS

Ticket (office)	*Kippu (uriba)*
A single ticket to Sendai, please.	*Sendai made, katamichi ichi-mae kudasai.*
Two returns to Nikko, please.	*Nikkomade, ofuku ni-mae kudasai.*
Reserved seat	*Shitei seki*
Unreserved seat	*Jiyuseki*
First class car	*Guriin* (Green) *sha*
Which platform does the train for Nagoya leave from?	*Nagoya yuki wa namban sen desuka?*
Thank you (very much)	*(Domo) arigato gozaimasu* (informally, *"Domo"* is enough)
Thank you for the meal.	*Gochisosama deshita.*
Don't mention it.	*Doitashimashite*
Here you are.	*Dozo*
After you.	*Dozo*
Sure, go ahead.	*Dozo* (In answer to "May I....?")

You will notice that *"Dozo"* is a rather useful word. It is normally translated as "Please" in phrasebooks, which is misleading. To a question like "Would you like a cup of coffee?" (*Kohi wa ikaga desuka?*), you should answer, *"Hai, onegaishimasu"* or *"Hai, itadakimasu."* *"Dozo"* would be used if *you* were handing someone else a cup of coffee. Some cynical foreigners in Japan claim that you can easily survive knowing only the words *"Dozo"* and *"Domo"*!

TIME OF THE DAY

(On) Sunday	*Nichi-yobi (ni)*
(Next) Monday	*(Raishuno) Getsu-yobi*
(Last) Tuesday	*(Senshuno) Ka-yobi*
(Every) Wednesday	*(Maishu) Sui-yobi*
(This) Thursday	*(Konshuno) Moku-yobi*
Friday	*Kin-yobi*
Saturday	*Do-yobi*
Yesterday	*Kino*
Today	*Kyo*
This morning	*Kesa*
This evening	*Konya*
Tomorrow	*Ashita*
What time is it?	*Nan-ji desuka?*

RESTAURANTS

Water	*Mizu*
Beef	*Gyuniku*
Pork	*Butaniku*
Chicken	*Toriniku*
Fish	*Sakana*
Salad	*Sarada*
Beer	*Biiru*
Grilled	*Yaite*
Boiled	*Nite*
Fried	*Itamete*
Raw	*Nama*

NUMBERS

Counting is very complicated in Japanese! Counting up to ten on their fingers, the Japanese will go: *ichi, ni, san, shi (yon), go, roku, shichi* (or *nana*), *hachi, ku* (or *kyu*), *ju.* If they are counting bottles, they will go: *ip-pon, ni-hon, sam-bon, yon-hon, go-hon, rop-pon, nana-hon, hap-pon, kyu-hon, jup-pon.* Depending on what is being counted, the suffix will change. A complete explanation is beyond the scope of this book, and, in any case, choosing the wrong counter suffix simply causes amusement: it does not seriously impair understanding. If you are buying or ordering something, you will be fairly safe with the following list:

One	*Hitotsu*
Two	*Futatsu*
Three	*Mittsu*
Four	*Yottsu*
Five	*Itsutsu*
Six	*Muttsu*
Seven	*Nanatsu*
Eight	*Yattsu*
Nine	*Kokonotsu*
Ten	*To*

If you want five of something, simply point at it and say *"Itsutsu kudasai"*.

FURTHER READING

HISTORY & CULTURE

Barr, Pat. *The Coming of the Barbarians: A Story of Western Settlement in Japan 1853-1870*. Penguin Books. 1988.

Borton, Hugh. *Japan's Modern Century*. The Ronald Press. 1955.

Dunn, Charles J. *Everyday Life in Traditional Japan*. Charles E. Tuttle Company, Ltd. 1987

Frederic, Louis. (Translated from the French by Eileen M. Lowe) *Daily Life in Japan at the Time of the Samurai*. Charles E. Tuttle. 1972.

Fukutake, Tadashi. *The Japanese Social Structure: Its Evolution in the Modern Century* (2nd ed.). University of Tokyo Press. 1989.

Kaempfer, Englebert. *The History of Japan*. (3 volumes). James MacLehose and Sons. 1906.

Meech-Pekarik, Julia. *The World of the Meiji Print: Impressions of the Meiji Print*. Weatherhill. 1986.

Neary, Ian. *Political Protest and Social Control in Prewar Japan: The Origins of Buraku Liberation*. Manchester University Press. 1989.

Reischauer, Edwin O. & Fairbank, John K. *East Asia: The Great Tradition*. Houghton Mifflin Co. 1960.

Sansom, Sir George B. *Japan, A Short Cultural History*. Appleton-Century-Crofts, Inc. 1943.

Sansom, Sir George B. *The Western World and Japan*. Alfred A. Knopf, Inc. 1950

Schiffer, Robert L. (Text). Cooke, Jerry (Photographs). *The Exploding City*. St. Martin's Press. 1989.

Seidensticker, Edward. *Low City, High City: Tokyo From Edo to the Earthquake*. Charles E. Tuttle Company. 1983.

Tanizaki, Jun'ichiro. *In Praise of Shadows. (In'ei Raisan)*. (Translated by Thomas J. Harper and Edward G. Seidensticker. Charles E. Tuttle Co. 1984.

Tsunoda, de Bary and Keene. *Sources of the Japanese Tradition*. (2 volumes)

Yazaki, Takeo. *Social Change and the City in Japan: From earliest times through the Industrial Revolution*. Japan Publications, Inc. 1968.

GENERAL

Waley, Paul. *Tokyo Now & Then: An Explorer's Guide*. Weatherhill. 1984.

Popham, Peter. *Tokyo: The City at the End of the World*. Kodansha International Ltd. 1985.

Heibonsha 1986. *Atlas Tokyo: Edo/Tokyo Through Maps* (bilingual).

Kodansha 1987. *Tokyo: A Bilingual Atlas*.

John Turrent/Jonathan Lloyd-Owen. *Around Tokyo: A Day-Tripper's Guide*. The Japan Times 1982.

Kennedy, Rick. *Good Tokyo Restaurants*. Kodansha 1985.

Ashby, Janet. *Gaijin's Guide*. The Japan Times 1985.

Pia Co. Ltd. *Tokyo Eating Out* (bilingual). 1988.

Japan Travel Bureau. *Japan In Your Pocket* (series).

Stuart, Paul Meredith. *NihONSENSE*. The Japan Times 1987.

Gunji, Masakutsu. *The Kabuki Guide*. Kodansha International 1987.

Walters, Gary D.A. *Day Walks Near Tokyo*. Kodansha International 1988.

Mitsubishi Corporation. *Japanese Business Glossary Parts I & II*. Toyo Keizai Shinposha 1983.

Kenny, Don. *A Guide To Kyogen*. Hinoki Shoten 1968.

O'neill, P.G. *A Guide To No*. Hinoki Shoten 1953.

Elkin, Judith. *Japanese Family*. A. & C. Black 1986.

Condon, Camy & Nagasawa, Kimiko. *Kites, Crackers and Craftsmen*. Shufunotomo 1974.

USEFUL ADDRESSES

TOURIST INFORMATION

Japan National Tourist Organization (**JNTO**) & Tourist Information Center (**TIC**). Narita Tel: (0476) 32-8711; Tokyo Tel: (03) 502-1461

Information service (English)
Tokyo Tel: (03) 201-1010
Yokohama Tel: (045) 322-1010
Narita Tel: (0476) 28-1010

TELL (Tokyo English Life Line)
Tel: (03) 264-4347

English Advisory Service
Tel: (03) 211-4433
1 p.m. to 4 p.m. (Mon. and Thu.)

Welcome Furoshiki
This is a free welcoming and orientation service. They will visit your hotel or home.
Tel: (03) 352-0765

Yokohama Information Corner
Tel: (045) 671-7209
10 a.m.to 4 p.m. (Mon., Wed. and Fri.)

Travel Phone
(For travel information and language problems.) Hours: 9 a.m. to 5 p.m. daily.
Tel: (03) 502-1461

AIRLINE OFFICES

Aeroflot
Dai-ni Motsuda Bldg.,
3-4-8 Toranomon, Minato-ku
Tel: (03) 434-9680

Air Canada
New Akasaka Bldg.,
3-2-3 Akasaka, Minato-ku
Tel: (03) 586-3891

Air France
Shin Aoyama Bldg., Nishi-kan, 15th Fl.,
1-1-1 Minami Aoyama, Minato-ku
Tel: (03) 475-1511

Air India
Hibiya Park Bldg.,
1-8-1 Yurakucho, Chiyoda-ku
Tel: (03) 214-1981

Air Lanka
Dowa Bldg.,
7-2-22 Ginza, Chuo-ku
Tel: (03) 573-4261

Air New Zealand
Shin Kokusai Bldg.,
3-4-1 Marunouchi, Chiyoda-ku
Tel: (03) 287-1641

Alitalia
Tokyo Club Bldg.,
3-2-6 Kasumigaseki, Chiyoda-ku
Tel: (03) 580-2242

All Nippon Airways
Kasumigaseki Bldg.,
3-2-5 Kasumigaseki, Chiyoda-ku
Tel: International (03) 272-1212

Domestic (03) 552-6311

American Airlines
Kokusai Bldg.,
3-1-1 Marunouchi, Chiyoda-ku
Tel: (03) 212-0861

Bangladesh Biman
Kasumigaseki Bldg.,
3-2-5 Kasumigaseki, Chiyoda-ku
Tel: (03) 593-1252

British Airways
Hibiya Park Bldg.,
1-8-1 Yurakucho, Chiyoda-ku
Tel: (03) 214-4161

Canadian Airlines
Hibiya Park Bldg.,
1-8-1 Yurakucho, Chiyoda-ku
Tel: (03) 281-7426

Cathay Pacific Airways
Toho Twin Towers Bldg.,
1-5-2 Yurakucho, Chiyoda-ku
Tel: (03) 504-1531

China Airlines
Matsuoka Tamuracho Bldg.,
5-22-10 Shimbashi, Minato-ku
Tel: (03) 436-1661, (03) 747-4942 (Haneda)

Continental Airlines
Sanno Grand Bldg.,
2-14-2 Nagatacho, Chiyoda-ku
Tel: (03) 592-1631

Delta Airlines
Kokusai Bldg.,
3-1-1 Marunouchi, Chiyoda-ku
Tel: (03) 213-8781

Egypt Air
Palace Bldg.,
1-1-1 Marunouchi, Chiyoda-ku
Tel: (03) 211-4521

Finnair
NK Bldg.,
2-14-2 Kojimachi, Chiyoda-ku
Tel: (03) 222-6801

Garuda Indonesian Airways
Kasumigaseki Bldg.,
3-2-5 Kasumigaseki, Chiyoda-ku

Tel: (03) 593-1181

Hawaiian Airlines
New Kokusai Bldg.,
3-4-1 Marunouchi, Chiyoda-ku
Tel: (03) 214-4774

Iberia Airlines
Ark Mori Bldg.,
1-12-32 Akasaka, Minato-ku
Tel: (03) 582-3631

Iran Air
Akasaka Habitation Bldg.,
1-3-5 Akasaka, Minato-ku
Tel: (03) 586-2101

Iraqi Airways
Akasaka Matsudaira Bldg.,
3-4-1 Akasaka, Minato-ku
Tel: (03) 586-5801

Japan Air Lines
Tokyo Bldg.,
2-7-3 Marunouchi, Chiyoda-ku
Tel: Tokyo (03) 457-1121,
Narita (0476) 32-3125

KLM Royal Dutch Airlines
Yurakucho Denki Bldg.,
1-7-1 Yurakucho, Chiyoda-ku
Tel: (03) 216-0771

Korean Air
Shin Kokusai Bldg.,
3-4-1 Marunouchi, Chiyoda-ku
Tel: (03) 211-3311

Kuwait Airways
1-1-2 Yurakucho,
Chiyoda-ku
Tel: (03) 597-0625

LOT Polish Airlines
Yamauchi Bldg.,
3-24-8 Nishi Shimbashi, Minato-ku
Tel: (03) 437-5741

Lufthansa German Airlines
Tokyo Club Bldg.,
3-2-6 Kasumigaseki, Chiyoda-ku
Tel: (03) 580-2111

Malaysian Airlines
Hankyu Kotsusha Bldg.,

3-3-9 Shimbashi, Minato-ku
Tel: (03) 503-5961

Northwest Airlines
5-12-12 Toranomon,
Minato-ku
Tel: (03) 432-6000

Pakistan International Airlines
Hibiya Park Bldg.,
1-8-1 Yurakucho, Chiyoda-ku
Tel: (03) 216-6511

Pan American Airlines
Hibiya Kokusai Bldg.,
2-2-3 Uchisaiwaicho, Chiyoda-ku
Tel: (03) 508-2211

Qantas Airways
Urban Toranomon Bldg.,
1-16-4 Toranomon, Minato-ku
Tel: (03) 593-7000

Sabena Belgian Airlines
Address Bldg.,
2-2-19 Akasaka, Minato-ku
Tel: (03) 585-6151

Scandinavian Airlines
Toho Twin Tower Bldg.,
1-5-2 Yurakucho, Chiyoda-ku
Tel: (03) 503-8101

Singapore Airlines
Yurakucho Bldg.,
1-10-1 Yurakucho, Chiyoda-ku
Tel: (03) 213-3431

Swissair
Hibiya Park Bldg.,
1-8-1 Yurakucho, Chiyoda-ku
Tel: (03) 212-1011

Thai Airways
Asahi Seimei Hibiya Bldg.,
1-5-1 Yurakucho, Chiyoda-ku
Tel: (03) 503-3311

Trans World Airlines
Kokusai Bldg.,
3-1-1 Marunouchi, Chiyoda-ku
Tel: (03) 212-1477

United Airlines
Kokusai Bldg.,

3-1-1 Marunouchi, Chiyoda-ku
Tel: (03) 817-4411

UTA French Airlines
Kasumigaseki Bldg.,
3-2-5 Kasumigaseki, Chiyoda-ku
Tel: (03) 593-0773

Varig Brazilian Airlines
Palace Bldg.,
1-1-1 Marunouchi, Chiyoda-ku
Tel: (03) 211-6751

Virgin Atlantic Airways
Mori Bldg. 30, 4th Fl.,
3-2-2 Toranomon, Minato-ku
Tel: (03) 435-8330

Tokyo City Terminal Information Office
42-1 Nihombashi, Hakozakicho, Chuo-ku
Tel: (03) 665-7156

COURIER SERVICES

DHL
Sumitomo Seimei Higashi Kanda Bldg.,
1st Fl., 2-5-15 Higashi Kanda, Chiyoda-ku
Tel: (03) 865-2580

Federal Express
Shin Tokyo Bldg., 1Fl.,
3-3-1 Marunouchi, Chiyoda-ku
Tel: (03) 201-4320

OCS (Overseas Courier Service Co., Ltd.)
2-9-12 Shibaura, Minato-ku
Tel: (03) 5476-8111

Nippon Express
7-6-19 Roppongi, Minato-ku
Tel: (03) 408-1501

World Courier
Kawashima Hoshin Bldg., 5th Fl.,
2-2-2 Shimbashi, Minato-ku
Tel: (03) 508-9281

COMMUNITY ORGANIZATIONS

America-Japan Society
Marunouchi Bldg., 3rd Fl.,
2-4-1 Marunouchi, Chiyoda-ku
Tel: (03) 201-0780

American Center
ABC Kaikan,
2-6-3 Shibakoen, Minato-ku
Tel: (03) 436-0901

ACCJ (American Chamber of Commerce in Japan)
Fukide Bldg., No.2,
4-1-21 Toranomon, Minato-ku
Tel: (03) 433-5381

Asia Center of Japan
8-10-32 Akasaka, Minato-ku
Tel: (03) 402-6111

British Council
1-2 Kagurazaka, Shinjuku-ku
Tel: (03) 235-8031

Foreign Correspondents' Club of Japan
Yurakucho Denki Bldg., 20th Fl.,
1-7-1 Yurakucho, Chiyoda-ku
Tel: (03) 211-3161

Institute Franco-Japonais
15 Funagawaracho,
Ichigaya, Shinjuku-ku
Tel: (03) 260-7224

Italian Institute of Culture
2-1-30 Kudan Minami, Chiyoda-ku
Tel: (03) 264-6011

Tokyo German Culture Center
7-5-56 Akasaka, Minato-ku
Tel: (03) 584-3201

Japan Chamber of Commerce
Tokyo Kaijo Bldg., #311,
3-2-2 Marunouchi, Chiyoda-ku
Tel: (03) 213-8585

JETRO (Japan External Trade Organization)
2-2-5 Toranomon, Minato-ku
Tel: (03) 582-5511

AA (Alcoholics Anonymous)
Tel: (03) 431-8357

Amnesty International
Dai San Yamatake Bldg., 3rd Fl.,
2-3-22 Nishi Waseda, Shinjuku-ku
Tel: (03) 203-1050

International Feminists of Japan
Tel: (03) 904-2646

Tokyo Gay Support Group
Tel: (03) 453-1618

EMBASSIES & CONSULATES

All consulates and embassies are open from Mon. to Fri. If you need to visit one of the offices, please call to check the office hours, as they are all slightly different.

Argentine Embassy
Chiyoda House, 2-17-8
Nagatacho, Chiyoda-ku
Tel: (03) 592-0321

Australian Embassy
1-1-12 Shibakoen, Minato-ku
Tel: (03) 435-0971

Austrian Embassy
1-1-20 Moto Azabu, Minato-ku
Tel: (03) 451-8281

Belgian Embassy
5-4 Nibancho, Chiyoda-ku
Tel: (03) 262-0191

Bangladesh Embassy
2-7-45 Shirogane, Minato-ku
Tel: (03) 442-1501

Bolivian Embassy
No. 38 Kowa Bldg.,
4-12-24 #804 Nishi-Azabu, Minato-ku
Tel: (03) 499-5441

Brazilian Embassy
2-11-12 Kita Aoyama, Minato-ku
Tel: (03) 404-5211

British Embassy
1 Ichibancho, Chiyoda-ku
Tel: (03) 265-5511

Brunei Embassy
6-5 Kita Shinagawa, Shinagawa-ku
Tel: (03) 447-7997

Bulgarian Embassy
5-36-3 Yoyogi, Shibuya-ku
Tel: (03) 465-1021

Burmese Embassy
4-8-26 Kita Shinagawa, Shinagawa-ku
Tel: (03) 441-9291

Canadian Embassy
7-3-38 Akasaka, Minato-ku
Tel: (03) 408-2101

Chilean Embassy
Nihon Seimei Akabanebashi Bldg.,
3-1-14 Shiba, Minato-ku
Tel: (03) 452-7561

Chinese Embassy
3-4-33 Moto Azabu, Minato-ku
Tel: (03) 403-3380

Czechoslovakian Embassy
2-16-14 Hiro-o, Shibuya-ku
Tel: (03) 400-8122

Danish Embassy
29-6 Sarugakucho, Shibuya-ku
Tel: (03) 496-3001

Dominican Rep. Embassy
No. 38 Kowa Bldg.,
4-12-24 Nishi Azabu, Minato-ku
Tel: (03) 499-6020

Egyptian Embassy
1-5-4 Aobadai, Meguro-ku
Tel: (03) 770-8021

Finnish Embassy
3-5-39 Minami Azabu, Minato-ku
Tel: (03) 442-2231

French Embassy
4-11-44 Minami Azabu, Minato-ku
Tel: (03) 473-0171

German Embassy
4-5-10 Minami Azabu, Minato-ku
Tel: (03) 473-0151

Greek Embassy
3-16-30 Nishi Azabu, Minato-ku
Tel: (03) 403-0871

Hungarian Embassy
2-17-14 Mita, Minato-ku
Tel: (03) 798-8801

Iceland Consulate
c/o Shintozai Co., Ltd.
1-5-17 Harumi, Chuo-ku
Tel: (03) 531-8776

Indian Embassy
2-2-11 Kudan Minami, Chiyoda-ku
Tel: (03) 262-2391

Indonesian Embassy
5-2-9 Higashi Gotanda, Shinagawa-ku
Tel: (03) 441-4201

Iranian Embassy
3-10-32 Minami Azabu, Minato-ku
Tel: (03) 446-8011

Iraqi Embassy
8-4-7 Akasaka, Minato-ku
Tel: (03) 423-1727

Irish Embassy
No. 25 Kowa Bldg.,
8-7 Sanbancho, Chiyoda-ku
Tel: (03) 263-0695

Israeli Embassy
3 Nibancho, Chiyoda-ku
Tel: (03) 264-0911

Italian Embassy
2-5-4 Mita, Minato-ku
Tel: (03) 453-5291

Jordanian Embassy
Chiyoda House,
2-17-8 Nagatacho, Chiyoda-ku
Tel: (03) 580-5856

Korean Embassy
1-2-5 Minami Azabu, Minato-ku
Tel: (03) 452-7611

Laotian Embassy
3-3-21 Nishi Azabu, Minato-ku
Tel: (03) 408-1166

Malaysian Embassy
20-16 Nanpeidaicho, Shibuya-ku
Tel: (03) 770-9331

Mexican Embassy
2-15-1 Nagatacho, Chiyoda-ku
Tel: (03) 581-1131

Nepalese Embassy
7-14-9 Todoroki, Setagaya-ku
Tel: (03) 705-5558

Netherlands Embassy
3-6 Shibakoen, Minato-ku
Tel: (03) 431-5126

New Zealand Embassy
20-40 Kamiyamacho, Shibuya-ku
Tel: (03) 467-2271

Norwegian Embassy
5-12-2 Minami Azabu, Minato-ku
Tel: (03) 440-2611

Oman Embassy
Silva Kingdom,
3-16-3 Sendagaya, Shibuya-ku
Tel: (03) 402-0877

Pakistan Embassy
2-14-9 Moto Azabu, Minato-ku
Tel: (03) 454-4861

Panama Embassy
No. 38 Kowa Bldg.,
4-12-24 Nishi Azabu, Minato-ku
Tel: (03) 499-3741

Peruvian Embassy
4-4-27 Higashi, Shibuya-ku
Tel: (03) 406-4240

Philippine Embassy
11-24 Nanpeidaicho, Shibuya-ku
Tel: (03) 496-2731

Polish Embassy
2-13-5 Mita, Meguro-ku
Tel: (03) 711-5224

Portuguese Embassy
6-31-21 Jingumae, Shibuya-ku
Tel: (03) 400-7907

Romanian Embassy
3-16-19 Nishi Azabu, Minato-ku
Tel: (03) 479-0311

Saudi Arabian Embassy
153 Azabu Nagasakacho, Minato-ku
Tel: (03) 589-5241

Senegal Embassy
1-3-4 Aobadai, Meguro-ku
Tel: (03) 464-8451

Singapore Embassy
5-12-3 Roppongi, Minato-ku
Tel: (03) 586-9111

Spanish Embassy
1-3-29 Roppongi, Minato-ku
Tel: (03) 583-8531

Sri Lanka Embassy
1-14-1 Akasaka, Minato-ku
Tel: (03) 585-7431

Swedish Embassy
No. 25 Mori Bldg.,
1-4-30 Roppongi, Minato-ku
Tel: (03) 582-6981

Swiss Embassy
5-9-12 Minami Azabu, Minato-ku
Tel: (03) 473-0121

Taiwan Visitor's Association
Imperial Tower, A-9 5th Fl.,
Imperial Hotel, 1-1-1 Uchisaiwaicho,
Chiyoda-ku
Tel: (03) 501-3591

Thailand Embassy
3-14-6 Kami Osaki, Shinagawa-ku
Tel: (03) 441-7352

Turkish Embassy
2-33-6 Jingumae, Shibuya-ku
Tel: (03) 470-5131

U.S.S.R Embassy
2-1-1 Azabudai, Minato-ku
Tel: (03) 583-4224

United Arab Emirates Embassy
Kotsu Anzen Kyoiku Center Bldg.,
3-24-20 Nishi Azabu, Minato-ku
Tel: (03) 478-0659

Uruguay Embassy
No. 38 Kowa Bldg.,
4-12-24-804 Nishi-Azabu, Minato-ku
Tel: (03) 486-1888

U.S.A. Embassy
1-10-5 Akasaka, Minato-ku
Tel: (03) 224-5000

Yugoslavia Embassy
4-7-24 Kita Shinagawa,
Shinagawa-ku
Tel: (03) 447-3571

Vatican Holy See Embassy
9-2 Sanbancho, Chiyoda-ku
Tel: (03) 263-6851

Vietnamese Embassy
50-11 Motoyoyogicho, Shibuya-ku
Tel: (03) 466-3311

ART/PHOTO CREDITS

INDEX

289